International Anesthesiology Clinics

International Anesthesiology Clinics (ISSN 0020-5907). Published quarterly by Little, Brown and Company, 34 Beacon Street, Boston, Massachusetts 02108-1493. Send address changes and subscription orders to Little, Brown and Company, Journals Subscription Department, 34 Beacon Street, Boston, MA 02108-1493. Subscription rates per year: personal subscription, U.S. and possessions, $149; foreign (includes Mexico), $171; Canada, $165 (PLEASE ADD 7% CANADIAN GST FOR ALL CANADIAN SUBSCRIPTIONS [Registration No. R128537917]); institutional, U.S., $165; foreign, $213; Canada, $182. Special rates for students, interns, and residents per year: U.S., $109; foreign, $132; Canada, $127. Single copies: $39. In Japan please contact our exclusive agent: Medsi, 1-2-13 Yushima, Bunkyo-ku, Tokyo 113, Japan. Subscription rates per year in Japan: individual, ¥23,100; institutional, ¥33,900 (for faster air cargo service add ¥1,600). Second-class postage paid at Boston, Massachusetts, and at additional mailing offices.

Postmaster: Send address changes to International Anesthesiology Clinics, 34 Beacon Street, Boston, MA 02108-1493.

International Anesthesiology Clinics is indexed in *Index Medicus, Current Contents/Clinical Medicine, Excerpta Medica,* and *Current Awareness in Biological Sciences.*

International Anesthesiology Clinics

Topics in Neuroanesthesia

Volume 34
Number 4
Fall 1996

Edited by

Richard A. Jaffe, MD, PhD

Associate Professor, Department of Anesthesia, Stanford University School of Medicine, Stanford, California

Rona G. Giffard, MD, PhD

Assistant Professor, Department of Anesthesia, Stanford University School of Medicine, Stanford, California

Little, Brown and Company
Boston / New York / London / Toronto

Editor in Chief
Thomas W. Feeley, MD
Professor of Anesthesia
Stanford University School of Medicine

Editorial Office
Department of Anesthesia H3580
Stanford University School of Medicine
Stanford, California 94305-5115

Associate Editor
David Royston, MB, ChB, FFARCS
Consultant in Cardiothoracic Anaesthesia
Department of Anaesthesia
Harefield Hospital
Harefield, Middlesex UB9 6JH
United Kingdom

Publisher
Little, Brown and Company
Boston, Massachusetts

Publishing Staff

Associate Publisher
Nancy Megley

Managing Editor
Rebecca H. Malone

Sales and Marketing Manager
Anne Orens

Contents

Contributing Authors

Verna L. Baughman, MD
Department of Anesthesiology, Michael
Reese Hospital, Chicago, Illinois

Traian T. Cojocaru, MD
Assistant Professor, Department of
Neurosurgery, Loma Linda University,
Loma Linda, California; Attending
Neurosurgeon, Jerry L. Pettis Memorial
Veterans Hospital, Loma Linda,
California

Daniel J. Cole, MD
Associate Professor of Anesthesiology,
Loma Linda University, Loma Linda,
California; Attending Anesthesiologist,
Department of Anesthesiology, Loma
Linda University Medical Center, Loma
Linda, California

Michael J. Cousins, AM, MD, FANZCA
Department of Anesthesia and Pain
Management, Royal North Shore
Hospital, St. Leonards, Australia;
University of Sydney, Sydney, Australia

Stephen P. Fischer, MD
Assistant Professor, Department of
Anesthesiology, Stanford University
School of Medicine, Stanford, California

Gregory B. Hammer, MD
Assistant Professor, Department of
Anesthesia, Stanford University Medical
Center, Stanford, California

Patricia D. Hurn, PhD
Assistant Professor, Department of
Anesthesiology, Johns Hopkins Medical
Institution, Baltimore, Maryland

Jeffrey R. Kirsch, MD
Director of Resident Education/Associate Professor, Department of Anesthesiology, Johns Hopkins University School of Medicine and Hospital, Baltimore, Maryland

Heidi M. Koenig, MD
Department of Anesthesiology, Michael Reese Hospital, Chicago, Illinois

Elliott J. Krane, MD
Department of Anesthesia, Stanford University Medical Center, Stanford, California

William L. Lanier, MD
Professor of Anesthesiology, Mayo Medical School, Rochester, Minnesota; Consultant in Anesthesiology, Mayo Clinic, Rochester, Minnesota

C. Philip Larson, Jr, MD
Professor of Clinical Anesthesiology, University of California, Los Angeles School of Medicine, Los Angeles, California; University of California, Los Angeles Center for the Health Sciences, Los Angeles, California

Jaime R. Lopez, MD
Department of Neurology and Neurological Sciences, Stanford University Medical Center, Stanford, California

Linda J. Mason, MD
Associate Professor of Anesthesiology and Pediatrics, Loma Linda University, Loma Linda, California; Attending Anesthesiologist, Department of Anesthesiology, Loma Linda University Medical Center, Loma Linda, California

Lawrence Molton, JD
Bishop, Barry, Howe, Haney, & Ryder, San Francisco, California

Alexander M. Norbash, MD
Assistant Professor, Department of
Radiology, Stanford University School of
Medicine, Stanford, California

Dale A. Pelligrino, PhD
Associate Professor, University of Illinois
at Chicago, Chicago, Illinois;
Department of Anesthesiology, Michael
Reese Hospital, Chicago, Illinois

Stanley I. Samuels, MB, FFARCS
Professor, Department of Anesthesia,
Stanford University School of Medicine,
Stanford, California

Robert J. Singer, MD
Fellow, Interventional Neuroradiology,
Stanford University School of Medicine,
Stanford, California; Resident,
Department of Neurosurgery, Vanderbilt
University School of Medicine,
Nashville, Tennessee

Richard J. Traystman, PhD
Vice Chairman for Research/Professor,
Department of Anesthesiology/Critical
Care Medicine, The Johns Hopkins
University School of Medicine and
Hospital, Baltimore, Maryland

Hamed S. Umedaly, MD, FRCPC
Department of Anesthesia and Pain
Management, Royal North Shore
Hospital, St. Leonards, Australia;
University of Sydney, Syndey, Australia

C. Thomas Wass, MD
Instructor in Anesthesiology, Mayo
Medical School, Rochester, Minnesota;
Consultant in Anesthesiology, Mayo
Clinic, Rochester, Minnesota

Preface

There are several excellent textbooks devoted to the practice and principles of neuroanesthesiology, and it is our hope that this volume will serve as a useful and timely supplement to those texts. In planning for this issue of *International Anesthesiology Clinics* we sought to achieve two goals. The first goal was to present those topics we believed deserved more consideration than they have traditionally been given; for example, historical aspects of neuroanesthesia, preoperative evaluation and intraoperative monitoring of the neurosurgical patient, pediatric neuroanesthesia, giant aneurysms, pain management following neurosurgery, and a primer on malpractice. The second goal was to present current reviews of recent developments of importance to the neuroanesthesiologist; for example, nitric oxide, mild hypothermia, cerebral protection, surgery for Parkinson's disease, and a discussion of interventional neuroradiological procedures.

To the extent that we have achieved these goals, we are entirely indebted to our outstanding group of contributors, who generously gave their time and shared their knowledge so that we all could become better informed anesthesiologists.

R.A.J.
R.G.G.

History of Neuroanesthesia: A Contemporary Review

Stanley I. Samuels, MB, FFARCS

It seems to me that only a purist of the order of Plato (assuming he had the time or interest) would argue that the specialty of neurosurgery began in the neolithic age. However, this argument could be based on the fact that neolithic man seemed to spend a goodly part of his time engaged in the practice of trephining his fellow neolithic man's skull. Evidence of this early surgical handiwork has been uncovered not only all over Europe, but in parts of Africa, Asia, and the Americas [1]. However, it is very unlikely that these early trephiners were assisted in their endeavors by a specialized group of neolithic neuroanesthesiologists. Rather, we must look back to the end of the 18th and the early part of the 19th century to detect the beginnings of neurosurgery and neuroanesthesia. At that time, the pioneer neurosurgeons were making their mark both in Europe and in the United States. This small group were well served (relatively speaking) by advances in aseptic techniques, diagnostic procedures, and a greater understanding of the pathology, anatomy, and physiology of the nervous system. However, it is fair to say that neurosurgery could not have advanced without the development of anesthesia.

This chapter will look back at these early giants of neurosurgery and anesthesia and examine the historical basis for modern day neuroanesthesia practice. In this context, liberal use will be made of articles and discussions found in contemporary medical journals. While sometimes extremely loquacious in the use of the English language, often tortuous in their circumlocutions, and frequently amusing in the use of 19th century grammar, one hopes that these writings are still of interest to the modern reader. It should come as no surprise that the anesthetic and surgical techniques we now take for granted are due, in no small measure, to these early pioneers who laid the groundwork for the modern practice of anesthesia and surgery.

■ The Pioneers

It is probably fair to say that those of us practicing anesthesia in the developing world live and work in a time of plenty. It seems that hardly a month goes by that some new anesthetic drug or appliance is not unveiled on the marketplace. Contrast this to the turn of the century when drugs and equipment available to the pioneer anesthetists were few in number. Politically insensitive as it may be, and without treading on too many toes, the terms anesthetist and anesthesiologist will be used interchangeably throughout this text. The latter term did not come into general usage until about 1902 [2].

To paraphrase the white queen in Alice in Wonderland, let us begin at the beginning. Our historical review really begins with Sir Humphrey Davy (1778–1829) who in 1798 suggested that nitrous oxide (laughing gas) inhalations might be used to relieve the pain of surgery. He described this as follows: "On the day when the inflammation was most troublesome, I breathed three large doses of nitrous oxide. The pain always diminished after the first four or five respirations" [3]. As is so often the case, this work was not followed up, and it was not until 1844 that Horace Wells (1813–1848) received nitrous oxide and had one of his own teeth removed. Gardner Quincy Colton was the anesthetist, John Riggs the dentist, and Horace Wells the patient. "A new era in tooth pulling," declared Wells after the successful experiment [2].

The *Boston Medical and Surgical Journal* put it somewhat more eloquently in June of 1845: "The nitrous oxide gas has been used in quite a number of cases by our dentists during the extraction of teeth, and has been found by its excitement perfectly to destroy pain. The patients appear very merry during the operation, and no unpleasant effects follow." Wishing for a wider audience, Wells then demonstrated its use (unsuccessfully) at Harvard Medical School in the same year. This failure was devastating to him, but he continued to use nitrous oxide in his practice. Gardner Quincy Colton established its use again in 1867 in New York, and T. W. Evans (another dentist) introduced the use of nitrous oxide to London in 1868.

The popularity of nitrous oxide waned following the introduction of ether by Dr Crawford Long (1815–1878). In 1842, he removed a tumor of the neck from James Venable. The surgery was described as pain free. Unfortunately, his successful use of ether as an anesthetic was not published until 1849 [4], and by that time, William Thomas Green Morton (1819–1868) had been given the chief credit for the introduction of ether as an anesthetic agent. In 1846, Massachusetts General Hospital, which had been the venue for the unsuccessful demonstration of nitrous oxide, was now the venue for William Morton's demonstration of the new agent, ether. This time there were no errors and its use spread quickly to London and Paris. It was in that year in 1846 that Oliver Wendell Holmes suggested the use of the term anesthesia rather than Morton's etherisation.

In 1902, ether, like nitrous oxide, was soon to be overshadowed by a newer agent, chloroform, introduced in 1847 by Sir James Young Simpson (1811–1870). This drug had been discovered somewhat unusually by three investigators working independently of each other in Germany, New York, and France. The year was 1831. Sir James Young Simpson and his assistants, Mathews Duncan and George Keith, introduced and popularized chloroform in 1847 in Edinburgh, Scotland. Not surprisingly, chloroform was widely in use in its birthplace of Scotland, as well as all over Europe and the southern states of America [5]. In 1848, ethyl chloride was introduced and was used mainly as an induction agent, particularly for children. Ethyl chloride seemingly had its own safety problems, as a description of ethyl chloride collapse attests to:

> If this occurs in a young child suspend child by its feet and withdraw tongue while an assistant manually compresses the chest. Sharp slapping of the precordium with a moist towel may stimulate the heart and respiration. If this does not rapidly improve the picture, the child should have an airway inserted (if necessary) and the anesthetist should have an airway either from the reservoir bag of a gas machine, or from his own lungs, via a face-mask. Time should not be wasted over endotracheal intubation. True cardiac arrest must be treated by cardiac compression [6].

Because of the dangers associated with chloroform anesthesia, Vernon Harcourt began work on a chloroform inhaler that would provide safe and accurate concentrations. His inhaler was introduced into clinical practice in 1904, replacing the open drop technique of chloroform anesthesia [7]. On a personal note, the author, like his uncles before him (all equally terrified of anesthesia and anesthetics), vividly remembers giving open drop chloroform whilst a medical student in Dublin. This was usually carried out under the direction of a senior obstetric nurse or resident. "In the country of the blind the one eyed man is king."

As we have seen, these early anesthetists had at their disposal a limited number of drugs and only simple anesthetic apparatus for delivery of such drugs to their patients. As we have seen, chloroform was widely used in its birthplace, Scotland, as well as all over Europe and the southern states of America. Ether was the agent used mainly in England and the northern states of America. These pioneer anesthetists had simple tools available for the practice of anesthesia, but, in order for the specialty of neuroanesthesia to flourish, it required the advent of surgeons with a special interest in brain surgery. As if on cue, these pioneer neurosurgeons stepped out of the wings to establish the new specialty of neurosurgery. They were both European and American.

It was in 1879 that Sir William Macewen (1848–1924) performed the first craniotomy for removal of a tumor [8], surprisingly enough carried out under endotracheal anesthesia. At that time it was the custom to place a tracheotomy for head or neck surgery. He described his experiences with endotracheal intubation the following year [9]. From a 20th century perspective, the passage of an endotracheal tube is simplicity itself, but to our predecessors these were giant steps:

> A few facts concerning the introduction of tubes passed through the natural passages into the trachea, instead of having recourse to operations for opening the windpipe through the neck, are considered worthy of attention; and in presenting these, it is thought advisable to confine the remarks as far as practicable to the relation of facts, refraining from entering into the merely discursive side of the question.
>
> In considering the practicability of such a procedure, facts were looked at from various sources. Post mortem experience showed that instruments of the tube kind could, after a little practice, be passed with facility through the mouth into the trachea. This was accomplished by introducing the finger into the mouth, depressing the epiglottis on the tongue, and so guiding the tube over the back of the finger into the larynx. In experimenting with various instruments, it was found more easy to introduce those of a large calibre, such as Nos. 18 and 20, than instruments of the size of 8 to 10 catheters—the latter being more liable to catch on the various irregularities on the internal laryngeal surface [9].

He then goes on to describe a series of successful cases using tracheal tubes during the year 1878. His house surgeon, a Dr Symington, administered the chloroform. The following deductions were drawn from the use of tracheal tubes:

> 1. Tubes may be passed through the mouth into the trachea not only in chronic, but also in acute affections—such as oedema glottidis; 2. They can be introduced without placing the patient under an anaesthetic; 3. The respirations can be perfectly carried on through them; 4. The expectoration can be expelled through them; 5. Deglutition can be carried on during the time the tube is in the trachea; 6. Though the patient at first suffers from a painful sensation, yet this passes off, and the parts soon became tolerant of the presence of the tube; 7. The patient can sleep with the tube in situ; 8. The tubes, in these cases at least, were harmless; 9. The ultimate results were rapid, complete, and satisfactory; 10. Such tubes may be introduced in operations on the face and mouth, in order to prevent blood from gaining access to the trachea, and for the purpose of administering the anaesthetic, and they answer this purpose admirably [9].

These tubes were made of either flexible brass or gum elastic.

However, Sir William's interest in anesthesia was not just technical. Macewen and the staff at Glasgow Royal Infirmary actively promoted the idea of teaching and educating medical students in the art of anesthesia. This endeavor was begun in 1884 [10]. The anesthetic of choice was chloroform, as he was aware of the stimulatory effects of ether on both heart and salivary glands. Morphine premedication was sometimes used, though this technique of premedication was not to come into general use until about 1920.

The use of the endotracheal tubes advocated by Sir William did not gain popularity, and Dr A. W. Adson writing in 1919 gave as his opinion that "intratracheal anesthesia has a definite, but limited field of usefulness. Only a short time ago its use was advocated in operations on the oral cavity, tongue, larynx, chest, and brain, but a comparison of the inhalation drop method, with intrapharyngeal and the intratracheal method, has resulted in the gradual abandonment of the latter except in an occasional chest operation, and in operations on the cerebellum, pons, and medulla" [11]. It would take another decade before Sir Ivan Magill and Stanley Rowbotham popularized the use of endotracheal anesthesia [12]. William Macewen was a general surgeon who had an interest in neurosurgery. His distinguished contemporary in London, England, was Sir Victor Horsley (1857–1916), who in 1886 was appointed as surgeon to the Hospital for Paralysis and Epilepsy, subsequently the Hospital for Nervous Diseases, Queen Square, London. Not only did Sir Victor specialize in neurosurgery, but in a similar fashion to his contemporaries, Cushing and Macewen, he had a deep interest in anesthesia. His scientific curiosity was such that he experimented with the use of chloroform, ether, and nitrous oxide using himself as the subject. As he put it, "to become familiar with the effects of different agents and observe the physical and mental phenomena they provided before consciousness was lost" [13]. It would appear that such self-experimentation was much easier to carry out in the more relaxed medicolegal climate of the 1880s. One can readily imagine the fate of a 20th century Horsley found inhaling or injecting anesthetic agents in an effort to become familiar with their effects. Horsley investigated the effects of ether, chloroform, and morphine on the intracranial contents. His studies took place during 1883–1885 and led him to conclude that the agent of choice was chloroform and that morphine had some value because of its cerebral constriction effects. Ether, he faulted due to its potential to cause a rise in blood pressure, excessive bleeding, and postoperative nausea, vomiting, and excitement. In 1888 in a paper in the *British Medical Journal*, he described his anesthesia technique for brain surgery as follows:

Anaesthetic—The method of narcotising the patient is most important, and consists of administration by hypodermic injection, of a quarter of a grain of morphine, after which the patient is chloroformed. The object of giving the morphine is two-fold. In the first place, as is well known, it allows of the performance of a prolonged operation, without the necessity of giving a large amount of chloroform. In fact, the amount actually used in an operation lasting two hours, I have found to be very small. The second reason for employing morphine is, perhaps, the more important, since it is based upon the fact determined by Professor Schäfer and myself, from experiments on monkeys—namely, that this drug causes well-marked contraction of the arterioles of the central nervous system; and that consequently, an incision into the brain is accompanied by very little oozing if the patient be under its influence. I have not employed ether in operations on man, fearing that it would tend to cause cerebral excitement; chloroform, of course, producing, on the contrary, well marked depression. Naturally, if there existed any heart-complication, the above theoretical considerations would be disregarded in favour of the safer narcotic. . . . In a case where considerable heart-mischief exists, no doubt an operation of the kind might be done under the influence of cocaine. If this be attempted, care must be taken to employ a very strong solution when the dura mater is exposed, since that membrane is extremely sensitive (being supplied by branches of the fifth cranial nerve), a fact which appears to be unknown to clinicians, although it is obviously of immense importance in considering the causation of intracranial pain, cranial tenderness, etc. [14].

He omitted morphine from his surgical regimen because of its effect as a respiratory depressant. He like Feodor Krause (1857–1937), the German neurosurgeon, advocated the use of hypotension to reduce bleeding. This was carried out by an increase in the concentration of chloroform. All these surgeons were aware of the need for deepening anesthesia at specific times during craniotomies, that is, the scalp, periosteum and dura required deeper anesthesia than the brain substance, which was insensitive to pain. At that time, deaths from chloroform were a major cause for concern. Sir Victor, perhaps because of his interest in anesthesia, was appointed to the Special Chloroform Committee. The committee began its work in 1901 and its conclusions made public in 1904 [15]. An editorial entitled "The Work of the Chloroform Committee Forum" (1911) in the *British Medical Journal* commented on the final report as well as adding some salutary comments on the teaching of anesthesia [16]. No apologies are made for reprinting it in its entirety, its content may still be appropriate after all these years.

For better or worse chloroform has been placed in the foremost rank of general anaesthetics; the benefit its use has bestowed on mankind has been lessened, however, by many fatalities associated with its employment. The number of these has bulked large in countries where full publicity is accorded to such accidents, but no corresponding record has been kept of the successful cases. The British Medical Association, in a former report drawn up by a committee, attempted with some measure of success to obtain the required statistics, and after analyzing 25,000 cases showed that while the incidence of death was highest for chloroform and chloroform-containing mixtures, it was comparatively small. The actual mortality has been stated to be on the increase, but whether this is so or not cannot be shown by such data as we at present possess. But even so, the patient who has to face the ordeal, and even the doctor who is compelled to accept the risk, are not willing to be content with even a minimal chance of fatality. Until comparatively of late years, little if any systemic teaching of anaesthetics has been attempted, and even now in the stress of an over-filled curriculum the student, as a rule, learns the subject of anaesthetics purely as a handicraftsman. In later life, when the responsibility of giving anaesthetics is brought home to him, he seeks salvation by reading some textbook on the subject. This perhaps confirms his fears of chloroform, and so incidentally renders him nervous, and induces him to seek methods which are vaunted as being less open to exception than, it is averred, is chloroform. If he has leisure to travel farther afield, he plunges into count-less monographs, physiological and pharmacological, which either narrate experiments explaining the action of chloroform on the circulatory or nervous control apparatus, or indulge in a minimum of research and a maximum of polemic. The pilgrim's progress towards the realm of safe anaesthesia is slow, and his burden grows heavier the farther his steps advance. Admitting his guides are accurate, he inquires of them how he is to apply his hardly-gained knowledge, and frequently asks in vain. The multifarious methods are set before him, but to him is left the choice of the path along which he must go. It is at this point that the report before us appears to supply a key to the problem. It admits that chloroform may be dangerous, and has been proved to be so in the past, but it supplies the remedy [16].

And the remedy was how to give chloroform with safety. While the report advises dosimetry, it is not content with offering advice; it selects out of many, one that had the added advantages of compatibility and safety. As we have seen, the one recommended was the Vernon-Harcourt inhaler.

Meanwhile on the other side of the Atlantic, the Committee on Anes-thesia of the American Medical Association gave us this opinion in 1912.

The use of chloroform for major operations is no longer justifiable. Necro-sis of the liver follows its use in a by no means inconsiderable percentage of cases, while as the mode of causation of this sequel is unknown, there are no precautions that can intelligently be taken against it. The surgeon whose patient dies in this manner must face the responsibility of having knowingly taken a chance and lost. . . . It is a mistake to think that a fatality is necessarily due to an unusually large administration of the anaes-thetic, the subject is liable to collapse under a small dosage. . . . We see no reason to believe that in respect of toxicity there is more than a slight quantitative difference between chloroform alone, and mixtures such as A.C.E. and etc. . . . For minor operations also the use of chloroform should cease.

Paluel Flagg in his book *The Art of Anesthesia* written in 1916 stated his view very clearly on the use of chloroform:

To reiterate. Chloroform, while ideal in efficiency, is a dangerous poison. In the light of present-day pathology, chloroform should cease to be used in obstetrics. Combined with ether, chloroform is quite efficient and less dangerous. Chloroform kills if pushed in the face of masseteric spasm. Delayed chloroform poisoning is a fact and argues for the complete replacement of the drug by safer anaesthetic agents. Chloroform, is used at all, should be taken from a freshly opened receptacle. The administration should invariably be performed in the prone position. The mortality of chloroform is variably estimated as 1-1000, 1-3000 [17].

And so on both sides of the Atlantic the great debate continued with regard to the relative merits of ether and chloroform.

In the interim, what had become of the neurosurgeons? So far the advent of neurosurgery has been seen mainly from a European perspective, but in the United States another giant of neurosurgery was stirring who gave tremendous impetus to both the fields of anesthesiology and neurosurgery in a similar fashion to his contemporaries Macewen and Horsley.

Harvey Cushing (1869–1939), together with a fellow student at Harvard School of Medicine, Amory Codman, designed the first charts for recording pulse, temperature, and respiration during anesthesia. These ether charts were introduced in 1894. In 1900, Cushing, whilst on a visit to Italy, saw the Riva-Rocci blood pressure apparatus in use in Padua. On his return to the United States, blood pressure recordings were added to his new anesthesia record [18, 19]. It is amusing to read that shortly after his innovation, the Harvard School of Medicine decided that the skilled finger was of much greater value clinically than any pneumatic instrument [20].

Meanwhile in Paris the French neurosurgeon, Thierrey de Martel (1876–1940), had adopted a surgical technique that was to bedevil neuroanesthetists to the present day. Namely, the use of the sitting position for brain surgery. In 1913, de Martel combined the sitting position with local anesthesia for all major intracranial and spinal surgery. At that time, his colleagues were divided between the use of the lateral and prone positions for surgery. Frazier preferred the lateral position with head up tilt (Fig 1). Cushing favored the prone position with head up tilt and designed a special outrigger to support the patient's head and shoulders. W.J. Gardener at the Cleveland Clinic championed the use of the sitting position [21]. Given the disadvantages of the sitting position (hypotension, venous air embolism) plus the present day medicolegal climate on both sides of the Atlantic, it may be that the sitting position will go the way of ether, chloroform, and ethyl chloride.

Patient positioning was just one of the many problems faced by these early neurosurgeons. Cushing and others were well aware of the danger inherent in having an anesthetist who was unversed in the ways of neurosurgery. In an article written in 1909, he described anesthesia as follows:

> Among the numerous details of a cranial operation there is one thing I particularly wish to dwell on—the administration of the anesthetic. In cranial operations in particular, not only because of the cramped field and the need of a covering for the anesthetist, but also because the cardiorespiratory centers in the medulla are often already embarrassed through

Fig 1. *Patient positioned for posterior fossa surgery.*

pressure, anesthetization by an expert is absolutely essential. There are trials enough for the surgeon in these cases without the added anxiety in regard to narcosis. For the past few years Dr. S. Griffith Davis, who devotes his time almost exclusively to this work, has greatly lightened these responsibilities for me by anesthetising all my neurologic patients. It is due entirely to his skill that in over three hundred cranial operations there has been complete absence of calamities usually assigned to anesthesia. Owing to the difficulty in cranial work of shutting of the anesthetist from the operative field, many have advocated rectal or other bizarre forms of administering the various drugs employed for this purpose; but we have been so free from accidents on this score and have learned to arrange so securely the operative sheets as to make a hood which effectually conceals the anesthetist and leaves exposed only the immediate small field of operation, that we have clung to the more familiar and, I think safer method of inhalation anesthesia [22].

In the same article, he goes on to say:

With a patient in this prone position it is difficult for the anesthetist to gauge fully the variations in cardiac action, and during the past six months Dr. Davis has employed in these, as in all other operations indeed, a simple device, so satisfactory that we wonder why it has not long since come into general use—namely, the continuous auscultation of cardiac and respiratory rhythm during the entire course of anesthesia. The idea arose from a practice in the Hunterian Laboratory of auscultating the heart during the production of experimental valvular lesions, and like other things has been carried from laboratory to clinic. The transmitter of a phonendo-

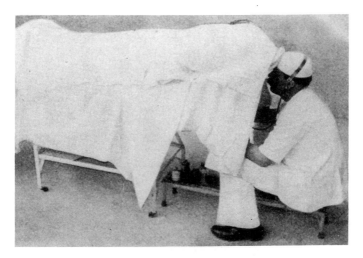

Fig 2. *Note use of phonendoscope for continuous auscultation of cardiac and respiratory rhythm.*

scope is secured by adhesive strips over the precordium and connects by a long tube with the anesthetist's ear, where the receiver is held by a device similar to a telephone operator's headgear. Uninterrupted information of the patient's condition is thus given, and the anesthetist need not disengage a hand for the occasional palpation of the pulse, which is all that he is usually expected to do (Fig 2). On several occasions, by the prompt appreciation of change in heart beat or respiration thus acquired, it has been possible to avert what otherwise might have been surgical disasters, owing to the immediate warning which led to the cessation of certain disturbing manipulations [22].

The remarks directed toward bizarre ways of administering ether may have referred to another giant of neurosurgery, Dr Charles Frazier (1870–1936). In an article on cranial surgery (1909), Dr Frazier writes:

In operations on the central nervous system and, more particularly, in subtentorial lesions, with the cardia and respiratory centers often just on the verge of a breakdown, so that even comparatively slight insults are not tolerated, a greater responsibility rests on the anesthetizer than in any other class of cases, except perhaps in those grave toxemias, as of peritonitis. So important in this feature of cranial operations that under no circumstances should an operation be undertaken unless the services of a skilled anesthetizer are available. This problem has been met in my service at the University Hospital by the appointment of a permanent salaried official, a graduate nurse, who gives her entire time to the work and has proved eminently satisfactory. In addition to the anesthetizer, the operating staff includes an assistant, whose duty it is solely to observe and record the blood pressure at frequent intervals throughout the operation. With these precautions one may proceed with the operation with the fullest assurance that the condition of the patient is being carefully watched and that one's attention will be drawn at once to the first suggestion of any alarming symptoms [23].

Like Cushing, he again recognized the importance of having a dedicated anesthetizer. In his case it was Miss Leta Hitz who proposed colonic ether as a suitable method of anesthesia for operations on brain and spinal cord. This method was enthusiastically taken up by Dr Frazier [24].

It was believed that women anesthetists would be more reliable than their male physician counterparts and William Bingham in his review article on the early history of neurosurgical anesthesia, describes a report to the staff of the Pennsylvania Hospital in 1910:

> The Surgical Staff . . . are unanimously agreed that the best interests of the Hospital should be served by employing a woman anaesthetist. She should not be a physician because any physician so employed only takes the position and holds it as a means of further advancement and drops it as soon as she can better herself, and a woman other than a physician so employed would feel that it was a permanent occupation and would conscientiously advance in usefulness [25].

In 1901 a Miss Ross was selected to become the first nurse anesthetist at the Hospital of the University of Pennsylvania and unknowingly began a schism between two branches of our profession, the nurse anesthetist and the anesthesiologist. The term anesthesiology was coined by Seifert in 1902, but it was not until 1945 that the title, American Society of Anesthetists Inc. was changed to the American Society of Anesthesiologists. In the United Kingdom, this division never occurred as anesthesia was always administered by physicians. However, it was readily apparent that the early neurosurgeons recognized the need for an expert anesthetizer, male or female, nurse or physician, who would be dedicated to the field of neurosurgery.

When Harvey Cushing left Johns Hopkins in 1912 to go to the Peter Brent Bingham, his anesthesiologist, Dr Davis, remained at Baltimore, and Dr Walter Boothby became Cushing's chief anesthetist. In turn Dr Boothby was succeeded by Miss Gertrude Gerrard who remained with Dr Cushing until his retirement in 1932 [26].

With regard to anesthetic agents, Cushing and his contemporaries preferred ether over chloroform. However, Cushing was unhappy with ether because of its obvious drawbacks such as bleeding, excitement, headache, and postoperative vomiting. Chloroform, on the other hand, produced a fall in blood pressure, minimal headache, and virtually no postoperative vomiting, and thus, he moved away from general anesthesia and toward regional anesthesia for his craniotomies [27]. The following was written in 1918:

During the shaving of the head, possibly an hour before the patient's turn will come, a sedative is given, a third of a grain of omnopon usually being sufficient, though this may be repeated if the patient is very restless or obstreperous. Then fifteen or twenty minutes before the operations, in the lines of proposed incision, the scalp is infiltrated with a 1 per cent novocain and adrenalin (15 drops to 30c.cm) solution, injected in the subaponeurotic layer.

There exists a difference of opinion regarding the relative merits of a general versus local anesthesia for cranial operations. The writer confesses to an original prejudice in favour of inhalation narcosis, but experience has led him completely to alter this view.

General narcosis increases intracranial tension, which exaggerates the difficulties of an operation already difficult enough. It increases bleeding from the scalp, which, with the adrenalin-novocain solution, is rendered negligible. It encourages the use of rougher methods, which a patient under local anesthesia would not tolerate, and which therefore are in all likelihood harmful. It encourages speed, which is to be decried if employed at the expense of delicacy. It leaves many patients, particularly those with threatened respiratory difficulties, in a condition in which inhalation troubles are prone to occur. . . . It is very rare, and then only in the case of semiconscious patients or those with restless irritability, that the operation cannot be carried through under local anesthesia, though this necessitates more gentle manipulations than those usually employed, particularly during the process of removing the area of cranial involvement [28].

His remarks on the speed of surgery are amusing in view of the comments of his contemporaries as will be seen later in this chapter.

In general the use of local anesthesia predominated for the next decade with Harvey Cushing and his contemporaries (De Martel, Dandy, Olivecrona, and Frazier) extolling the virtues of local anesthesia. At least a decade would pass before the pendulum would swing back and general anesthesia would become accepted as the method of choice for cerebral surgery.

These early surgeons realized that control of the airway and the remote location from the site of the operation were major problems facing the anesthetist. Rather than being at the head of the operating table with the patient supine, the anesthetist frequently was placed to the side of the patient and required to maintain the airway from there (Fig 3). A more unpleasant scenario has the patient prone so that the anesthetist would "often for keeping unobstructed respiration he will have to prop the chin up by a hand kept under the towels throughout, and a small prop between the patient's teeth may be necessary to act as a fulcrum against which to exert the necessary pull on the lower jaw" [28]. As we will see later, in Dr Cushing's clinic the anesthetist was completely shut off from the surgical field by drapes. To make matters somewhat worse, as Dr Langton Hewer points out:

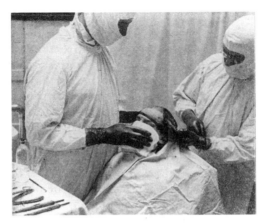

Fig 3. *Placement of anesthetist during craniotomy. Note gowned, gloved, and masked anesthetist (1909).*

the demands made by cranial surgery upon anaesthesia have increased very greatly in the last few years. When the late Sir Victor Horsley first made craniotomy a relatively safe operation in this country, a duration of half an hour was rarely exceeded, and chloroform was a perfectly satisfactory anaesthetic. This "rapid" technique was developed by the late Sir Percy Sargent and others who extended the scope of cranial surgery considerably, and though extensive tumours were removed, the time of operation was usually under one and a half hours. Ether, generally administered by the endotracheal route, gave excellent results in such cases. More recently, however, the "slow" method, in which Dr. Harvey Cushing has taken such a prominent part, has, to a certain extent, come into vogue. In one well-known clinic the average duration of major cranial operations is five hours, whilst a time of twelve hours has on occasion been exceeded. The vexed question as to whether the end-results justify the immense time taken by surgeons of the "slow" school is of great interest, but cannot with propriety be discussed in a book of this nature. There is no doubt, however, that these excessively long operations have profoundly modified anaesthetic technique, since the continued use of lipid soluble drugs, such as chloroform or ether, is not permissible, as severe toxic symptoms may ensue. The other difficulties which confront the anaesthetist are the impossibility of approaching the face when the operation has started and the patient's position, which may be extremely awkward [29].

Prior to the use of insufflation anesthesia and then subsequently the advent of endotracheal anesthesia, the mechanics of keeping the mask applied to the patient's face must have been extremely difficult to say the least. As Blomfeld writes in his text: "The surgeon's arrangements frequently make the use of a drop bottle highly inconvenient, if not impossible, for head operations. Either a Vernon Harcourt with long tube, or some form of pumping apparatus separated from its face-mask by a long tube is necessary" [28]. Even with this arrangement it was still necessary for the anesthesiologist to be close to the patient in order to control the airway. The stage was set for respiratory obstruction with concomitant hypoxia and hypercarbia and obviously less than ideal operating conditions for the surgeon. However, our pioneer anesthesia colleagues were nothing if not resourceful, and they improvised various methods of keeping the airway open, such as pulling the tongue forward, by use of a tongue clip or a suture. It was not until 1909 that Hewitt's pharyngeal airway was introduced.

As we have seen despite early work by Macewen and others, endotracheal intubation had not proved popular. In 1909 Meltzer and Auer described a method whereby a continuous stream of oxygen and air plus anesthetic vapor is blown into the trachea through a small bore tube [30]. It rapidly became the gold standard for anesthesiologists practicing in the era 1910–1940. Like everything else in life, insufflation anesthesia had its downside. For example, it could not guard the trachea against aspiration of blood, secretions, and foreign bodies. There was also the ever present danger of pressure build-up should the exit path of the gases be blocked, which could lead to overinflation and possible rupture of the lungs. However, insufflation anesthesia was a great step forward for our anesthesia colleagues, and the next step was to be a move away from endotracheal insufflation to endotracheal intubation following on the work by Rowbotham and Magill in England in 1921 [12]. The years 1928–1932 saw the decline of insufflation anesthesia and its replacement by endotracheal anesthesia. In England, Challis and his colleagues were the first to use endotracheal inhalation for neurosurgery in 1933 at the London Hospital. The advantage of the cuffed endotracheal tube in giving patients a clear airway would have brought tears of delight to those early neurosurgeons who stressed the importance of an adequate airway.

A fascinating read can be culled from the discussion on anesthetics in intracranial surgery published in 1933 [31]. It should be noted that for reasons that are particularly English, surgeons in the United Kingdom are known by the title Mr, all other physicians are called doctor. This discussion provides an interesting review of the anesthesia for cranial surgery in the United Kingdom. Mr Norman M. Dott records his practice:

> During ten years' work in connection with cerebral surgery, the methods which I have employed have been: from 1923 to 1925, ether vapour for inhalation; in 1926 local infiltration with novocain-adrenalin was added to the general anaesthesia; from 1926–1928, ether, mainly by the rectal route; 1929, local novocain-adrenalin anaesthesia with morphia; in 1929 and 1930 we returned to rectal ether; 1931, local novocain with morphia again; 1932 avertin with ether vapour; routine cocainization of throat added; 1932 and 1933 avertin-morphia. Naturally we made occasional trials of other methods, such as intravenous nembutal, gas-and-oxygen,

with various adjuvants, etc., but these methods were so much less satisfactory that they were never extensively employed.

To begin with we depended entirely on ether, administrated as vapour by a nasal or tracheal tube, to produce full surgical anaesthesia.

The few cases operated on under local anaesthesia soon taught us the local haemostatic advantage of novocain-adrenalin infiltration and we began to use it routinely along with ether. This was a real advance both for haemostasis and because a much lighter general anaesthesia could be used.

I must say that with inhalation ether we were not troubled by chest complication or by much post-anaesthetic vomiting, but ether anaesthesia often had to be carried to a depth otherwise unnecessary in order to abolish laryngeal irritation by the vapour.

This led us to give the ether per rectum, and after a short time preliminary rectal injection of paraldehyde was added to our practice. This produced a primary drowsiness and an amnesia greatly facilitating induction, and it also gave some hours of drowsiness after operation with a quiet awakening. The rectal ether gave a smooth light anaesthesia without laryngeal irritation. We became increasingly impressed with the slack, easily mobilized brain and the absence of congestion in cases in which we tried local anaesthesia. We began to realize that ether, increasing the secretion of cerebrospinal fluid and often increasing the blood-pressure, was inimical to satisfactory conditions for cerebral operations, more especially when there was already increased intracranial pressure, and when exposure of the lesion required cerebral retraction, as in cerebella-pontile-angle or pituitary cases.

There are two classes of cases to which we have not yet extended the avertin-morphia method. Trigeminal neuralgia cases are operated on in semi-sitting posture and with head erect; most of the patients are elderly, and many have some degree of arteriosclerosis. In these conditions we have feared the consequences of the artificial fall in blood-pressure caused by avertin, and meantime we continue to use rectal ether or local anaesthesia in these cases also.

The avertin referred to is tribromethanol introduced in 1927. Its use was supplanted by the introduction of thiopental in 1934.

Dr Zebulon Mennell, perhaps the first British neuroanesthetist, was fortunate in being the anesthetist for Victor Horsley and Percy Sargent. It should be noted that the ambidextrous Horsley seldom took more than half an hour for his cranial cases, while Sargent took somewhat more time. One is left in awe. It was their successors who adopted the much decried slower methods of operating, described by Mennell as "slow motion" surgery. For this type of surgery, he switched to endotracheal inhalation using nitrous oxide and oxygen. His comments on speed of surgery make fascinating reading for those of us who routinely sit through 6- to 8-hour craniotomies. He bemoans the slow technique of some surgeons in the following extract:

Most of my work in the connection during the past thirty years has been done with the late Sir Percy Sargent, who had actually promised to take part in the present discussion. The slow technique adopted by some surgeons in recent years has altered the anaesthetist's outlook and methods. I represent work done in conjunction with the more rapid type of surgery, and it is, perhaps, difficult to accommodate my ideas and practice to the slower type. It is impossible to combine the two methods satisfactorily, either from the anaesthetist's or the patient's point of view. Anything taking over an hour or, at the outside, and a half, is what I call slow, and requires a different type of anaesthesia.

Chloroform was perfectly safe and satisfactory for Horsley, who never took over half an hour. Ether was best for Sargent, who never took over an hour and a half. But neither of these anaesthetics is satisfactory for the lengthy operations of from two to six hours, which are becoming commonplace.

Ether given by the plenum method, either intratracheal or intrapharyngeal, is my anaesthetic of choice for the quick operations. I recommend the use of atropine in large doses, and the avoidance of morphine.

In 1912–1914 I used intravenous hedonal for over two hundred head cases. My experience of this barbiturate did not make me give up ether, and when the intratracheal method was introduced into this country I discontinued hedonal entirely. The more modern nembutal and pernocton have not altered my opinion of the use of the barbiturates in head work. . . . For operations lasting longer than one and a half hours the choice must lie between continuous nitrous oxide, preferably by the intratracheal method, or local analgesia both necessitating previous medication. I think it does no harm giving some ether in the earlier stages of continuous gas-oxygen, and it is astonishing with modern machinery how quiet it is possible to keep patients, and, of course, the nitrous oxide has practically no effect on their condition.

The cases which are still a problem to me are those dreadful cases of extreme pressure, when it is almost impossible to induce anaesthesia on account of the shallow respiration. In such a case I use chloroform in high concentration, and directly there is relaxation, pass a catheter and use ether.

Mennel worked at the National Hospital for Nervous Diseases in London. It has now been renamed the National Hospital for Neurology and Neurosurgery (Fig 4). An English neuroanesthetist, Dr Stuart Ingram, tells the story of how his father-in-law, a retired thoracic surgeon, was taught anesthesia by Dr Mennel at St Thomas Hospital in London. In these days Mennel instructed the house staff in the art of anesthesia before they were let loose on the public. Mennel insisted that they use only ether, but it was well known to the house staff that Mennel added a goodly measure of chloroform to the inhaler. This of course had the effect of smoothing out his induction of anesthesia when demonstrating before his students [32].

Dr J.F. Ryan was also fortunate in working mainly with fast surgeons.

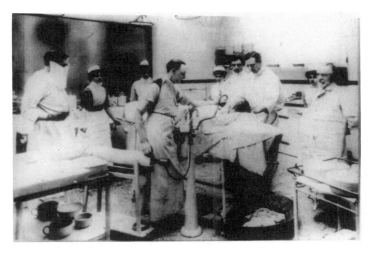

Fig 4. *Operating room scene (1906) at the National Hospital for Nervous Diseases, Queen Square, London. Dr Llewelyn Powell is seen using the Vernon-Harcourt inhaler. Also included are Dr Victor Horsley at left and Professor Theodore Kocher to right. Photograph by kind permission of Dr Stuart Ingram and the National Hospital for Nervous Diseases now called National Hospital for Neurology and Neurosurgery.*

His comments on manipulation in the region of the medulla are still pertinent today.

My experience of anaesthetics in cranial surgery has been confined almost entirely to the more rapid type of operation. I have given anaesthetics in more than 400 of these cases, most of them at the National Hospital, Queen Square. In about 300 of them endotracheal ether was used.

The type of anaesthesia is essentially a very light one; this is made possible by the perfect airway afforded by the intratracheal catheter whatever the position of the patient, and by the constant strength of ether vapour which can be delivered quietly and under low pressure by means of a motor pump. If the catheter is securely fixed so that it remains perfectly still between the vocal cords, it is surprising how very light an anaesthesia it is possible to maintain without the assistance of any pre medication, except, of course, the usual dose of atropine. Any movement of the catheter will produce coughing which is not permissible in these cases; it can be stitched in position to the angle of the mouth, or it is quite easily held there by means of a towel clip. The use of the intratracheal method has the obvious advantage of providing for the immediate delivery if required, of oxygen or of carbon dioxide and oxygen. If by any chance the anaesthesia becomes too light, it is quite a simple matter to increase the concentration of the ether vapour in the presence of a little carbon dioxide without causing the patient to cough. Apart from passing interference with the rhythm of respiration, due to manipulation in the region of the medulla or to alteration of intracranial tension on opening the dura, only one of my cases caused anxiety from the point of view of respiratory failure.

The chief criticisms which have been offered to ether anaesthesia in cranial surgery are that it causes: (1) Swelling and increased vascularity of the brain due to congestion following induction and to the direct irritant effect of ether. (2) Increase of shock from the amount of ether used. (3) Vomiting with the possible risk of producing bleeding in a previously dry operative field. (4) Post-Anaesthetic chest complications. The swelling and congestion of the brain can well understand if the anaesthesia is an uneven one, given in the presence of an imperfect airway, possibly after a bad induction.

Of interest are his comments on patient comfort. "The personal comfort of the patient is of little importance in head cases, for the majority of these patients worry very little about the anaesthetic or the operation, a considerable number of them being in too confused a state to worry much about anything and the others glad to have something done for them." The less caring and less sensitive part of one's nature wonders as to how easy it must have been to practice anesthesia in that era.

Dr J.H.T. Challis, who extolled the virtues of adding carbon dioxide to an anesthetic mix but for some reason did not approve of cocainizing the airway, did have some pertinent comments regarding accessibility of the patient:

> The intratracheal tube, having been introduced, is attached to a Magill bag and outlet valve connected with any gas-oxygen-ether apparatus available. Boyle's with dry flow meter, being that of choice.
>
> Once the patient is arranged for operation, it is only with the utmost difficulty that one can get a good look at his face, as the eyes are covered with gutta-percha, and the whole head and face—with the exception of the nose and mouth—are draped in sterile towels. One hand and arm are left exposed to enable the anesthetist to obtain various data throughout the operation. As early as possible he proceeds to record blood-pressure and pulse and respiration rates, and he continues to chart his reading every five minutes during the operation. Depth of anaesthesia is judged entirely by the movements of the Magill bag and by the colour of the exposed hand and of the site of the operation.
>
> After the operation is concluded, if there has been no undue loss of blood or shock during its performance, the patient should cough on removal of the intratracheal tube and respond to requests to open his eyes, or to put out his tongue, within five minutes of the discontinuance of the anaesthetic.

The discussion ended with Mr Cecil P.E. Wakeley stating that he used local anesthesia combined with ether intratracheal gas and oxygen and avertin for all his neurological operations. This 1933 discussion could well be described as the watershed in the development of neuroanesthesia, for "the best is yet to come" could well have been the unspoken thoughts of our neurosurgical and anesthesia colleagues as the 1930s drew to a close. The next decades would see radical changes in the diagnosis and treatment of lesions of the central and peripheral nervous systems. Electrodiagnostic studies would become part and parcel of daily life in the neurosurgical operating rooms. Electroencephalograms, evoked potentials, electromyography, etc, would all move from the laboratory and clinic setting to the operating rooms. Neuroradiology would make enormous progress with the increasing use of computerized axial tomography, magnetic resonance imaging, myelography, and angiography. To this list can be added the introduction of the operating room microscope and the advent of stereotactic brain surgery and radio surgery. At the same time, the anesthesia world was also enjoying its own boom. Thiopental was introduced in 1934, and as we have seen, endotracheal anesthesia had been introduced and would be increasingly and widely used following the arrival of curare in 1942. With the introduction of halothane in 1952, neuroanesthesiologists now had some marvelous clinical tools. However, it was the introduction of a quantitative method to measure cerebral blood flow and metabolic cerebral rates in man (1945) by Kety and Schmidt [33] together with intracranial pressure measurement introduced by Lundberg [34] that put neuroanesthesia practice on a scientific foundation and opened the doors to neuroanesthesia research.

Given all the advances in the fields of interventional radiology, stereotactic surgery, and now endoscopic surgery, it could be that craniotomy as we know it may become an operation of the past, and future generations of anesthesiologists may look back in wonderment when they read of the anesthetic accomplishments required of their predecessors.

■ References

1. O'Connor D, Walker AE. Prologue. In: Walker AE, ed. A history of neurological surgery. Baltimore: The Williams and Wilkins Company, 1951:1–22
2. Lee JA, Atkinson RS. A synopsis of anesthesia. 6th ed. Bristol: John Wright and Sons, Ltd, 1968
3. Researches. Chemical and philosophical; chiefly concerning nitrous oxide. London: J. Johnson, 1800
4. Long CW. An account of the first use of sulphuric ether by inhalation as an anaesthetic in surgical operations. South Med Surg J 1849;5:705–713
5. Sykes WS. Essays on the first hundred years of anaesthesia. Edinburgh: E. & S. Livingstone 1961; Vols I and II
6. Lee JA, Atkinson RS. A synopsis of anesthesia. 6th ed. Bristol: John Wright & Sons, Ltd, 1968:177–186
7. Harcourt AG Vernon. Discussion on chloroform and anaesthesia. Br Med J 1903; 2:142
8. Macewen W. Intracranial lesions. Lancet 1881;2:581–583. Reprint: J Neurosurg 1962;19:803
9. Macewen W. Clinical observations on the introduction of tracheal tubes by the

mouth instead of performing tracheotomy or laryngectomy. Brit Med J July 24, 1880

10. Frost EAM. After 1880. The developers. In: Atkinson RS, Boulton TB, eds. The history of anesthesia. Camforth Lancs: Royal Society of Medicine Services and The Parthenon Publishing Group, 1987: chap 25

11. Adson AW. Observations of intratracheal anesthetics in neurologic surgery. Am J Surg Anesthesia Supplement 1919;XXXIII:123

12. Rowbotham ES, Magill IW. Anaesthetics in the plastic surgery of the face and jaws. Proc Roy Soc Med 1921;14:17

13. Holmes G. The National Hospital, Queen's Square 1860–1948 Edinburgh: Livingstone, 1954

14. Horsley V. Brian surgery. Brit Med J 1886;2:670–675

15. Special Chloroform Committee of the British Medical Association. Third report of proceedings. Brit Med J 1904;2:161–171

16. The work of the Chloroform Committee Forum. Brit Med J July 22, 1911:178–179

17. Flagg PJ. The art of anesthesia. 2nd ed. Philadelphia & London: J.B. Lippincott, 1919

18. Cushing HW. On avoidance of shock in major amputations by cocainization of large nerve trunks preliminary to their division. With observations on blood pressure changes in surgical cases. Ann Surg 1902;36:321–345

19. Cushing HW. On routine determinations of arterial tension in operating room and clinic. Boston Med Surg J 1903;148:250–256

20. Fulton JF. Harvey Cushing—a biography. Springfield, IL: Charles C. Thomas, 1946:69

21. Gardner WJ. Intracranial operations in the sitting position. Ann Surg 1935;101:138–145

22. Cushing H. Some principles of cerebral surgery. JAMA 1909;184–194

23. Frazier C. Problems & procedures in cranial surgery. JAMA 1909;52:1805–1813

24. Frazier C. Colonic anaesthesia in operations upon brain and spinal cord. Ann Surg 1928;87:161–172

25. Bingham W. The early history of neurosurgical anesthesia. J Neurosurg 1973;39:

26. Thatcher VS. History of anesthesia. Philadelphia: Lippincott, 1953:568–584

27. Cushing H. Notes on penetrating wounds of the brain. Brit Med J 1918;1:221

28. Blomfield J. Anaesthetics in practice and theory. London: Wm. Heinman, 1922:256

29. Hewer L, ed. Recent advances in anesthesia and analgesia. 2nd ed. London: J. & A. Churchill Ltd, 1937; Chap 14:169–173

30. Meltzer SJ, Auer J. Continuous respiration without respiratory movements. J Exp Med 1909;11:622

31. Section on anaesthetics discussion on anaesthesia in intracranial surgery. Proc R Soc Med 1933;954–958

32. Ingram S. Personal communication, 1996

33. Kety SS, Schmidt CF. The determination of cerebral blood flow in man and the use of nitrous oxide in low concentrations. Am J Physiol 1945;143:53

34. Lundberg N. Continuous recording and control of ventricular fluid pressure in neurosurgical practice. Acta Psychiatr Neurol Scand 1960;36:(suppl 149):10–193

Preoperative Evaluation of the Adult Neurosurgical Patient

■ Stephen P. Fischer, MD

Preoperative knowledge of the pathophysiological characteristics of neurosurgical disorders is essential for the formulation of an anesthetic plan for intra- and postoperative patient management. The goal of this chapter is to provide the clinical information needed to rationally approach the preoperative evaluation of the neurosurgical patient. Several associated medical conditions such as cardiac dysfunction and hemodynamic changes may occur with primary neurosurgical disorders and will be reviewed. A suggested protocol for screening and enhanced preoperative neurological examinations will be presented together with suggested preoperative laboratory and diagnostic studies for the neurosurgical patient.

■ Preoperative Neurological Examination

The purpose of the neurological examination for the anesthesiologist is: (1) to determine the general location and extent of the neurological lesion, (2) to document in the anesthesia record the presence or absence of nervous system malfunction for perioperative comparison, (3) to determine and record the patient's preoperative physical status and stability, and (4) to develop an appropriate anesthesia management plan. Preoperative neurological assessment involves evaluation of both peripheral and central nervous system function. The neurological examination should be performed in exactly the same manner each time, proceeding from higher to lower levels of integration so that no step is omitted. Very little specialized equipment is required and a portion of the examination, for example, tests for general cerebral function, can be accomplished while taking the patient's history. The preoperative physical examination of other organ systems (e.g., pulmonary, cardiac, etc) should be done before the neurological examination in order to integrate other physical findings with the presenting neurological abnormality. For example, a patient hyperventilating secondary to severe emphysema may have neurological evidence of altered mental status, paresthesias, carpopedal spasm, tetany, and dizziness. The primary medical disorder in this case is pulmonary and not neurological.

The Screening Neurological Examination

An abbreviated neurological evaluation for the patient without apparent neurological disease should be performed in all patients undergoing anesthesia. If an anesthesia technique (general or regional) can affect an organ system, then that organ system should be evaluated and documented preoperatively by the anesthesiologist. To screen the musculoskeletal or motor system, observe the patient's gait, ability to perform toe and heel walk, and ability to maintain the arms held forward and evaluate the patient's grip strength. Sensory system screening includes the physical distinction of vibration, pain, and light touch on the patient's hands, feet, and limbs. Superficial reflexes and reflexes of the deep tendons can be assessed easily and quickly. Cranial nerve abnormalities can often be elicited by patient history and by observation. Mental status (appearance, mood, thought processes, cognitive function) and speech pattern are typically revealed by interaction with the patient.

The Enhanced Neurological Examination

A focused neurological exam for patients who are known to have neurological disorders is described in this section.

Tests for Cerebral Function General cerebral abnormalities may cause disturbances in emotional status, communication, intellectual performance, behavior, and level of consciousness. Specific cerebral function testing such as sensory interpretations (the recognition of objects by sight, sound, and touch), motor integration (the ability to carry out a purposeful physical action), and language (the understanding and communication in spoken or written form) can reveal specific cortical areas of dysfunction (e.g., frontal, parietal, temporal, or occipital lobes).

Cranial Nerve Evaluation Detailed testing of all twelve cranial nerves (CN) can be reviewed in a standard medical textbook. Six of the cranial nerves when dysfunctional can affect patient management during anesthesia.

The olfactory nerve (CN I) controls the sensation of smell. The loss of smell (anosmia) without nasal disease or inflammation suggests a frontal lobe or pituitary lesion, meningitis, hydrocephalus or an anterior fossa skull fracture. Anesthesia implications include increased intracranial pressure (ICP), cerebral hemorrhage, and signs and symptoms of meningeal infection.

Testing: Evaluate each nostril separately, asking the patient to identify some common odors.

The oculomotor nerve (CN III) controls pupillary size and the response to light. Preoperative pupil size should be recorded to provide baseline data for subsequent assessment of anesthetic depth, narcotic effect, and for comparison with postoperative pupil changes.

Testing: Perform a bilateral comparison of pupil size and reaction of both pupils to a bright light.

Patients with trigeminal neuralgia (CN V) have unilateral symptoms usually confined to the second (maxillary) or third (mandibular) division of this nerve. Symptoms are characterized by sudden, lightening-like paroxysms of severe pain. Most trigeminal neuralgia is probably caused by compression of the nerve by tortuous posterior fossa arteries. The anesthesiologist can precipitate an attack of pain if the face mask touches trigger zones around the lips or buccal cavity. Severe pain and deviation of the mandible to one side can occur with mouth opening in patients with trigeminal neuralgia. Consequently, patients may be reluctant to open their mouth fully during examination or at the time of anesthesia induction.

Testing: Motor—examine bilateral strength of temporal and masseter muscles while the patient clenches his or her teeth.
Sensory—with the patient's eyes closed, test forehead, cheeks, and jaw for light touch and temperature (alcohol wipe) sensations.

The facial nerve (CN VII) innervates muscles for facial expression, mobility, and symmetry and provides sensory innervation for taste sensation. The facial nerve may be damaged by face mask pressure, surgery, or positioning. A baseline evaluation and documentation of any abnormality is appropriate prior to anesthesia induction.

Testing: Motor—evaluate patient's ability to raise eyebrows, frown and smile, close eyes tight, and puff cheeks.

The glossopharyngeal nerve (CN IX) supplies sensory fibers to the mucosa of the pharynx and soft palate. Glossopharyngeal dysfunction can cause severe pain that is similar to trigeminal neuralgia. The trigger zone lies in the posterior pharynx and tonsillar area. Stimulation of this area with an oral airway or laryngoscope can result in severe pain locally that spreads toward the angle of the jaw and ear. Additionally, patients with CN IX disorders can experience reflex bradycardia and hypotension during pain episodes, secondary to intense afferent discharge of the glossopharyngeal nerve.

Testing: Palatal reflex—stroke each side of the mucous membrane of the uvula. The side touched should rise if the nerve is intact.
Pharyngeal gag reflex—touch posterior pharynx with tongue depressor to elicit gag.

The vagus nerve (CN X) supplies motor fibers to the pharynx, soft palate, larynx, and trachea. The motor and sensory supply of the trachea and larynx are the superior and recurrent laryngeal branches of the vagus nerve. Hoarseness of the voice may indicate vocal cord paralysis. The anesthesiologist may observe tachycardia in patients with a damaged vagus nerve.

Testing: Observe patient's ability to swallow and speak without hoarseness and the movement of the patient's soft palate symmetrically when saying "ah."

Cerebellar Function   Balance and coordination are controlled by the cerebellum. Disturbance in physical movements, tremor, and ataxia suggest cerebellar insult (tumor, ischemia, infarction). Evidence of cerebellar damage is suggested when a patient demonstrates ataxia especially with the eyelids opened.

The Motor System   Muscle strength, tone, and size should be evaluated for asymmetry. Additionally, increased resistance to passive muscle stretching is observed in upper motor neuron lesions and in Parkinson's disease. There are anesthesia management concerns in patients with upper motor neuron diseases, hemiplegia, and paraplegia. For example, succinylcholine given to these patients may precipitate a hyperkalemic response.

The Sensory System   Evaluation of the peripheral sensory system is important before any regional anesthetic technique. The patient's ability to discriminate temperature and pinprick sensation will be used to determine if a regional procedure is successful. A patient with diabetes, for example, may have impaired sensation, especially in the lower extremities. Upper or lower extremity dysfunction (motor or sensory) may suggest that a regional anesthesia technique is undesirable.

Reflex Testing   There are three types of muscle reflexes, categorized as deep, superficial, and pathological. The site of the reflex stimulus and response corresponds to a specific central nervous system (CNS) segment. The deep tendon reflexes, including biceps (cervical level 5, 6), patellar (lumbar level 2, 3, 4), and achilles (sacral level 1, 2), are easily tested. Superficial reflexes also delineate CNS segment functionality and are tested by stroking the skin with an object such as a tongue depressor. For example, the upper abdominal reflex corresponds to thoracic segments 7, 8, and 9. The lower abdominal reflex relates to thoracic segments 11 and 12. Increased reflexes are observed in patients with hyperthyroidism and upper motor neuron disease. Decreased reflexes such as a slowed relaxation phase in the ankle reflex are observed in hypothyroidism. Patients with clinical signs and symptoms of hypo- and hyperthyroidism present an increased concern for the anesthesiologist.

The most common pathological reflex is the Babinski sign, which is performed by stroking the lateral aspect of the sole of the foot. In pyramidal tract or upper motor neuron disease, a dorsiflexion of the big toe occurs (in addition to fanning of the toes) indicating the presence of the Babinski reflex.

■ Craniotomy for Intracranial Tumors

Preoperative Evaluation

Intracranial tumors present preoperatively according to their growth rate, size, location, and the consequences of intracranial pressure [1]. Slow growing tumors may present with few symptoms. A rapidly expanding mass often evokes acute neurological compromise with readily apparent symptoms. The preoperative assessment of a patient presenting with an intracranial tumor is directed toward determining if increased ICP is present. Table 1 lists the etiologies of increased intercranial pressure.

Signs and symptoms of increased ICP include: (1) nausea and emesis, (2) headache, often worsened by cough, (3) altered mental status, (4) decreased alertness, (5) hypertension, (6) seizures, (7) visual disturbances, (8) papilledema, (9) unilateral pupillary dilation, (10) abducens (CN VI) or oculomotor (CN III) palsy, and (11) neck rigidity. If the abducens nerve is involved, the patient will be unable to look laterally with the involved eye. Oculomotor nerve dysfunction prevents the patient from looking down, up, or medially.

As ICP continues to increase, there may be evidence of brain herniation, manifested by: (1) apnea, (2) dilated and unreactive pupils, (3) contralateral hemiplegia, (4) decreased consciousness, and (5) bradycardia. A preoperative neurological assessment should be documented, and an electrocardiogram should be obtained to document bradycardia or other rate-related cardiac changes suggesting ischemia or conduction deficits.

The preoperative evaluation for pituitary tumors [2] should include

Table 1. *Etiologies of Increased Intracranial Pressure*

Cerebrovascular hemorrhage
Intracranial tumor
Head trauma
Infection
Hypertensive and metabolic encephalopathy
Hydrocephalus
Cerebral ischemia (with cerebral edema)

assessment of endocrine dysfunction, fluid and electrolyte status, visual loss, headache, and cardiac disease. There is an increased association of coronary artery disease and cardiac hypertrophy in patients with pituitary tumors. Patients may also manifest signs and symptoms of Cushing's disease, which includes hypertension, diabetes, mental status changes, and muscle weakness. Patients may already be taking corticosteroids, diuretics, and anticonvulsant medications to decrease the potential for increased ICP. Each of these drugs can have an effect on the anesthesia perioperative management plan.

Many neurological procedures require unusual patient positions such as prone or sitting [3, 4]. The sitting position, as with posterior fossa surgery, presents the potential for postural hypotension in patients who are often volume depleted from diuresis and fluid restriction. Preoperative evaluation of the patient's volume status is imperative.

■ Craniotomy for Vascular Diseases

Preoperative Evaluation

Neurosurgical vascular lesions include intracranial aneurysms and arteriovenous malformations (AVM). The patient with an intracranial aneurysm [5] may demonstrate preoperative signs and symptoms of a nonspecific nature, depending on whether or not the aneurysm has previously bled. Patients may report headaches, orbital pain, dizziness, and mild sensory or motor abnormalities. With the rupture of an intracranial aneurysm, the presenting signs and symptoms are usually similar to hemorrhage in the subarachnoid space [6–8] or of a rapidly expanding intracranial tumor. A patient may manifest signs and symptoms of: (1) increased ICP secondary to hemorrhage, (2) focal neurological signs, (3) a depressed level of consciousness, (4) nausea and emesis, (5) hypothermia, (6) the triad of meningeal irritation (photophobia, headache, and meningismus), (7) cranial nerve palsies, and (8) seizures. Additionally, a ruptured intracranial aneurysm with increased ICP may affect the electrocardiogram causing ST-segment elevation or depression, the presence of U waves, a prolonged QT interval and T-wave inversion or flattening. These changes usually do not correlate with cardiac instability during the neurosurgical procedure [9, 10]. Preoperatively, the primary focus should be directed toward controlling systemic hypertension. Additional laboratory findings of coagulopathies [11], leukocytosis, glycosuria, and proteinuria may occur in these patients.

The preoperative evaluation of patients with arteriovenous malformations is similar to patients with aneurysms. The anesthesiologist inquires about a history of seizures, the signs and symptoms of intracranial hemorrhage, and hypertension. Occasionally, a large AVM can precipitate high output cardiac failure secondary to high AVM flow.

■ Carotid Thromboendarterectomy

Preoperative Evaluation

Patients presenting with carotid artery [12, 13] or vertebrobasilar arterial disease usually have manifested signs or symptoms of either a transient ischemic attack (TIA) or a completed stroke [14, 15]. There is an associated higher incidence of hypertension and coronary artery and valvular heart disease in patients presenting with cerebrovascular occlusive disorders. A careful cardiovascular evaluation is imperative, including comparison of the current electrocardiogram with previous tracings. Uncontrolled systemic hypertension should be treated preoperatively without lowering blood pressure to a level that precipitates ischemic symptoms. There is also an association of cerebrovascular occlusive disease with diabetes mellitus [16]. Cerebral and lacunar infarction occurs with the thrombotic or embolic occlusion of a cerebral vessel. The neurological deficits are related to the particular vessel(s) involved and the extent of any collateral circulation. TIAs are characterized by focal ischemic deficits that usually last from minutes up to 2 hours [17, 18]. Approximately 30% of patients with a history of stroke have had TIAs. Table 2 reviews the clinical findings of a patient with TIAs. Since TIAs are transient, patients may have a normal exam at the time of their assessment.

Patients with cerebral infarction secondary to carotid artery occlusion may present various neurological deficits including: (1) contralateral extremity motor and sensory loss, (2) vertigo, (3) diplopia, (4) amnesia, (5) presence of a contralateral grasp reflex (a clawing movement of the patient's fingers to stroking the palmar surface), and (6) behavioral changes (often best described by the family). Patients who progress to a completed intercerebral stroke secondary to embolic ischemia or hemorrhage may manifest additional signs of increased ICP, cerebral edema, coagulopathies, stupor, or coma [19].

Patients may have symptoms of TIAs with certain head and neck positions. These patients usually have a history of severe cervical arthritis and

Table 2. *Signs and Symptoms of Transient Ischemic Attacks*

Carotid Territory	Vertebrobasilar Area
Contralateral arm, leg, face weakness with paresthesias or numbness	Weakness, paresthesias, or numbness in either or both sides
Dysphasia	Dysarthria
Monocular visual loss (contralateral to the affected limbs)	Diplopia, visual dimness, or blurring
Hyperreflexia	Ataxia
Extensor plantar response on the affected side	Drop attacks or falling to floor from leg weakness
	Vertigo

spondylosis. In the operating room, careful head positioning is essential to avoid precipitating cerebral ischemia. A carotid bruit may be present or absent in these patients [20, 21]. The diseased carotid artery should not be palpated during an examination to avoid the possibility of dislodging and embolizing a carotid plaque. Patients may indicate awareness of TIA symptoms associated with lowered blood pressure, for example, when taking antihypertensive medications. This information can provide the anesthesiologist with a lower blood pressure limit during surgery, to avoid the potential for cerebral ischemia.

■ Spinal Neuroanesthesia

Preoperative Evaluation

Spinal neurosurgery includes several operative procedures secondary to injury, tumor, spinal stenosis, and aging. There are similarities in the preoperative evaluation of these patients with signs and symptoms attributed to spinal cord or nerve root compression [22–24]. Often these patients are healthy and their first complaint is localized spinal segmental pain with or without radiation to an extremity. Patients with spinal nerve compression develop weakness and atrophy in muscle groups of the affected extremity. Patients should be evaluated preoperatively for changes in motor and sensory function in the affected extremities for postoperative comparison.

■ Craniotomy for Head Trauma

Preoperative Evaluation

The assessment of a patient presenting with a head injury is often influenced by the extent of the injury and whether it has caused open or closed skull trauma [25–27]. Associated trauma such as abdominal injuries and long bone fractures may be present. Patency of the airway, ventilation, and treatment of shock are the initial focus of the anesthesiologist. The preoperative evaluation is then primarily directed toward the absence or presence of increased ICP.

The Glasgow coma scale [28] (Table 3) can assist the anesthesiologist in head trauma patient evaluation and suggests the urgency of a patient's need for intubation and neurosurgical intervention [29]. The Glasgow coma scale assigns a score to functions of verbal response, motor response, and eye opening. Total points are utilized to indicate the status of a patient's neurological function and deficits.

In patients with acute head trauma, the preoperative evaluation must proceed concomitantly with management of unstable or urgent conditions [30]. Seizures may accompany cerebral trauma and suggest the expansion of an intracranial hematoma. Both hypertension and hypotension [31] are manifestations of head injuries and require immediate treatment. Comatose patients with decerebrate or decorticate posturing have severe hemispheric dysfunction and deterioration and probably require intubation.

Table 3. *Glasgow Coma Scale*

Response	Score*
Eye Opening	
Spontaneous	4
To speech	3
To pain	2
None	1
Best Motor Response	
Obeys	6
Localizes	5
Withdraws (flexion)	4
Abnormal flexion	3
Extensor response	2
None	1
Verbal Response	
Oriented	5
Confused conversation	4
Inappropriate words	3
Incomprehensible sounds	2
None	1

*Patients with a scale score less than 7 usually require intubation and hyperventilation. Approximately 50% of these patients die or remain in a vegetative state.

The preoperative assessment may be limited by the extreme urgency to proceed to the operating room. In addition to laboratory and diagnostic tests, a drug screen [32–34] should be performed in head trauma patients since illegal and prescription drugs may influence intra- and postoperative anesthesia management.

■ Cost-Effective Preoperative Laboratory and Diagnostic Testing

The value and utility of preoperative diagnostic studies have become a central issue in evaluating cost-effective health care in the surgical patient [35–40]. It is estimated that up to three billion dollars are spent in the United States annually in preoperative laboratory and diagnostic studies. The use of preoperative testing as a screening tool to detect disease and to determine stability of a patient for surgery has been the focus of numerous studies. These studies have compared the clinical yield from indicated versus unindicated preoperative testing for electrocardiograms [41], chest roentgenograms [42, 43], blood chemistries, and hematological studies [44, 45]. Additionally, the value of preoperative pulmonary function testing and the utility of bleeding time determination [46] has been questioned. Most studies conclude that unwarranted preoperative tests do not change perioperative care [41–47] and substantially contribute to increased hospital costs. Unnecessary testing is inefficient, expensive, and requires additional technical resources. Inappropriate studies may lead to evaluation of

Table 4. *Guidelines for Laboratory and Diagnostic Studies in Otherwise Healthy Neurosurgical Patients*

| | General Anesthesia | |
Age	Men	Women
12–39 y	None	CBC
		? Pregnancy test
40–49 y	Electrocardiogram	CBC
		? Pregnancy test
50–64 y	CBC	CBC
	Electrocardiogram	? Pregnancy test
		Electrocardiogram
65–74 y	CBC	CBC
	Electrocardiogram	Electrocardiogram
	Creatinine/BUN	Creatinine/BUN
	Glucose	Glucose
>74 y	CBC	CBC
	Electrocardiogram	Electrocardiogram
	Creatinine/BUN	Creatinine/BUN
	Glucose	Glucose
	? Chest roentgenogram	? Chest roentgenogram

Note: For operative procedures with anticipated significant blood loss, coagulation testing and a CBC are appropriate in all patients.
CBC = complete blood count; BUN = blood urea nitrogen.
Source: Modified from Roizen MF, Fischer SP. Preoperative evaluation for adults and children. In: Paul White, ed. Ambulatory anesthesia and surgery. London: Saunders, 1996 (in press).

borderline or false/positive laboratory abnormalities. This may result in unnecessary operating room delays, cancellations, and potential patient risks through additional testing and follow-up.

The neurosurgical patient will require preoperative laboratory and diagnostic studies consistent with his or her medical history, the proposed operative procedure, and potential for blood loss. Table 4 summarizes the recommended preoperative tests for the neurosurgical patient.

■ Summary

The purpose of this chapter is to provide the anesthesiologist with a focused review of the information needed to rationally approach the preoperative evaluation of the neurosurgical patient. The anesthesia preoperative assessment is a neuromedical evaluation of the patient's current condition integrated with the anesthesiologist's knowledge of the potential clinical and operative events that may occur.

The neurosurgical patient presents the anesthesiologist with significant clinical challenges in providing the most appropriate care and the best outcome possible. The foundation of this challenge begins with the anesthesia preoperative evaluation.

■ References

1. Black PM. Brain tumors. N Engl J Med 1991;324(21):1471–1476
2. Matjasko J. Perioperative management of patients with pituitary tumors. Seminars in Anesth 1984;111:155–167
3. Kenning JA, Toutant SM, Saunders RL. Upright patient positioning in the management of intracranial hypertension. Surg Neurol 1981;15:148–152
4. Lipe HP, Mitchell PH. Positioning the patient with intracranial hypertension: how turning and head rotation affect the internal jugular vein. Heart Lung 1980;9:1031–1037
5. Whittle IR, Dorsch NW, Besser M. Giant intracranial aneurysms: diagnosis, management, and outcome. Surg Neurol 1984;21(3):218–230
6. Doshi R, Neil-Dwyer G. A clinicopathological study of patients following a subarachnoid hemorrhage. J Neurosurg 1980;52:295–301
7. Jones NR, Blumberg PC, North JB. Acute subdural hematomas. Aetiology, pathology and outcome. Aust NZ J Surg 1986;56:907–913
8. Vander Ark GD. Cardiovascular changes with acute subdural hematoma. Surg Neurol 1975;3:305–308
9. Cruikshank JM, Neil-Dwyer G, Brice J. Electrocardiographic changes and their prognostic significance in subarachnoid hemorrhage. J Neurol Neurosurg Psychiatry 1974;37:755–759
10. Miner ME, Allen SJ. Cardiovascular effects of severe head injury. In: Frost E, ed. Clinical anesthesia in neurosurgery. Butterworth, MA: Stoneham, 1991:439–445
11. Cully MD, Larson CP Jr, Silverberg GD. Hetastarch coagulopathy in a neurosurgical patient. Anesth 1987;66(5):706–707
12. Steinberg GK, Anson JA. Carotid endarterectomy: update. Western J Med 1992;158:64–65
13. Hobson RW II, Weiss DG, Fields WS, et al. Efficacy of carotid endarterectomy for asymptomatic carotid stenosis. The Veterans Affairs Cooperative Study Group. N Engl J Med 1993;328(4):221–227
14. Cebul RD, Whisnant JP. Carotid endarterectomy. Ann Intern Med 1989;111:660–671
15. Kempczinski R. Discussion of "Carotid endarterectomy in a metropolitan community: the early results after 8535 operations, by Rubin JR et al." J Vasc Surg 1988;7:259–268
16. Pulsinelli WA, Levy DE, Sigsbee B, et al. Increased damage after ischemic stroke in patients with hyperglycemia with or without established diabetes mellitus. Am J Med 1983;74:540–544
17. Koudstaal PJ, Van Gijn J, Staal A, et al. Diagnosis of transient ischemic attacks: improvement of interobserver agreement by a check-list in ordinary language. Stroke 1986;17(4):723–726
18. Whisnant JP. Epidemiology of stroke: emphasis on transient cerebral ischemic attacks and hypertension. Stroke 1974;5:68–75
19. Teasdale G, Jennett B. Assessment of coma and impaired consciousness. A practical scale. Lancet 1974;2:81–89
20. Chambers BR, Norris JW. Clinical significance of asymptomatic neck bruits. Neurology 1985;35:742–752
21. Chambers BR, Norris JW. Outcome in patients with asymptomatic neck bruits. N Engl J Med 1986;315:860–865
22. Bryson BL, Mulkey M, Mumford B, et al. Cervical spine injury: incidence and diagnosis. J Trauma 1986;26:669–677

23. Evans DE, Kobrine AI, Rizzoli HV. Cardiac arrhythmias accompanying acute compression of the spinal cord. J Neurosurg 1980;52:52–59

24. Fraser A, Edmonds-Seal J. Spinal cord injuries: a review of the problems facing the anaesthetist. Anaesth 1982;37:1084–1098

25. Choi SC, Muizelaar JP, Barnes TY, et al. Prediction tree for severely head-injured patients. J Neurosurg 1991;75:251–289

26. Miller JD, Jennett WB. Complications of depressed skull fracture. Lancet 1968;2:991–995

27. Frost EAM, Kim BY, Thiagarajah S. Anesthesia and outcome in severe head injury. Br J Anaesth 1981;53(3):310–315

28. Teasdale G, Jennett B. Assessment of coma and impaired consciousness: a practical scale. Lancet 1974;2:81–95

29. Changaris DG, McGraw CP, Richardson JD, et al. Correlation of cerebral perfusion pressure and Glasgow coma scale to outcome. J Trauma 1987;27:1007–1015

30. Becker DP, Miller JD, Ward JD, et al. The outcome from severe head injury with early diagnosis and intensive management. J Neurosurg 1977;47:491–550

31. Andrews BT, Levy ML, Pitts LH. Implications of systemic hypotension for the neurological examination in patients with severe head injury. Surg Neurol 1987;28:419–425

32. Kraus JF, Morganstern H, Fife D, et al. Blood alcohol tests: prevalence of involvement and early outcome following brain injury. Am J Public Health 1989;79:294–299

33. Galbraith S, Murray WR, Patel AR, et al. The relationship between alcohol and head injury and its effect on the conscious level. Br J Surg 1976;63:128–130

34. Cregler LL, Mark H. Medical complications of cocaine abuse. N Engl J Med 1986;315(23): 1495–1500

35. Fischer SP. Development and effectiveness of an anesthesia preoperative evaluation clinic in a teaching hospital (special article). Anesthesiology 1996;85:196–206

36. Macario A, Roizen MF, Thisted R, et al. Reassessment of preoperative laboratory testing has changed the test-ordering patterns of physicians. Surg Gynecol Obstet 1992;175: 539–547

37. Roizen MF, Cohn S. Preoperative evaluation for elective surgery—what laboratory tests are needed? In: Stoelting RK, ed. Advances in anesthesia. St. Louis, MO: Mosby-Year Book, 1993;10:25–47

38. Macpherson DS, Snow R, Lofgren RP. Preoperative screening: value of previous tests. Ann Intern Med 1990;113:969–973

39. Turnbull JM, Buck C. The value of preoperative screening investigations in otherwise healthy individuals. Arch Intern Med 1987;147:1101–1105

40. Roizen MF, Kaplan EB, Schreider BD, et al. The relative roles of the history and physical examination, and laboratory testing in preoperative evaluation for outpatient surgery: the "Starling" curve of preoperative laboratory testing. Anesthesiol Clin North Am 1987;5: 15–34

41. Gold BS, Young ML, Kinman JL, et al. The utility of preoperative electrocardiograms in the ambulatory surgical patient. Arch Intern Med 1992;152:301–305

42. Charpak Y, Blery C, Chastang C, et al. Prospective assessment of a protocol for selective ordering of preoperative chest x-rays. Can J Anaesth 1988;35:259–264

43. Tape TG, Mushlin AI. The utility of routine chest radiographs. Ann Intern Med 1986; 104:663–670

44. Kaplan EB, Sheiner LB, Boeckmann AJ, et al. The usefulness of preoperative laboratory screening. JAMA 1985;53:3576–3581

45. McKee RF, Scott EM. The value of routine preoperative investigations. Ann R Coll Surg 1987;69:160–162

46. Rohrer MJ, Michelotti MC, Nahrwold DL. A prospective evaluation of the efficacy of preoperative coagulation testing. Ann Surg 1988;208:554–557

47. Narr BJ, Hansen TR, Warner MA. Preoperative laboratory screening in healthy Mayo patients: cost-effective elimination of tests and unchanged outcomes. Mayo Clin Proc 1991; 66:155–159

Intraoperative Neurophysiological Monitoring

Jaime R. Lopez, MD

Intraoperative neurophysiological monitoring (IOM) represents the application of electrophysiological techniques to detect changes in the functional state of the nervous system consistent with ischemia or injury. Electrophysiological techniques may assist in localizing neural structures, identifying specific cortical functional areas, and delineating epileptogenic cortex. The information obtained may also determine the mechanism of injury and prevent damage by detecting dysfunction prior to reaching an irreversible stage. IOM using electroencephalography (EEG) was first used in 1965 [1]. Subsequently, other electrophysiological techniques such as somatosensory evoked potentials (SSEPs), brain stem auditory evoked potentials (BAEPs), visual evoked potentials (VEPs), electromyography (EMG), and peripheral nerve compound action potentials have gradually come into use. This review of the subject will focus on the intraoperative application and clinical utility of EEG, BAEPs, VEPs, SSEPs, and EMG in neurosurgical procedures.

EEG is produced by the spontaneously generated electroencephalographic brain wave activity and is easily recorded, requiring no stimulus. However, evoked potential (EP) recordings can only be generated by applying an external stimulus. In general, stimulation is provided using peripheral nerve electrical stimulation for SSEPs, auditory clicks for BAEPs, and light flashes for VEPs. Standardized recording sites along the neural pathways are used to assess different components of the EP waveform (i.e., latency, amplitude, and morphology). Averaging of 50–1000 responses is necessary in order to be able to record the EP from the background EEG and electrical noise. In addition to recording EPs, spontaneous or stimulus-triggered EMG can be recorded from muscle using either intramuscular or surface electrodes. Electrical or magnetic stimulation of peripheral nerves, nerve roots, spinal cord, cranial nerves, or cortical structures can generate a motor-evoked response that can be recorded from a muscle or nerve.

■ Ischemia and Electrophysiological Studies

Different techniques have been used to identify and attempt to prevent damage caused by cerebral ischemia. The most extensively studied and commonly used techniques are EEG and SSEPs. The rationale for employing electrophysiological techniques as a marker for ischemia is the good correlation between these techniques and regional cerebral blood flow (rCBF). Sundt and colleagues [2–4] demonstrated that in patients undergoing carotid endarterectomies (CEA), major EEG changes occurred with rCBF <10 ml/100 g/min, and less severe EEG changes were seen with rCBF between 10–18 ml/100 g/min, with the critical level defined as 15 ml/100 g/min. In contrast, primate studies show that SSEPs are maintained at levels of rCBF of ≥16 ml/100 g/min but absent at levels below 12 ml/100 g/min; while at levels between 14–16 ml/100 g/min, there is a sharp decline in the amplitude of the evoked response with a 50% amplitude reduction corresponding to rCBF of 16 ml/100 g/min [5–8]. In addition to altering the SSEP amplitude, ischemia also appears to prolong the central conduction time (CCT) with a threshold of rCBF (<15 ml/100 g/min) similar to those previously reported on the basis of amplitude reduction [9, 10]. Interestingly, there is experimental evidence suggesting a decreasing susceptibility to local ischemia as one descends the neuraxis, demonstrated by persistence of electrophysiological function during systemic hypotension [7].

There clearly seems to be a threshold relationship between cerebral blood flow and alteration of the EEG and SSEP. There is also a good deal of experimental evidence for a rCBF threshold and cellular membrane failure [8, 11]. Branston and colleagues [6] found that at rCBF levels between 12–16 ml/100 g/min the SSEP was abolished and small self-limiting increases in extracellular potassium activity were detected. This study further demonstrated that the rCBF threshold range for a massive irreversible rise in extracellular potassium, associated with structural changes of infarction, occurred between 7.6–11.4 ml/100 g/min. In baboon chronic stroke models following middle cerebral artery (MCA) occlusion, areas of infarction corresponded to blood flow levels of 10 ml/100 g/min or less [8, 12]. In acute stroke (primate) models, infarction occurred only in areas in which rCBF measured ≤12 ml/100 g/min [13, 14]. Thus, these findings suggest that significant (50%) reduction in amplitude of the SSEP, which corresponds to a rCBF of 14–16 ml/100 g/min, is indicative of ischemia and represents a warning of possible progression from reversible to irreversible cell damage.

■ Carotid Endarterectomy

CEA was first successfully introduced in 1953 as treatment for intermittent neurological symptoms secondary to cerebral ischemia as a result of internal carotid artery (ICA) stenosis [15]. The use of CEA rose dramatically through the mid-1980s, even though no controlled trials had been performed. However, in 1991 the North American Symptomatic Carotid Endarterectomy Trial (NASCET) [16] unequivocally demonstrated the benefit of CEA over medical management in symptomatic patients with high-grade stenosis ($\geq 70\%$). More recently, a more modest benefit of CEA (versus medical therapy) has been demonstrated in asymptomatic patients with high-grade carotid stenosis ($\geq 60\%$) [17]. The NASCET trial also emphasized the importance of maintaining a low perioperative complication rate, since complication rates $>5.8\%$ (strokes and death) significantly diminished the benefit of CEA. Indications for surgery were defined as: severe (70%–99%) carotid stenosis in patients with recent hemispheric and retinal transient ischemic attacks or nondisabling strokes, carotid stenosis of $>60\%$ in asymptomatic patients, and ulcerative carotid plaques ($<60\%$) as a source of emboli. CEA can be performed under general or regional anesthesia [18]. However, in most centers the preferred mode remains general anesthesia because it allows for a more controlled surgical environment and provides easier and more accurate manipulation of physiological parameters [19].

Intraoperative Considerations

Possible brain ischemia as a direct result of CEA is an important factor that requires special attention, since cross-clamping of the common carotid artery is an unavoidable component of CEA. If collateral circulation is inadequate, then ipsilateral hemispheric ischemia is the result of carotid cross-clamping. With this in mind, a variety of techniques have been used to identify cerebral ischemia. In general, techniques such as stump pressure measurements, radionuclide cerebral blood flow measurements, and transcranial Doppler assess cerebrovascular integrity; whereas, EEG and cortical SSEPs indirectly measure cerebral ischemia by means of assessing cerebral function. Based on the changes seen during IOM, some surgeons will request induced systemic hypertension and/or use intraluminal shunting as strategies to reverse cerebral ischemia. Unfortunately, there is no clear consensus regarding the necessity for an indwelling arterial shunt during CEA. Surgeons will usually belong to one of three groups: those who always shunt, those who never shunt, and those who selectively shunt based on results of IOM [19, 20]. The routine use of shunts in CEA is controversial, since it is not devoid of complications; it carries the risk of embolization and possible stroke [21, 22] as well as possible arterial damage [23]. In addition, shunt malfunctions from various causes have been reported [18, 24].

Continuous EEG Monitoring   EEG monitoring during CEA has been in use for over 30 years. Initial studies compared EEG changes with postoperative neurological deficits [1]. Subsequently, EEG monitoring grew in popularity because of readily available equipment, familiarity with technique, ease of set-up, and reliability in determining carotid artery cross-clamp–dependent ischemia. The ability to detect ischemia and predict postoperative neurological deficits reliably with EEG was shown in several studies [3, 4, 25, 26]. Patients with EEG changes during CEA were found to have a higher incidence of stroke as opposed to patients who did not develop changes. In a series of 293 CEAs, Redekop and Ferguson [27] noted that the postoperative neurological deficit risk was much higher in the subgroup with major EEG changes (18%) as opposed to those without changes (2%). In a separate study, Zampella and associates [28] reported that 43 of 59 patients developed EEG changes and 17% (10/59) developed postoperative complications. Sundt and colleagues [4] reported that in 1145 consecutive CEAs they had "never had a patient emerge from anesthesia with a new deficit that was not predicted by the EEG." The use of EEG monitoring has also allowed for reduction in the frequency of carotid shunts and improved neurological outcome [25, 26]. Assessment of the EEG data from the different studies suggests that EEG is very sensitive in detecting cerebral ischemia and useful in predicting outcome.

Intraoperative EEG Changes   Intraoperative EEG changes may be due to several different factors.

Ischemia   The two major changes are generalized as slowing with decreased amplitude in the ischemic hemisphere [1, 29] and attenuation of the anesthetic-induced fast rhythms [30]. As expected, ipsilateral hemispheric EEG changes are the most common findings during ischemia after unilateral carotid cross-clamping (Fig 1). However, bilateral EEG changes have been reported in patients with compromised collateral circulation [30]. Patients were also noted to have a higher frequency of intraoperative EEG changes if their preoperative EEG was abnormal [4].

Anesthesia   Anesthetics have a significant effect on the EEG, typically producing rhythmic beta activity. Initially during induction, 12–18 Hz (beta) activity appears over the anterior hemispheres. At lighter levels of steady state anesthesia, the amplitude increases, becomes widespread, and slows to 8–14 Hz. Intermittent delta may also be seen anteriorly. Burst suppression pattern can be seen with high doses of many anesthetics, including isoflurane, halothane, and enflurane as well as barbiturates [31]. EEG changes due to anesthesia are bilateral and symmetrical (Fig 2).

Mean Arterial Pressure (MAP)   In some cases, bilateral or unilateral (ipsilateral to the diseased carotid) EEG changes consistent with ischemia can be seen when the MAP drops below a certain critical level dependent on the patient's baseline MAP (personal observation).

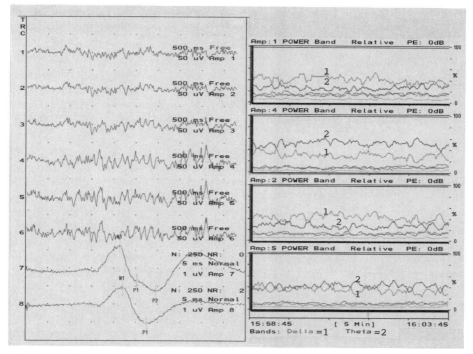

Fig 1. *Left hemispheric ischemic changes characterized by attenuation of the raw electroencephalogram and increase in the compressed spectral array delta frequency during left carotid endarterectomy. Note the morphological asymmetry of the left cortical somatosensory evoked potential (trace 8, right median nerve stimulation). Traces 1–3: Left hemisphere F3/C3/P3 referenced to linked ears; Traces 4–6: Right hemisphere F4/C4/P4 referenced to linked ears.*

Interventions Ipsilateral EEG changes after carotid artery cross-clamping are due to reduced cerebral perfusion. Thus, in order to reverse cerebral ischemia, surgeons who use IOM will shunt once the EEG shows major changes. There is clinical evidence to suggest that shunting those cases leads to improved overall neurological outcome [4, 26, 31, 32]. In a study comparing neurological outcome in two groups of CEAs performed either with or without EEG IOM, Cho and coworkers [26] found that the use of IOM and selective shunting reduced the frequency of carotid shunts from 49% to 12% and decreased major neurological morbidity and mortality from 2.3% to 1.1%.

Computer Processed EEG Conventional intraoperative EEG generates a large amount of data and requires the use of large complex equipment, precise time-consuming electrode placement, and trained personnel to continuously interpret the EEG data. Therefore, in an attempt to facilitate IOM with EEG, digitally processed EEG methods have been developed [30, 33]. Myers and colleagues [33] performed spectral analysis of EEG

38 ■ Lopez

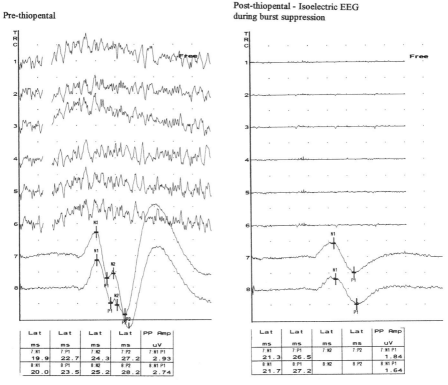

Pre-thiopental

Post-thiopental - Isoelectric EEG
during burst suppression

Lat	Lat	Lat	Lat	PP Amp
ms	ms	ms	ms	uV
7:N1	7:P1	7:N2	7:P2	7:N1 P1
19.9	22.7	24.3	27.2	2.93
8:N1	8:P1	8:N2	8:P2	8:N1 P1
20.0	23.5	25.2	28.2	2.74

Lat	Lat	Lat	Lat	PP Amp
ms	ms	ms	ms	uV
7:N1	7:P1	7:N2	7:P2	7:N1 P1
21.3	26.5			1.84
8:N1	8:P1	8:N2	8:P2	8:N1 P1
21.7	27.2			1.64

Fig 2. *Anesthetic (thiopental) effects on electroencephalogram and median nerve cortical somatosensory evoked potentials (SSEPs). Traces 1–3: Left parasagittal (F3, C3, P3 to linked
ears); Traces 4–6: Right parasagittal (F4, C4, P4 referenced to linked ears); Trace 7: Left median nerve stimulation; Trace 8: Right median nerve stimulation. Note the symmetrical amplitude reduction and morphology change in SSEP wave forms.*

data by digitizing analog EEG signals and, using a computer to perform a
Fourier analysis, produced a power versus frequency display. Once the
EEG has been digitized and computer processed, it can be displayed in
different formats, including compressed spectral array (CSA) or by areas
of density (intensity) termed density-modulated spectral array (DSA) [34].
These types of displays allow for easier interpretation of the EEG, showing
ischemic changes as loss of amplitude in the power spectrum for all fre-
quencies and a shift of the EEG spectrum to the lower frequency range.
Several studies using computerized EEG analysis have found the technique
useful in identifying cerebral ischemia and predicting neurological outcome following CEA [30, 35, 36]. In fact, some have claimed that computer
processed EEG proved more useful than analog EEG [30, 36]. However,
Kearse and associates [37], in a prospective study of 103 patients undergoing CEA monitored with analog EEG and DSA, concluded that DSA was

not sufficiently sensitive in detecting mild cerebral ischemia associated with analog EEG changes. Thus, it appears that there is a role for computerized EEG analysis during CEAs, with the caveat being that it may lack sensitivity in detecting mild EEG pattern changes consistent with cerebral ischemia.

Somatosensory Evoked Potentials

There is a strong correlation between SSEPs and cerebral ischemia, and SSEPs have gained popularity as a useful IOM technique to assess cerebral function during cerebrovascular surgery. Median nerve SSEPs reflect the cerebral functional status of the primary sensory cortex, which is supplied by the MCA and thus at risk during carotid cross-clamping (Fig 3). There are also several technical advantages of SSEPs over EEG for IOM, such as relative resistance to general anesthesia, fewer electrode sites, easier recording and interpretation, and serial comparison [38].

Moorthy and colleagues [39] were the first to report the use of median nerve SSEPs during CEA and to correlate SSEP changes with neurological deterioration. Subsequently, Markand and coworkers [40] reported on 38 CEAs monitored with SSEP. One patient had a sudden loss of consciousness and loss of the cortical SSEP following carotid cross-clamping. The SSEP changes were reversed, and the patient regained consciousness after

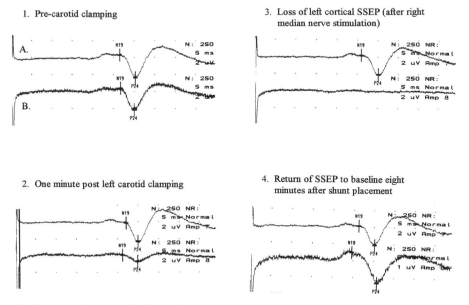

Fig 3. *Transient loss of right median nerve cortical somatosensory evoked potential is reversed after placement of shunt during left carotid endarterectomy: (A) left median nerve stimulation and (B) right median nerve stimulation.*

shunt placement. In three other cases, SSEP changes were reversed by shunting. Other investigators have reported on the reliability and accuracy of SSEPs in CEAs [41–46]. However, at least one study has concluded that SSEPs are not sufficiently sensitive to detect the onset of cerebral ischemia, since neither 50% amplitude reduction nor increase in CCT has been established as a physiological marker of intraoperative ischemia [47]. In this study, SSEP criteria were measured against the EEG gold standard instead of using neurological outcome as the endpoint. The investigators found that 10 out of 23 patients with EEG evidence of ischemia after cross-clamping had prolongation of the CCT but that only 1 had an amplitude reduction of 50% or more. In contrast, Amantini and associates [44] felt that there is a higher incidence of false positives with EEG and, subsequently, the use of shunts, since there is less agreement in identifying EEG evidence of ischemic risk as compared to SSEPs. Although SSEP criteria for cerebral ischemia are not uniform and differ among various investigators, with some using amplitude reduction, latency delay, prolongation of CCT, or a combination of the three to signify cerebral ischemia, most studies have found that a 50% amplitude reduction of the N19-P24 wave or a 1 millisecond delay of the CCT correlates best with postoperative neurological deficits [37, 41–43, 46, 48, 49].

Fisher and coworkers [20] reviewed seven studies comprising 3028 patients. The cumulative results revealed that 170 patients (5.6%) had a significant decline in intraoperative SSEPs (due to surgical manipulation), and 34 (20%) of the 170 patients developed significant postoperative deficits. In addition, Lam and colleagues [47] reviewed the reported sensitivity and specificity in six studies (including theirs) between 1985 and 1991. The sensitivities ranged from 83%–100% and specificities from 83%–99%. They concluded that in their study comparing conventional EEG and SSEP monitoring during CEAs both modalities had similar sensitivity and specificity. In a separate study, Brinkman and associates [48] found that intraoperative SSEP amplitude decrements of 50% or more were associated with worsening of neurological function, determined by comparing pre- and postoperative neurophysiological testing. These findings suggest that SSEP IOM is useful in improving neurological outcome during CEA.

Nonischemic Factors Affecting SSEPs Hypothermia can prolong the latencies of all peaks and needs to be taken into consideration because surgery frequently leads to a 1°C–3°C drop in the core body temperature.

Hypotension can lead to amplitude reduction and/or delay in the cortical SSEP latencies. The critical level depends on the patient's preoperative blood pressure.

■ Intracranial Neurovascular Surgery

EEG, SSEPs, and BAEPs have been used to monitor cerebral function, since a well established correlation exists between ischemia and decreased electrophysiological function. The type of electrophysiological technique to be used depends on several factors, such as type of surgery, anatomic location, intracranial vascular supply at risk, and preoperative neurological deficits. EEG has had limited use in aneurysm surgery because craniotomy and brain relaxation produce air spaces between dura and arachnoid that interfere with EEG recording from the underlying cortex [50].

MCA and ICA vascular territories can be monitored with median nerve SSEPs, since the somatosensory cortex representing the hand is supplied by the MCA (Fig 4). In addition, median nerve SSEPs also provide information on the posterior cerebral artery [51] since it supplies the thalamic segment of the somatosensory pathway. Several studies have shown the utility of median nerve SSEPs in predicting postoperative neurological outcome [52–60]. In reviewing the reported clinical outcomes of 10 studies involving MCA aneurysm surgery, Palatinsky and associates found the reliability of median nerve SSEPs in predicting outcome ranged between 78%–100% [60a]. Ducati and colleagues [61] monitored 50 aneurysms (12 MCA) and reported that a CCT greater than 9 msec correlated with postoperative neurological deficits. In addition to prolongation of the CCT, Friedman and associates [54] (1987) found that decrease in cortical SSEP amplitude or disappearance of the cortical SSEP accurately predicted postoperative deficits. In a study of 53 MCA aneurysm procedures, Friedman and associates [59] (1991) found new postoperative deficits in 4 out of 4 patients with significant change in SSEP and incomplete return to baseline or loss of the SSEP and 1 out of 5 patients with significant SSEP changes that returned to baseline, while only 1 out of 37 patients without SSEP changes developed a new postoperative deficit. Symon and coworkers [55] monitored 37 patients undergoing aneurysm surgery (17 MCA) and concluded that preservation of conduction, even if CCT increased to 10 msec, was associated with good outcome. However, prompt disappearance of the N20 wave (within 1 minute) as well as slow recovery of the SSEP (>20 minutes) was associated with new postoperative deficits.

In an attempt to determine the permissible temporary occlusion time in aneurysm surgery, Mizoi and Yoshimoto [62] retrospectively analyzed the results of IOM with median nerve SSEPs in 97 patients undergoing MCA and ICA surgery. They reported loss of the SSEP in 42 patients during temporary occlusion; all but 3 recovered the SSEP back to baseline levels after recirculation. All of the 3 patients who did not recover their SSEP experienced a rapid loss of the SSEP (between 1 and 5 minutes) and developed postoperative deficits. One patient without SSEP changes developed postoperative hemiplegia. The authors concluded that tempo-

1. First vascular clip placed.

Time: 13-JAN-1996 15:31:55

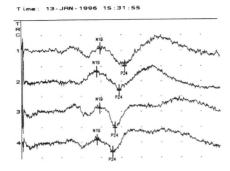

3. Loss of right cortical SSEPs (after left median nerve stimulation).

Time: 13-JAN-1996 15:35:22
IOM Note: 15:36:28   SURG. YES

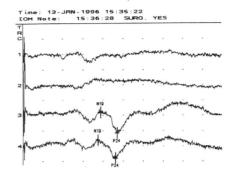

2. Second vascular clip placed adjacent to right MCA. Surgeon alerted of SSEP change.

Time: 13-JAN-1996 15:34:04
IOM Note: 15:36:15   SURGEON ALERT=

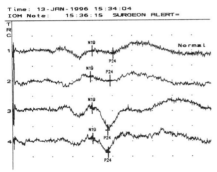

4. Return of SSEP to baseline level 10 minutes after removal of clip.

Time: 13-JAN-1996 15:48:23

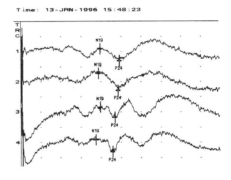

Fig 4. *Transient loss of right cortical median nerve somatosensory evoked potential (SSEP) during intracranial aneurysm clipping. Postoperatively the patient remained neurologically normal. MCA = middle cerebral artery.*

rary vascular occlusion is relatively safe for a period of approximately 10 minutes after gradual loss of the SSEP.

In addition to providing information about the development of cerebral ischemia during temporary clipping, SSEPs are useful in identifying significant ischemia due to accidental clipping of blood vessels, manipulation of brain structures, and excessive retraction [58, 60]. In a study of 134 aneurysms (39 ICA and 40 MCA), Schramm and colleagues [58] reported loss or alteration of SSEPs in 12 cases of temporary occlusion, 2 cases of accidental clipping, 1 case of permanent occlusion, and 1 case each of retraction of the MCA and cerebellar retraction. In 15 out of 17 instances of SSEP changes, the surgical course was altered. Changes included repositioning of vascular clips and repositioning of retractors. In rare instances, cortical SSEP changes may identify a peripheral ischemic process such as a malfunctioning blood pressure cuff causing arm ischemia [59].

Anterior Cerebral Artery (ACA)

Grundy and associates [63] (1982) were the first to report successful use of posterior tibial SSEP monitoring in ACA territory arteriovenous malformation surgery. Momma and coworkers [57] found median nerve SSEPs to be poor indicators of ischemia in ACA vascular territory surgery. Most likely this is because the ACA vascular distribution does not supply the median nerve somatosensory cortex, and the cortical generators of the P40-N45 posterior tibial SSEPs lie within the vascular territory of the ACA. Schramm and colleagues [58] (1990) recommended SSEP monitoring using posterior tibial nerve stimulation combined with median nerve stimulation, since posterior tibial nerve SSEPs are inadequate in detecting ischemia in the recurrent artery of Heubner, which supplies only the anterior limb of the internal capsule.

Posterior Circulation

Several investigators have found IOM of vertebral basilar aneurysms with SSEPs and BAEPs to be unreliable [57, 59, 64], possibly because ischemia due to basilar perforator occlusion may not affect the brain stem auditory or somatosensory pathways [50, 59]. However, Manninen and associates [65] (1994) found that dual modality monitoring (SSEPs and BAEPs) was useful during posterior fossa aneurysm surgery. They looked at a total of 70 patients with aneurysms of the vertebral basilar circulation and found that 10 patients had a change in their BAEP with 6 developing a postoperative neurological deficit. Fourteen patients had SSEP changes, and 8 of these had new postoperative deficits. All patients who had permanent EP changes developed postoperative neurological deficits. They also reported that the incidence of false negative and false positive results for both modalities was 20% and 30%, respectively. These findings suggest that identification of brain stem ischemia with IOM is enhanced by using a dual modality approach.

■ Spinal Surgery

The main use of IOM in which the spinal cord is at risk involves scoliosis surgery. However, some authors feel IOM should be used in any patient who is at risk for injury to the spinal cord during surgical procedures [66, 67]. The risk of postoperative paraplegia and paraparesis as a result of instrumentation procedures for correction of scoliosis has been reported to be 0.72% [68]. Spinal cord injury may result from several factors, including compression or traction of the cord, intraoperative vascular insufficiency, or trauma [20].

Several methods of monitoring spinal cord function have been used intraoperatively. The first technique employed was the intraoperative wake-up test, described by Vauzelle and coworkers [69] in 1973. The wake-up test is simple; anesthesia is discontinued at a critical stage during surgery (usually after distraction/derotation), and the patient is asked to wiggle his or her toes. Unfortunately, the wake-up test has several limitations. It requires a cooperative patient who can comprehend, hear, and follow simple commands, requires presurgical rehearsal, interrupts the surgical procedure, can take up to 15 minutes or more to complete, and may fail to detect spinal cord injury [70]. Furthermore, the wake-up test only provides a one-time neurological assessment and does not allow continuous monitoring. Theoretically, it is possible that by the time the wake-up test is performed damage to the spinal cord has long occurred and is irreversible. This subsequently led to the use of electrophysiological techniques that would allow continuous monitoring of spinal cord function. Different strategies in stimulation and recording have been used; typically, peripheral nerve or spinal epidural stimulation is performed, and recordings are obtained from epidural, interspinous ligaments, spinous process, or scalp sites [71]. The most commonly used methods are the spinal evoked potential (recorded from the skin, interspinous ligament, vertebrae, or epidural space) and the scalp recorded SSEP. Generally, tibial or peroneal nerve SSEPs are used to monitor below the C8 level, and median or ulnar nerve SSEPs are performed to monitor above the C8 level [72]. Although SSEPs do not monitor the central motor pathways, animal studies suggest that SSEPs are sensitive to acute spinal cord damage from either ischemic or mechanical insults to the spinal cord [73, 74].

Several studies have demonstrated the validity of SSEP monitoring in scoliosis surgery [75–77]. Nuwer and colleagues [77] performed a large multicenter survey of surgical outcome from centers that use SSEP monitoring in scoliosis surgery, obtaining data on 51,263 procedures, and found that experienced SSEP monitoring teams had fewer neurological deficits and that false negatives occurred in only 0.063% of patients. The authors recognized that intraoperative intervention (secondary to SSEP changes) may have prevented or reduced the severity of any postoperative deficit, thereby influencing the outcome and artificially raising the number of false positive cases and undercounting true positive cases. With this assumption, sensitivity and specificity of SSEP monitoring was calculated as 92% and 98.9%, respectively. They also found a negative predictive value of 99.33% but only a mediocre positive predictive value of 42%. They concluded that SSEP monitoring detects more than 90% of the intraoperative neurological deficits and that SSEP monitoring for scoliosis surgery is a clinically useful, valid procedure.

The use of SSEPs as a measure of spinal cord function is not limited solely to scoliosis surgery, but has also been found useful in other spinal surgical procedures such as spinal AVMs and tumors, unstable fractures, resection of syringomyelia, spinal decompression, embolization of spinal AVMs, and selective dorsal rhizotomy in children [20, 71]. Nash and Brown [67] (1989) stated that "it is standard practice to conduct some form of monitoring when performing any spinal operation that is associated with a high risk of neurological injury. Generally, operations are considered to carry such a risk when corrective forces are being applied to the spine, the patient has pre-existing neurological damage, the cord is being invaded, or an osteotomy or other procedure is being carried out in immediate juxtaposition to the spinal cord."

In spite of the impressive track record of SSEPs in monitoring spinal cord function, false negative cases have been reported and are of concern [20, 77]. The criticism of mixed nerve SSEP spinal cord monitoring is that it measures conduction in the ascending sensory pathways located in the posterior columns while the anterior, motor pathways remain unmonitored. Thus, several techniques have evolved in an attempt to monitor the spinal cord motor pathways. Motor evoked potentials (MEPs) can be generated by applying an electrical or magnetic stimulation transcranially to the motor cortex or to the spinal cord and recording distal to the spinal level of interest from the spinal cord, peripheral nerve, or muscle [78–80]. Unfortunately, the clinical utility of MEPs is limited due to the effect of anesthetic agents on the motor pathways causing severe reduction of MEP amplitude. However, different anesthetic techniques (e.g., total intravenous anesthesia) are currently being investigated that may facilitate recording of MEPs in the operating room. Transcranial electrical and magnetic stimulation is still considered experimental in the United States and the devices are not approved by the Food and Drug Administration.

■ Posterior Fossa and Cranial Nerve Surgery

Posterior fossa surgery presents difficult and unique challenges to the IOM team, since various types of surgery are performed, each requiring a different monitoring protocol. Thus, the IOM protocol is designed according to the neural structures at risk. The most commonly used modalities are BAEPs, spontaneous and triggered EMG and SSEPs [81]. It is common to use these modalities simultaneously, in order to monitor a larger group of neural structures (Fig 5). The most common use of IOM in posterior fossa surgery is for acoustic neuroma resections. However, monitoring is also utilized in surgeries for other types of tumors, hemifacial spasm, trigeminal neuralgia, and vascular structures.

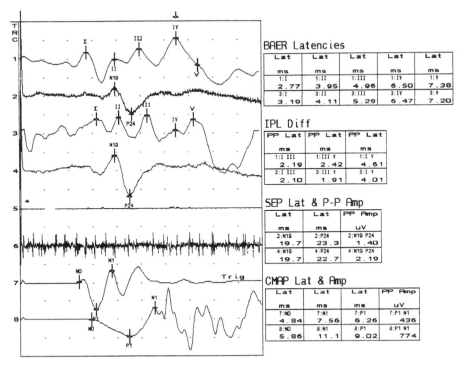

Fig 5. *Example of multimodality recording in posterior fossa surgery of brain stem arteriovenous malformation (AVM) resection. Trace 1 and 3: Left and right brain stem auditory evoked potential (BAEP), respectively; Trace 2 and 4: Cortical somatosensory evoked potential after left and right median nerve stimulation; Spontaneous electromyography (EMG) activity recorded from right masseter (trace 5) and right orbicularis oris (trace 6); Stimulation of brain stem nuclei generates a triggered EMG response from right masseter (trace 7) and right orbicularis oris (trace 8).*

Monitoring Cranial Nerves (CNs)

CN I Monitoring of the visual pathways has been attempted using VEPs. However, VEPs are very sensitive to technical, anesthesiological, temperature, blood pressure, and other surgical factors and are affected in an unpredictable manner [20, 82]. Strauss and associates [82] state that flash VEPs are not useful for IOM during removal of visual pathway lesions due to a combination of nonspecific findings with false positive and false negative cases.

CNs III–VII and IX–XII IOM of the motor component of any cranial (or peripheral) nerve is performed in essentially the same fashion. The basic principle involves EMG monitoring of spontaneous and triggered muscle activity. Obviously, the cranial nerve(s) at risk will determine

Table 1. *Muscles Accessible for Cranial Nerve EMG Monitoring*

Cranial Nerve	Muscles
III	Inferior rectus
IV	Superior oblique
V	Masseter
VI	Lateral rectus
VII	Frontalis, orbicularis oculi and orbicularis oris
IX	Posterior pharyngeal muscles
X	Cricothyroid or vocalis
XI	Sternocleidomastoid or trapezius
XII	Tongue

from which muscles to record (Table 1). Recordings can be obtained by placing two intramuscular wire electrodes within the muscle or using surface electrodes. Simultaneous spontaneous EMG and compound muscle action potential (CMAP) recordings can be obtained by using intramuscular wire and surface electrodes. Using intramuscular wire electrodes increases the sensitivity for detecting spontaneous EMG activity, while surface electrodes allow for more reliable monitoring of CMAP amplitude and morphology [83].

The rationale for using spontaneous EMG activity monitoring is based on the property that thermal, mechanical, or metabolic irritation of the intracranial portion of the motor CNs will lead to characteristic activity in the innervated muscles [81]. Daube and Harper [83] (1989) termed this activity "neurotonic discharges," defining them as "distinctive discharges of a motor unit potential in rapid irregular bursts." In contrast, CMAP monitors integrity and continuity of the nerve from the point of stimulation (proximal to the site of surgery) to the muscle. The onset latency of the CMAP indicates the conduction time of the fastest fibers, while its amplitude is approximately proportional to the number of available axons [84].

CN XIII The need to preserve hearing in surgeries of the cerebellopontine angle and in acoustic neuroma resections has led to a variety of auditory evoked potential techniques. The most commonly used recording technique is the BAEP; however, other less commonly used techniques such as electrocochleography (ECoG) and direct recording of nerve action potentials (NAP) are useful in assessing eighth nerve function. The advantage of the BAEP is that it reflects the electrical activity in the auditory nerve and auditory pathways of the brain stem in response to cochlear stimulation. Five distinct vertex positive waveforms can be recorded, with waves I, III, and V being the most significant for IOM purposes. Waves I and II originate from the auditory nerve at the level of the cochlea, wave

III within the lower pons, and wave V in the midbrain near the inferior colliculus [81]. Direct intracranial recordings of eighth NAPs can be obtained using a small cotton-wick electrode applied to the eighth nerve close to its entrance to the brain stem. The ECoG is the least commonly used modality and can be recorded using a needle electrode placed through the tympanic membrane and resting on the promontory of the middle ear. ECoG is used to document integrity of the cochlea.

In monitoring CN VIII function the BAEP seems to be the most comprehensive modality, since it assesses peripheral and central auditory pathways, has few technical limitations, can be used during the entire procedure, and has good correlation with postoperative hearing status [85]. In a study of 90 BAEP monitored patients compared with 90 unmonitored historical matched controls undergoing acoustic neuroma surgery, Harper and associates [86] (1992) found that BAEP monitoring reduced the risk of hearing loss in patients with acoustic neuromas <2 cm and was statistically significant for tumors <1.1 cm in diameter. In addition, BAEP monitoring improved the chance of preserving useful hearing.

■ Effects of Anesthesia on IOM

Anesthetic agents produce multiple effects and may influence IOM by a variety of mechanisms, including direct effects on the monitoring modality, effects on cerebral blood flow, systemic hypotension with secondary hypoperfusion of neural structures, hypothermia, and direct effects on cerebral metabolism [87]. In addition, synaptic transmission is affected to a greater degree as compared to axonal conduction. This differential effect of anesthetics is the reason why cortical EP and EEG are more suppressed than subcortical EP [88].

EEG Effects

Most anesthetic agents produce similar EEG patterns when used at concentrations below their minimal alveolar concentration (MAC) level. At subanesthetic concentrations, thiopental produces maximum beta (>13 Hz) in the anterior midline, while halothane, enflurane, isoflurane, and 50% nitrous oxide produce similar but less prominent beta activity [89]. Anesthetic induction is associated with widespread low amplitude beta activity followed by theta (4–7 Hz) and delta (0–3 Hz) activity dominating the recording as anesthetic depth increases. During this phase, a faster rhythm may be intermixed with bursts of high amplitude, frontal intermittent, rhythmic delta activity [88, 89]. When a light level steady state anesthetic level is reached, the characteristic pattern of anterior maximum, rhythmic fast pattern in the alpha-beta range is seen with all agents [89]. Burst suppression and electrocortical silence occur at sufficiently high

Table 2. *Anesthetic Effects on Evoked Potentials*

Drug	Cortical SSEP		BAEP	
	Latency	Amplitude	Latency	Amplitude
Isoflurane	Increase	Decrease	Increase	Decrease
Enflurane	Increase	Decrease	Increase	Decrease
Halothane	Increase	Decrease	Increase	Decrease
Nitrous oxide	Increase	Decrease	Increase	No change
Thiopental	Increase	Decrease	Increase	
Diazepam	Increase	Decrease		
Fentanyl	Slight increase	Slight decrease	No change	No change
Propofol	Increase	No change	Increase	
Ketamine	Increase	Increase	Increase	
Etomidate	Increase	Increase		

doses. Etomidate at low doses can activate the EEG and may increase epileptiform activity but at higher doses can produce burst suppression. Propofol can also lead to EEG activation with fast-wave activity [88].

SSEP Effects

Typically, anesthetics decrease the cortical SSEP amplitude and increase the latency (Table 2). All the volatile anesthetics depress the cortical SSEPs, each to an approximately equal degree. The combination of nitrous oxide and a volatile anesthetic tends to have a greater depressant effect than an equipotent administration of a single agent. In each agent, concentrations above 0.5 MAC cause sufficient latency and amplitude changes to interfere with IOM [88]. Barbiturates have effects similar to the volatile anesthetics. Usual therapeutic doses of narcotics have no significant effect on SSEP parameters. Ketamine can increase SSEP amplitude, and etomidate increases the amplitude and latency of the cortical SSEP [90].

BAEP Effects

In comparison to EEG and SSEP, BAEPs are much more resistant to anesthetic effects (see Table 2). Typically, latencies of waves III–V are the most affected. All the volatile anesthetics have similar effects.

■ Conclusion

The field of IOM is relatively new, is in constant development and evolution, and requires the understanding of clinical neurophysiological techniques across multiple disciplines. While some of these techniques are investigational, others are now standard protocol during certain surgical procedures; for example, in 1992 the Scoliosis Research Society issued a position statement that intraoperative neurophysiological monitoring during spinal cord surgery involving instrumentation is not investigational and is considered a viable alternative as well as an adjunct to the wake-up test [91].

Fisher et al [20], following an extensive review of the literature, as well as the Therapeutics and Technology Assessment Subcommittee of the American Academy of Neurology [92], in their position statement, concluded that the following monitoring procedures are useful and no longer investigational: (1) EEG, CSA, and SSEP in CEA and brain surgeries that potentially compromise cerebral blood flow, (2) BAEP and CN monitoring in surgeries performed in the region of the brain stem or inner ear, and (3) SSEP monitoring performed for surgical procedures potentially involving ischemia or mechanical trauma of the spinal cord. They also concluded that MEPs and VEPs are still investigational.

The tireless efforts of JoAnn Ceranski and Rita Sullivan in patient monitoring and data acquisition are greatly appreciated.

■ References

1. Perez-Borja C, Meyer JS. Electroencephalographic monitoring during reconstructive surgery of the neck vessels. Electroencephalogr Clin Neurophysiol 1965; 18:162–169
2. Sundt TM, Sharbrough FW, Anderson RE, Michenfelder JD. Cerebral blood flow measurements and electroencephalograms during carotid endarterectomy. J Neurosurg 1974;41:310–320
3. Sharbrough F, Messick J, Sundt TM. Correlation of continuous electroencephalograms with cerebral blood flow measurements during carotid endarterectomy. Stroke 1973;4:674–683
4. Sundt TM, Sharbrough F, Piepgras DG, et al. Correlation of cerebral blood flow and electroencephalographic changes during carotid endarterectomy with results of surgery and hemodynamics of cerebral ischemia. Mayo Clin Proc 1981;56:533–543
5. Branston NM, Symon L, Crockard HA, Pasztor E. Relationship between the cortical evoked potential and local cortical blood flow following acute middle cerebral artery occlusion in the baboon. Exp Neurol 1974;45:195–208
6. Branston NM, Strong AJ, Symon L. Extracellular potassium activity, evoked potential and tissue blood flow. Relationships during progressive ischaemia in baboon cerebral cortex. J Neurol Sci 1977;32:305–321
7. Branston NM, Ladds A, Symon L, Wang AD. Comparison of the effects of ischaemia on early components of the somatosensory evoked potential in brainstem, thalamus, and cerebral cortex. J Cereb Blood Flow Metabol 1984;4:68–81
8. Symon L. The relationship between CBF, evoked potentials and the clinical features in cerebral ischaemia. Proc 23rd Scand Neurol Congress. Acta Neurol Scand 1980; 62(Suppl):175–190

9. Hargadine JR, Branston NM, Symon L. Central conduction time in primate brain ischemia—a study in baboons. Stroke 1980;11:637–642

10. Lesnick JE, Michele JJ, Simeone FA, et al. Alteration of somatosensory evoked potentials in response to global ischemia. J Neurosurg 1984;60:490–494

11. Astrup J. Energy-requiring cell functions in the ischemic brain: their critical supply and possible inhibition in protective therapy. J Neurosurg 1982;56:482–497

12. Symon L, Crockard HA, Dorsch NWC, et al. Local cerebral blood flow and vascular reactivity in a chronic stable stroke in baboons. Stroke 1975;6:482–492

13. Morawetz RB, DeGiorlami U, Ojemann RG, et al. Cerebral blood flow determined by hydrogen clearance during middle cerebral artery occlusion in unanesthetized monkeys. Stroke 1978;9:143–149

14. Jones TH, Morawetz RB, Crowell RM, et al. Thresholds of focal ischemia in awake monkeys. J Neurosurg 1981;54:773–782

15. DeBakey ME. Successful carotid endarterectomy for cerebrovascular insufficiency: nineteen-year follow-up. JAMA 1975;233:1083–1085

16. North American Symptomatic Carotid Endarterectomy Trial Collaborators. Beneficial effect of carotid endarterectomy in symptomatic patients with high grade stenosis. N Engl J Med 1991;325:445–453

17. Executive Committee for the Asymptomatic Carotid Atherosclerosis Study. Endarterectomy for asymptomatic carotid artery stenosis. JAMA 1995;273:1421–1428

18. Whittemore AD. Carotid endarterectomy and alternative approach. Arch Surg 1980;115:940–942

19. Loftus CM, Quest DO. Technical issues in carotid artery surgery 1995. Neurosurgery 1995;36:629–647

20. Fisher RS, Raudzens P, Nunemacher M. Efficacy of intraoperative neurophysiological monitoring. J Clin Neurophysiol 1995;12:97–109

21. Fode NC, Sundt TM, Robertson JT, et al. Multicenter retrospective review of results and complications of carotid endarterectomy in 1981. Stroke 1986;17:370–376

22. Halsey JH. Risks and benefits of shunting in carotid endarterectomy. Stroke 1992; 23:1583–1587

23. Loftus CM, Dyste GN, Reinarz SJ, Hingtgen WL. Distal cervical carotid dissection after carotid endarterectomy: a complication of indwelling shunt? Neurosurgery 1986;19:441–445

24. Lindsey RL. A simple solution for determining shunt flow during carotid endarterectomy. Anesthesiology 1984;61:215–216

25. Wassmann H, Fischdick G, Jain KK. Cerebral protection during carotid endarterectomy-EEG monitoring as a guide to the use of intraluminal shunts. Acta Neurochir 1984;71:99–108

26. Cho I, Smullens SN, Streletz LJ, Fariello RG. The value of intraoperative EEG monitoring during carotid endarterectomy. Ann Neurol 1986;20:508–551

27. Redekop G, Ferguson G. Correlation of contralateral stenosis and intraoperative electroencephalogram changes with risk of stroke during carotid endarterectomy. Neurosurgery 1992;34:191–194

28. Zampella E, Morawetz RB, McDowell HA, et al. The importance of cerebral ischemia during carotid endarterectomy. Neurosurgery 1991;29:727–731

29. Trojaborg W, Boyson G. Relationship between EEG, regional cerebral blood flow and internal carotid artery pressure during carotid endarterectomy. Electroencephalogr Clin Neurophysiol 1973;34:61–69

30. Chiappa KH, Burke SR, Young RR. Results of electroencephalogram monitoring during 367 carotid endarterectomies: use of a dedicated minicomputer. Stroke 1979;10:381–388

31. Messick JM, Sharbrough F, Sundt T. Selective shunting on the basis of EEG and regional CBF monitoring during carotid endarterectomy. Int Anesthesiol Clin 1984;22:137–145

32. Sundt TM. The ischemic tolerance of neural tissue and the need for monitoring and selective shunting during carotid endarterectomy. Stroke 1983;14:93–98
33. Myers RR, Stockard JJ, Saidman LJ. Monitoring of cerebral perfusion during anesthesia by time-compressed fourier analysis of the electroencephalogram. Stroke 1977;8:331–337
34. Levy WJ, Shapiro HM, Maruchak G, Meathe E. Automated EEG processing for intraoperative monitoring: a comparison of techniques. Anesthesiology 1980;53:223–236
35. Rampil IJ, Holzer JA, Quest DO, et al. Prognostic value of computerized EEG analysis during carotid endarterectomy. Anesth Analg 1983;62:186–192
36. Ahn S, Jordan SE, Nuwer MR, et al. Computed electroencephalographic topographic brain mapping. A new and accurate monitor of cerebral circulation and function for patients having carotid endarterectomy. J Vasc Surg 1988;8:247–254
37. Kearse LA, Martin D, McPeck K, Lopez-Breshnahan M. Computer-derived density spectral array in detection of mild analog electroencephalographic ischemic pattern changes during carotid endarterectomy. J Neurosurg 1993;78:884–890
38. Markand ON. Continuous assessment of cerebral function with EEG and somatosensory evoked potential techniques during extracranial vascular reconstruction. In: Loftus CM, Traynelis VC, ed. Intraoperative monitoring techniques in neurosurgery. New York: McGraw-Hill, Inc, 1994:19–32
39. Moorthy SS, Markand ON, Dilley RS, et al. Somatosensory-evoked responses during carotid endarterectomy. Anesth Analg 1982;61:879–883
40. Markand ON, Dilley RS, Moorthy S, Warren C. Monitoring of somatosensory evoked responses during carotid endarterectomy. Arch Neurol 1984;41:375–378
41. Gigli GL, Caramia M, Marciani MG, et al. Monitoring of subcortical and cortical somatosensory evoked potentials during carotid endarterectomy: comparison with stump pressure levels. Electroencephalogr Clin Neurophysiol 1987;68:424–432
42. Haupt WF, Horsch S. Evoked potential monitoring in carotid surgery: a review of 994 cases. Neurology 1992;42:835–838
43. Schweiger H, Kamp HD, Dinkel M. Somatosensory-evoked potentials during carotid artery surgery: experience in 400 operations. Surgery 1991;109:602–609
44. Amantini A, Bartelli M, de Scisciolo, et al. Monitoring of somatosensory evoked potentials during carotid endarterectomy. J Neurol 1992;239:241–247
45. Tiberio G, Floriani M, Giulini SM, et al. Monitoring of somatosensory evoked potentials during carotid endarterectomy: relationship with different haemodynamic parameters and clinical outcome. Eur J Vasc Surg 1991;5:647–653
46. Kearse LA, Brown EN, McPeck K. Somatosensory evoked potential sensitivity relative to electroencephalography for cerebral ischemia during carotid endarterectomy. Stroke 1992;23:498–505
47. Lam AM, Manninen PH, Ferguson GG, Nantua W. Monitoring electrophysiologic function during carotid endarterectomy: a comparison of somatosensory evoked potentials and conventional electroencephalogram. Anesthesiology 1991;75:15–21
48. Brinkman SD, Braun P, Ganji S, et al. Neuropsychological performance one week after carotid endarterectomy reflects intra-operative ischemia. Stroke 1984;15:497–503
49. De Vleeschauwer P, Horsch S, Matamoros R. Monitoring of somatosensory evoked potentials in carotid surgery: results, usefulness and limitations of the method. Ann Vasc Surg 1988;2:63–68
50. Emerson RG, Turner CA. Monitoring during supratentorial surgery. J Clin Neurophysiol 1993;10:404–411
51. Buchtal A, Belopavlovic M. Somatosensory evoked potentials in cerebral aneurysm surgery. Eur J Anaesth 1992;9:493–497
52. McPhearson RW, Niedermeyer EF, Otenasek RJ, Hanley DF. Correlation of tran-

sient neurological deficit and somatosensory evoked potentials after intracranial aneurysm surgery. J Neurosurg 1983;59:146–149

53. Symon L, Wang AD, Costa E, et al. Perioperative use of somatosensory evoked responses in aneurysm surgery. J Neurosurg 1984;60:269–275

54. Friedman WA, Kaplan BL, Day AL, et al. Evoked potential monitoring during aneurysm operation: observations after fifty cases. Neurosurgery 1987;20:678–687

55. Symon L, Momma F, Murota T. Assessment of reversible cerebral ischaemia in man: intraoperative monitoring of the somatosensory evoked response. Acta Neurochir 1988;42(Suppl):3–7

56. Buchtal A, Belopavlovic M, Mooij JJA. Evoked potential monitoring and temporary clipping in cerebral aneurysm surgery. Acta Neurochir 1988;93:28–36

57. Momma F, Wand AD, Symon L. Effects of temporary occlusion on somatosensory evoked responses in aneurysm surgery. Surg Neurol 1987;27:343–352

58. Schramm J, Koht A, Schmidt G, et al. Surgical and electrophysiological observations during clipping of 134 aneurysms with evoked potential monitoring. Neurosurgery 1990;26:61–70

59. Friedman WA, Chadwick MA, Verhoeven FJ, et al. Monitoring of somatosensory evoked potentials during surgery for middle cerebral artery aneurysms. Neurosurgery 1991;29:83–88

60. Djuric S, Milenkovic Z, Klopcic-Spevak M, Spasic M. Somatosensory evoked potential monitoring during intracranial surgery. Acta Neurochir 1992;119:85–90

60a. Palatinsky E, DiScenna A, McDonald H, et al. SSEP and BAEP monitoring of temporary clip application and induced hypotension during cerebrovascular surgery. In: Loftus CM, Traynelis VC, ed. Intraoperative monitoring techniques in neurosurgery. New York: McGraw-Hill, 1994:61–71

61. Ducati A, Landi A, Cenzato M, et al. Monitoring of brain function by means of evoked potentials in cerebral aneurysm surgery. Acta Neurochir 1988;42(Suppl):8–13

62. Mizoi K, Yoshimoto T. Permissible temporary occlusion time in aneurysm surgery as evaluated by evoked potential monitoring. Neurosurgery 1993;33:434–440

63. Grundy BL, Nelson PB, Lina A, Heros RC. Monitoring of cortical somatosensory evoked potentials to determine the safety of sacrificing the anterior cerebral artery. Neurosurgery 1982;11:64–67

64. Little JR, Lesser RP, Luders H. Electrophysiological monitoring during basilar aneurysm operation. Neurosurgery 1987;20:421–427

65. Manninen PH, Patterson S, Lam AM, et al. Evoked potential monitoring during posterior fossa aneurysm surgery: a comparison of two modalities. Can J Anaesth 1994;41:92–97

66. Follett KA. Intraoperative electrophysiological spinal cord monitoring. In: Loftus CM, Traynelis VC, ed. Intraoperative monitoring techniques in neurosurgery. New York: McGraw-Hill, Inc, 1994:231–238

67. Nash CL, Brown RH. Current concepts review spinal cord monitoring. J Bone Joint Surg 1989;71:627–630

68. MacEwen GD, Bunnell WP, Sriram K. Acute neurological complications in the treatment of scoliosis: a report of the Scoliosis Research Society. J Bone Joint Surg 1975;57:404–408

69. Vauzelle C, Stagnara P, Jovinroux P. Functional monitoring of spinal cord activity during spinal surgery. Clin Orthoped 1973;93:173

70. Diaz JH, Lockhart CH. Postoperative quadriplegia after spinal fusion for scoliosis with intraoperative awakening. Anesth Analg 1987;66:1039–1042

71. Spielholz NI. Intraoperative monitoring using somato-sensory evoked potentials: a brief overview. Electromyogr Clin Neurophysiol 1994;34:29–34

72. Jacobson GP, Tew JM. Intraoperative evoked potential monitoring. J Clin Neurophysiol 1987;4:145–176

73. Nuwer MR. Evoked potential monitoring in the operating room. New York: Raven Press, 1986:188–219
74. Reuter DG, Tacker WA, Badylak SF, Voorhees WD, Konrad PE. Correlation of motor-evoked potential response to ischemic spinal cord damage. J Thorac Cardiovasc Surg 1992;104:262–272
75. Engler GL, Spielholz NI, Bernhard DN, et al. Somatosensory evoked potentials during Harrington instrumentation. J Bone Joint Surg 1978;60A:528–532
76. Nuwer MR, Dawson EC. Intraoperative evoked potential monitoring of the spinal cord: a restricted filter, scalp method during Harrington instrumentation for scoliosis. Clin Orthop 1984;183:42–50
77. Nuwer MR, Dawson EG, Carlson LG, et al. Somatosensory evoked potential spinal cord monitoring reduces neurologic deficits after scoliosis surgery: results of a large multicenter survey. Electroencephalogr Clin Neurophysiol 1995;96:6–11
78. Burke D, Hicks R, Stephen J, et al. Assessment of corticospinal and somatosensory conduction simultaneously during scoliosis surgery. Electroencephalogr Clin Neurophysiol 1992;85:388–396
79. Jellinek D, Jewkes D, Symon L. Noninvasive intraoperative monitoring of motor evoked potentials under propofol anesthesia: effects of spinal surgery on the amplitude and latency of motor evoked potentials. Neurosurgery 1991;29:551–557
80. Levy WJ, Kraus KH, Gugino LD, et al. Transcranial magnetic evoked potential monitoring. In: Loftus CM, Traynelis VC, ed. Intraoperative monitoring techniques in neurosurgery. New York: McGraw-Hill, Inc, 1994:251–255
81. Cheek JC. Posterior fossa intraoperative monitoring. J Clin Neurophysiol 1993;10: 412–424
82. Strauss C, Fahlbusch R, Nimsky C, Cedzich C. Monitoring of visual evoked potentials during para- and suprasellar procedures. In: Loftus CM, Traynelis VC, ed. Intraoperative monitoring techniques in neurosurgery. New York: McGraw-Hill, Inc, 1994:135–140
83. Daube JR, Harper CM. Surgical monitoring of cranial and peripheral nerves. In: Desmedt JD, ed. Neuromonitoring in surgery. Amsterdam: Elsevier, 1989:115–138
84. Kimura J. Electrodiagnosis in diseases of nerve and muscle: principles and practice. Philadelphia: FA Davis Company, 1989:81
85. Harper CM. Brain stem and cranial nerve monitoring. In: Daube JR, ed. Clinical neurophysiology. Philadelphia: FA Davis Company, 1996:451–456
86. Harper CM, Harner SG, Slavit DH, et al. Effect of BAEP monitoring on hearing preservation during acoustic neuroma resection. Neurology 1992;42:1551–1553
87. McPherson RW. General anesthetic considerations in intraoperative monitoring: effects of anesthetic agents and neuromuscular blockade on evoked potentials, EEG, and cerebral blood flow. In: Loftus CM, Traynelis VC, ed. Intraoperative monitoring techniques in neurosurgery. New York: McGraw-Hill, Inc, 1994:97–106
88. Russell GB, Allen GC, Jones JL. Pharmacologic effects of anesthesia on intraoperative neurophysiologic monitoring. In: Russell GB, Rodichok LD, ed. Primer of intraoperative neurophysiologic monitoring. Boston: Butterworth-Heinemann, 1995:227–240
89. Sharbrough FW. Cerebral function monitoring. In: Daube JR, ed. Clinical neurophysiology. Philadelphia: FA Davis Company, 1996:443–450
90. McPherson RW, Sell B, Traystman RJ. Effects of thiopental, fentanyl and etomidate on upper extremity somatosensory evoked potentials in humans. Anesthesiology 1986;65:584–589
91. Graybeal JM. Intraoperative neurophysiological monitoring: a historical perspective. In: Russell GB, Rodichok LD, ed. Primer of intraoperative neurophysiologic monitoring. Boston: Butterworth-Heinemann, 1995:9–14
92. Therapeutics and Technology Assessment Subcommittee of the American Academy of Neurology. Assessment: intraoperative neurophysiology. Neurology 1990;40: 1644–1646

Perioperative Care of the Neurosurgical Pediatric Patient

Gregory B. Hammer, MD
Elliot J. Krane, MD

■ Presurgical Care

Management of the pediatric neurosurgical patient demands a broad-based knowledge of general neurosurgical anesthesia and intensive care as well as an understanding of childhood anatomy and physiology. There are many anatomical and physiological differences between the newborn, infant, and young child and their adult counterparts. Maturational changes in pediatric circulatory, respiratory, and central nervous system physiology have profound impact on the diagnosis and treatment of the neurologically injured child.

The Respiratory System

Both hypoxia and hypercarbia are associated with untoward physiological consequences, particularly in patients with underlying neurological disease. The causes of respiratory failure in children and adults include impaired control of ventilation, neuromuscular disorders, structural impairment of the thorax, airway obstruction (extrathoracic and intrathoracic), and alveolar disease states.

Many of these conditions may be seen in patients with neurological disorders. Impaired control of ventilation may be secondary to head trauma, intracranial hemorrhage, elevated intracranial pressure (ICP), central nervous system (CNS) infection, status epilepticus, or drug intoxication. Trauma to the cervical cord or phrenic nerve may precipitate respiratory failure. Trauma to the chest may produce pneumothorax, hemothorax, or flail chest, causing structural impairment and consequent respiratory failure. Extrathoracic airway obstruction may be caused by trauma from a previously indwelling tracheal tube, resulting in edema, hemorrhage, stenosis, or vocal cord injury. Intrathoracic airway and parenchymal lung disease may be concomitant with neurological injury, including neurogenic pulmonary edema, aspiration of gastric contents, or pulmonary contusion or hemorrhage.

Many features of the anatomy and physiology of the pediatric patient may result in predisposition to respiratory failure. From the nares to the terminal bronchiole, the calibers of the airways in infants and children are small. Because the resistance to gas flow through airways is inversely proportional to the fourth power of their radius (Poiseuille's law), there is an inherently elevated resistance to gas flow in the airways of infants and children. Any lesion that causes further airway narrowing may raise gas-flow resistance to a critical level. This may limit gas flow such that adequate alveolar gas exchange cannot occur, thereby causing respiratory failure. Patients with normal CNS function will increase their effort of breathing in response to airway obstruction in an attempt to overcome elevated resistance to gas flow. Patients with CNS impairment, however, may have limited ability to increase their respiratory effort and may be especially predisposed to respiratory failure. Resulting hypoxia and hypercarbia may exacerbate existing CNS damage.

Infants are also predisposed to respiratory failure because of their increased metabolic requirements as compared with adults. Infants normally consume approximately 6–8 ml of O_2/kg body weight/min and produce about an equal amount of CO_2, compared with a normal minute O_2 consumption and CO_2 production of approximately 3 ml/kg body weight/min in the adult [1]. Conditions that cause reduced alveolar gas exchange in infants, therefore, produce a more precipitous drop in arterial oxygen tension (PaO_2) and elevation of arterial carbon dioxide tension ($PaCO_2$). Infants may, therefore, be especially predisposed to the secondary injury of hypoxia and/or hypercarbia during recovery from a primary CNS injury.

Examples of extrathoracic airway lesions that may cause elevated resistance to gas flow in pediatric patients include edema and hemorrhage of the nose, tongue, posterior pharynx, and supra- or subglottic tissues. These may be produced by trauma such as facial injuries incurred in a fall or motor vehicle accident. Patients with CNS injury may have diminished tone of the hypopharynx due to brain stem or lower cranial nerve dysfunction, contributing to inspiratory obstruction.

In the neurologically impaired pediatric patient, the diagnosis of respiratory failure must be made promptly and treated rapidly in order to avoid secondary neurological injury. The appearance of tachypnea, nasal flaring, exhalatory grunting, and intercostal retractions signal the need for immediate intervention in the infant or child with CNS injury. Alternatively, signs of respiratory depression, including decreased respiratory rate with somnolence, also merit urgent treatment. Respiratory failure may be accompanied by tachycardia or bradycardia and hypertension or hypotension, depending upon the underlying condition and age of the patient.

In the neonate and infant, for example, limited sympathetic tone may predispose to bradycardia secondary to hypoxia.

Monitoring of the neurologically impaired patient with respiratory compromise should include continuous electrocardiography, respiratory rate, and pulse oximetry, as well as frequent blood pressure measurements by automated cuff or continuous intra-arterial monitoring. Arterial CO_2 tension may be estimated with transcutaneous CO_2 monitoring or nasal capnometry [2, 3]. Except in the preterm infant at risk for retinopathy of prematurity, supplemental oxygen should be continuously administered to achieve oxygen saturation by pulse oximetry of 98%–100%. If the oxygen saturation cannot be maintained in this range (or $PaO_2 > 80$–100 mm Hg) despite an inspired oxygen concentration of >0.60, if respiratory acidemia exists, or if heart rate and/or blood pressure are adversely affected in the presence of respiratory distress, tracheal intubation should be performed and mechanical ventilation should be instituted. These modalities should also be utilized in the presence of impending or existing unconsciousness, absent protective airway reflexes, intracranial hypertension, or severe neuromuscular weakness.

The Circulatory System

The systemic arterial blood pressure is lower in the infant and increases to adult values by the time of adolescence. In the infant, stroke volume is limited, so that increased cardiac output is largely mediated by increased heart rate. Stroke volume and cardiac output increase with age, while the heart rate decreases with age. Other differences between the developing pediatric heart and that of the adult include oxygen consumption, response to hypoxemia, and autonomic innervation.

Acute hypoxia, like hypo- and hyperthermia, is a potent stimulus for a reactive increase in cardiac output. This increase in cardiac output is mediated in part by increased sympathetic stimulation [4]. The developing heart is better able to tolerate acute severe hypoxia than the adult heart. This is, at least in part, related to the increased capacity of the immature myocardium to maintain anaerobic metabolism due to improved glycolytic activity [5]. The infant's myocardium allows it to survive more prolonged exposure to acute severe hypoxia than the adult. Unfortunately, the infant brain does not appear to be similarly protected against hypoxic-ischemic injury. Therefore, among infants, there is a predisposition toward brain-injured survival following severe hypoxia as compared with adults.

Autonomic control of the heart and circulation is less well developed in the infant than the adult. The infant appears to have a relative predominance of parasympathetic neural tone. The infant may, for example, exhibit an exaggerated vagotonic response to hypoxemia, laryngoscopy, or gastroesophageal reflux, leading to bradycardia. Conversely, the infant may demonstrate increased sensitivity to exogenous catechols [6]. Physicians caring for critically ill pediatric patients should be aware that because of development differences pharmacological manipulation of the circulation may differ from that of the adult patient.

Therapies to ameliorate low cardiac output and hypertension in pediatric patients are similar in principle to those used in adults, however, important differences do exist. Inotropic drugs should be very carefully titrated in infants, as they may demonstrate pronounced sensitivity to these agents for reasons described above. Primary hypertension is uncommon in infancy and early childhood. In infants with hypertension secondary to brain injury, the primary cause of the hypertension (e.g., elevated intracranial pressure) should be aggressively treated before antihypertensive agents are invoked. Beta-blockers should be used with extreme caution in infants. These agents may cause a precipitous fall in cardiac output that is dependent on heart rate in the first years of life.

If a cardiac murmur is detected during preoperative auscultation of the heart, a formal cardiology evaluation may be indicated to rule out the existence of intracardiac shunting, which might lead to paradoxical air embolism [7] during craniotomies.

The Nervous System

The nervous system undergoes rapid developmental change during the first years of life, as reflected in the neurological examination of the infant and young child. While cranial nerves are myelinated at birth and can be readily examined, a detailed motor and sensory examination of the infant may be more difficult. An infant's tone when relaxed and the symmetric response to light, sound, and gentle touch may be revealing. Hand preference is uncommon during the first 18 months of age, and hypotonia, or flaccidity, are abnormal at any age [8]. Interpretation of the gross motor exam is guided by an understanding of normal motor developmental milestones (Table 1). Examination of reflex movements may be diagnostic. The newborn startle, or Moro's, reflex normally disappears after 6 months of age, whereas bilateral extensor plantar reflexes as well as ankle clonus are normal up to 1 year of age. Persistence or reappearance of these reflexes beyond 1 year of age may indicate intracranial pathology.

The normal infant skull has an open anterior fontanelle, soft calvaria, and open, moveable sutures. The posterior fontanelle normally closes in early infancy. The anterior fontanelle is usually closed by 12 months of age [9]. These features mitigate, but do not prevent, the increases in ICP associated with hydrocephalus and intracranial mass lesions. The anterior fontanelle is normally flat when the infant is upright and may be full and pulsatile with crying. A persistently tense, bulging fontanelle suggests elevated intracranial pressure. Gradual increases in intracranial volume

Table 1. *Motor Developmental Milestones in Infants and Toddlers*

Age	Milestone
1 week	Extends head in prone position
3–4 months	Has head control
5–6 months	Rolls prone to supine
6–7 months	Rolls supine to prone
7–8 months	Sits alone; transfers objects hand to hand
9–11 months	Stands while holding on
11–12 months	Walks with assistance
13–15 months	Walks by self
18 months	Climbs stairs with assistance
24 months	Runs

may be accommodated by expansion of the fontanelles and separation of the suture lines, resulting in an enlarging head circumference. This may be associated with subacute or chronic ICP elevation.

The relatively elastic infant skull may absorb some of the energy associated with head trauma. This may, however, allow more brain compression and distortion than the adult skull. In addition, the more compliant infant skull may allow more to-and-fro motion of the brain during shaking of the head. This may lead to tearing of the bridging veins between the cortex and the venous sinuses, resulting in subdural hemorrhage. Furthermore, the floor of the anterior and middle fossae are smoother than in the adult, providing less resistance to brain movement and further predisposing to subdural hematoma formation [10]. Bilateral retinal hemorrhages may also be associated with nonaccidental shaking injury and are suggestive of increased ICP [11].

Cerebrospinal fluid (CSF) production begins during the eighth week of embryonic development. CSF is produced primarily in the choroid plexus in the temporal horns of the lateral ventricles. CSF drains from the lateral ventricles via the foramen of Munro to the third ventricle, then into the fourth ventricle via the aqueduct of Sylvius. CSF then enters the cisterna magna via the lateral foramina of Luschka and the midline foramen of Magendie. After entering the cranial and spinal subarachnoid spaces, CSF is reabsorbed by the arachnoid villi. Newborn infants, especially those born prematurely, may develop intracranial hemorrhage due to inadequate autoregulation of cerebral blood flow (CBF) as well as diminished structural support of the microvasculature in the periventricular region. This may lead to impairment of CSF outflow and obstructive hydrocephalus. Obstructive hydrocephalus may also result from meningitis or congenital aqueductal stenosis. These lesions may all be associated with elevated ICP and require placement of ventriculoperitoneal shunts or other drain-

Table 2. *Cerebral Blood Flow (CBF) and Cerebral Metabolic Rate for Oxygen (CMRO$_2$) in the Neonate, Infant, and Adult*[19]

	CBF (ml/100 g/min)	CMRO$_2$ (ml O$_2$/100 g/min)
Neonate	40	2.3
Infant	90–100	5.0
Adult	53	3.0

age procedures. Atrophy of brain parenchyma may occur following neuronal cell death in infants, resulting in hydrocephalus ex vacuo. This condition is not generally associated with ICP elevation and does not require drainage.

Cerebral blood flow and cerebral metabolic rate for oxygen increase during infancy and early childhood before decreasing to adult values in later childhood (Table 2). Autoregulation of CBF must occur over a lower range of systemic blood pressure than in the adult, given that mean arterial blood pressure in the neonate may be as low as 35 mm Hg [1]. CBF increases from 40 ml/min/100 g to 90–100 ml/min/100 g during the first year of life. Cerebral function is impaired at CBF less than 15–20 ml/min/ 100 g, and brain infarction occurs at CBF less than 10 ml/min/100 g [12]. Autoregulation may be impaired in cases of cerebral hypoxia/ischemia (e.g., birth asphyxia, infant respiratory distress syndrome, persistent pulmonary hypertension), severe acidemia, neonatal sepsis, or meningitis. Newborns with impaired autoregulation of CBF may develop intracranial hemorrhage associated with acute hypertension (e.g., awake intubation).

The effect of PaCO$_2$ on CBF may be different in pediatric vs adult patients. While hyperventilation to a PaCO$_2$ less than 20 mm Hg does not appear to further diminish CBF in adults, CBF in children decreases until PaCO$_2$ reaches 15 mm Hg. In a newborn animal model, CBF continued to decrease to a PaCO$_2$ of 12–15 mm Hg [13]. Monitoring of arterial-jugular oxygen difference has been recommended in patients undergoing prolonged hyperventilation to a PaCO$_2$ less than 20 mm Hg, with the goal of maintaining the jugular venous O$_2$ tension greater than 20 mm Hg.

The effects of PaO$_2$ on CBF is also different in the newborn compared with adults. The neonate is adapted to a lower intrauterine arterial oxygen tension. Whereas CBF increases in older children and adults in response to PaO$_2$ values less than 50 mm Hg, CBF is not increased in newborns until the PaO$_2$ is less than 25 mm Hg [12].

The normal values for ICP are somewhat different in the pediatric patient compared with adults. Normal ICP is less than 2 mm Hg in the neonate, up to 6 mm Hg in the 1-year-old infant, and as high as 13 mm Hg in the older child [14]. ICP may be elevated due to congenital lesions, hydrocephalus, tumors, CNS infections, hemorrhage, hypoxia-ischemia,

Table 3. *Modified Coma Scale for Infants*

Response	Score[a]
Eye opening	
Spontaneous	4
To speech	3
To pain	2
None	1
Verbal	
Coos, babbles	5
Irritable cries	4
Cries to pain	3
Moans to pain	2
None	1
Motor	
Normal spontaneous movements	6
Withdraws to touch	5
Withdraws to pain	4
Abnormal flexion	3
Abnormal extension	2
None	1

[a]The range of scores is from 3 to 15. Though similar to the adult Glasgow Coma Scale, this system has not been validated as a predictor of outcome following head injury in children.

and head trauma. General measures utilized for control of ICP in adults are applied in children, including head elevation, sedation, neuromuscular blockade, avoidance of sympathetic stimulation, and hyperventilation. Extreme hyperventilation to $PaCO_2$ values as low as 12–15 mm Hg may be useful in infants and young children, but monitoring of jugular venous oxygen tension has been advocated in this setting [15]. The risks of treating infants and children with elevated ICP may be minimized by using a balanced approach, including isovolemic dehydration or osmolar therapy, hyperventilation, hypothermia, and judicious use of barbiturates.

Cortical brain injury may be assessed by scoring systems modified from those used in adults. Examples include the Modified Coma Scale for Infants (Table 3) and the Children's Coma Scale (Table 4) [11, 16]. As with the Glasgow Coma Scale (GCS) used in adults, these systems assign point values to indices of the motor, sensory, and ocular examinations. There is no consensus on the most appropriate scoring system for infants and young children. Regardless of which system is used, physicians and nurses must assess ocular function as well as verbal and motor responses in a frequent, consistent manner. Any deterioration in the examination should be met with immediate evaluation and intervention where appropriate.

Table 4. *Children's Coma Scale*[16]

Response	Score[a]
Ocular	
Pursuit	4
Extraocular muscles (EOM) intact and reactive pupils	3
Fixed pupils or EOM impaired	2
Fixed pupils and EOM paralyzed	1
Verbal	
Cries	3
Spontaneous respirations	2
Apneic	1
Motor	
Flexes and extends	4
Withdraws from painful stimuli	3
Hypertonic	2
Flaccid	1

[a]The range of scores is from 3 to 11.

As with adult patients, ICP may be monitored in infants and children with a variety of devices, including intraventricular catheters as well as subarachnoid and epidural monitors. In infants, several techniques have been developed for assessing ICP via the anterior fontanelle. These include pneumotonometry and a fiberoptic system [17, 18]. Electrical monitoring, using electroencephalography and evoked potentials, are also utilized extensively in pediatric patients, as are imaging with ultrasound, computed tomographic scanning, and magnetic resonance imaging. Interpretation of these studies requires special expertise and understanding of the anatomical and developmental changes that occur in newborns and infants.

The preoperative assessment of the patient should determine the presence or absence of intracranial hypertension, which may be deduced from the history. When the history is brief, as in the case of head trauma, the existence of intracranial hypertension may be difficult to assess. The Glasgow Coma Scale (or its modifications) is useful in the acute setting; in general, a GCS score of 6 or less suggests the presence of acute intracranial hypertension [19]. The elements of Cushing's triad—hyperventilation, bradycardia, and hypertension—are late signs and portend impending herniation. Other signs of herniation syndrome include pupillary asymmetry, dilation, or irregularity; cranial nerve palsies; asymmetric motor tone or strength; tendon reflex asymmetry; and respiratory irregularity. These are late signs and mandate immediate therapy to lower ICP, including hyperventilation and osmotherapy.

■ Anesthetic Management

OR Preparation

Operating theaters should be warmed to 75°C–80°C prior to bringing the patient into the room. The anesthesiologist must ensure that age-appropriate airway equipment is available and functioning and that an assortment of appropriately sized endotracheal tubes and vascular cannulae is available. The use of forced air warming devices aids in stabilizing children's temperatures during lengthy neurosurgical procedures and obviates the need to keep the operating theater uncomfortably warm for the surgical team after draping the patient.

Premedication

Sedative premedication is generally withheld from children with intracranial hypertension or space occupying lesions because of the risk of respiratory depression, hypercarbia, and attendant worsening of ICP. On the other hand, judicious use of benzodiazepine premedicants in a conscious, directly supervised child may alleviate anxiety, prevent agitation and hypertension (and their attendant elevation of ICP), and generally smooth the preoperative and anesthesia induction periods. An appropriate regimen would be the oral or rectal administration of midazolam, 0.5–0.7 mg/kg; this is generally not associated with respiratory depression provided that there is not recent or concomitant administration of opiates.

Children with vascular malformations who do not have increased ICP and who are at risk for bleeding should be well sedated to prevent systemic hypertension. An alternative to midazolam in this setting would be oral or rectal administration of pentobarbital, 4–5 mg/kg. Children (and adults) with vascular malformations being resected also benefit from the preoperative administration of beta-blockers, which prevent or mitigate the hemodynamic response to anesthesia induction, vascular access, and laryngoscopy. This may be accomplished by oral premedication with propranolol in a total dose of 1 mg/kg divided in 3 administrations in the 12 hours prior to surgery or by an intravenous esmolol infusion of 500 μg/kg.

Induction of Anesthesia

The goals for anesthesia induction include hemodynamic stability, prevention of sustained increases in ICP, and securing of the airway. In general, intravenous induction with a short-acting agent such as sodium thiopental (5–7 mg/kg) or propofol (3–4 mg/kg) will diminish ICP and allow the anesthesiologist to induce hyperventilation early in the anesthetic. The subsequent administration of a synthetic opiate such as fentanyl or sufentanil will blunt the hemodynamic response to airway instrumentation. Finally, laryngoscopy and intubation of the airway are facilitated by the administration of a neuromuscular blocking agent that does not release histamine such as pancuronium or vecuronium.

All patients with CNS injury and respiratory failure should be considered as having a full stomach. CNS injury and respiratory failure may each be associated with increased gastric acidity and volume. Therefore, patients with both disorders might logically be assumed to be at high risk for gastric regurgitation and pulmonary aspiration. Bag-and-mask ventilation may result in gaseous distention of the stomach, increasing this risk. The appropriate application of cricoid pressure during bag-and-mask ventilation and laryngoscopy reduces the likelihood of this potentially catastrophic event [20]. Cricoid pressure should be maintained until correct placement of the tracheal tube has been confirmed by auscultation.

Wherein rapid intubation of the airway is necessary to prevent aspiration of gastric contents, succinylcholine should be used in spite of the theoretical elevation in ICP that may occur in some patients [21]. The elevation of ICP is usually small, transient, and overshadowed by the adverse effects on ICP of coughing, aspiration, and hypoventilation that may occur with a more prolonged induction [22]. Alternatively, high dose rocuronium (0.9 mg/kg) will provide satisfactory intubating conditions in about 60 seconds, without alterations in hemodynamics or adverse changes in cerebral dynamics.

Tracheal Intubation

Preoperative indications for tracheal intubation in infants and children include maintenance of alveolar gas exchange and oxygenation, prevention of pulmonary aspiration of gastric contents, and control of intracranial pressure. Neurologically injured children may require tracheal intubation in the emergency department, pediatric intensive care unit, or pediatric ward as well as the operating room. Prior to tracheal intubation, bag-and-mask hyperventilation should be performed with 100% oxygen. A continuous oxygen source and bag-and-mask system with the appropriate size face mask for positive pressure ventilation should be maintained for this purpose at or near each patient's bedside. Circuits employing self-inflating bags or anesthesia bags may be utilized safely and effectively, as long as the operator is familiar with the specifications of the system in use. A range of oropharyngeal and nasopharyngeal airways should be readily available to maintain extrathoracic airway patency during bag-and-mask ventilation. As with adult patients, nasopharyngeal airways should not be employed in the presence of basilar skull fracture with possible discontinuity of the nasopharyngeal mucosa nor in patients with bleeding diatheses.

Anatomical features of the infant's airway may render tracheal intubation more difficult than in the adult patient. These features include large head size relative to neck, shoulders, and thorax; small mandibular size;

relatively large tongue; and a glottis that is displaced cephalad and anteriorly. Special equipment for performing tracheal intubation in infants and children includes appropriately sized laryngoscope blades and tracheal tubes. After confirmation of correct positioning of the tracheal tube, appropriate tube size must also be confirmed. During slow positive pressure inspiration, the neck overlying the trachea is auscultated. The inflating pressure at which a gas leak around the tracheal tube is first heard is noted. The tracheal tube size is generally appropriate if this initial leak occurs at between 10 and 35 cm H_2O. If the initial leak is at a pressure of 0–10 cm H_2O, the indwelling tube should be replaced with the next larger size (e.g., a 4.0-mm inside diameter (ID) tube is replaced with a 4.5-mm ID tube). If no leak occurs at an inflating pressure of 35 cm H_2O, a smaller tube should be inserted if the patient's clinical status permits.

Tracheal tubes should be secured with suture to the alveolar ridge in cases involving extensive craniofacial dissection in order to prevent accidental intraoperative dislodging of the airway. For other neurosurgical cases, the use of benzoin and waterproof tape is recommended.

Monitoring and Maintenance of Anesthesia

Routine monitors for all pediatric anesthesia cases include means of auscultating breath and heart sounds, pulse oximetry, capnometry, electrocardiography, and thermistry. The utility of continuous auscultation of the esophageal stethoscope cannot be overemphasized, given the frequency with which connections become dislodged, small endotracheal tubes become occluded by secretions, or even dislodged during the course of a long neurosurgical case. Monitoring of the depth of neuromuscular blockade with a peripheral nerve stimulator will reduce the risk of patient movement during the surgery and the risk of excessively deep blockade at the conclusion of surgery. All intracranial surgery and craniofacial surgery should involve the use of intra-arterial pressure monitoring both for second-to-second assessment of hemodynamics as well as for frequent arterial blood sampling for measurement of hemoglobin, glucose, and electrolytes. A precordial Doppler device will assist in detecting venous air emboli during siting craniotomies and craniofacial surgery [23, 24], while central venous cannulation via the jugular veins, subclavian veins, or femoral veins is further recommended for craniotomies in the siting position and for craniofacial surgery to permit the aspiration of venous air emboli from the heart. The optimal site for the tip of the cannula for this purpose is at the right atrial–superior vena cava junction [25], and appropriate positioning of the cannula can be confirmed radiographically prior to surgery.

The selection of anesthetic agents involves knowledge of the effects of these agents on intracranial blood flow and pressure, the pharmacokinetics of the agents, and the cost of the agents. These topics have been extensively reviewed elsewhere.

Table 5. *Pediatric Neuroanesthesia Drug Dosages*

Drug	Induction Dose	Maintenance Dose
Thiopental	5–7 mg/kg	
Propofol	2–3 mg/kg	100–250 μg/kg/hr
Fentanyl	5 μg/kg	1–3 μg/kg/hr
Sufentanil	0.25 μg/kg	0.2–0.6 μg/kg/hr
Succinylcholine	1 mg/kg	
Rocuronium	0.9 mg/kg	
Pancuronium	0.1 mg/kg	0.025–0.05 mg/kg/hr
Vecuronium	0.1 mg/kg	0.05–0.075 mg/kg/hr
Vancomycin	15 mg/kg over 60 min	Repeat q8h
Cephalosporins	25 mg/kg	Repeat q6h
Penicillins	25 mg/kg	Repeat q6h

All halogenated inhalation agents decrease cerebral metabolic rate but increase cerebral blood flow (and ICP) in a dose-dependent manner. These deleterious effects on ICP can be ameliorated by the concomitant use of hyperventilation to induce hypocapnia. Nevertheless, many anesthesiologists believe that halogenated agents should not be introduced if ICP is known to be elevated until the dura is open, so that the ICP response to the agent can be directly determined by observing the appearance of the brain through the wound.

Most pediatric anesthesiologists therefore choose a balanced anesthetic technique that combines nitrous oxide, an opiate (typically fentanyl) a relaxant (typically pancuronium or vecuronium) with the low-dose administration of a halogenated agent (generally isoflurane), to ensure amnesia and hypnosis. A balanced anesthetic technique is associated with more rapid awakening after lengthy neurosurgical procedures, therefore permitting more rapid assessment of the neurosurgical examination by the surgeon. Typical and reasonable dosage regimens for drugs used in pediatric neuroanesthesia are found in Table 5.

Emergence

Prompt arousal of the child after neurosurgery is the goal that permits neurological examination of the child and obviates the need for mechanical ventilation postoperatively. In order to accomplish this goal, several strategies are useful.

Opiates (fentanyl, sufentanil) should be withheld for the final 30–60 minutes of the anesthetic. Typically, wound closure and dressing take 30–60 minutes after major procedures; therefore, as the surgeon begins to prepare for closure, the anesthesiologist should administer the final dose of opiate. Similarly, it takes a lengthy period of time for the body to excrete the more soluble halogenated agents (halothane, isoflurane) after lengthy procedures, and even small alveolar concentrations of halogenated agents will impair arousal. Therefore, the beginning of closure is the appropriate time to discontinue these agents. Signs of light anesthesia during closure can then be managed with small intravenous doses of short-acting drugs such as propofol, a low-dose propofol infusion, or administration of one of the less soluble halogenated agents such as desflurane or sevoflurane. Extubation of the trachea is appropriate in children who were not obtunded or comatose preoperatively, who demonstrate stable hemodynamics, normal ICP, and intracranial dynamics, and who are free of excessive facial or airway edema. Extubation then should follow demonstration that the child is awake, has recovered full neuromuscular function, and is able to protect his/her airway.

Reversal of neuromuscular blockade is best demonstrated by recovery of the full train-of-four response and response to tetanic stimulus. A reliable clinical sign in the infant or toddler is the ability to flex the legs at the hip and maintain the legs in the air against gravity, a position most children reflexively assume during emergence. In the older child and teenager, sustained head flexion is a reliable sign of adequacy of neuromuscular function, as is the case in the adult. The most reliable signs that a child has regained sufficient consciousness for extubation is eye opening, forceful eye closing noted by wrinkling of the eyelids and bulging of the eyebrows, or reaching for the endotracheal tube with the hand. Upon observation of these indicators, the oral cavity may be suctioned free of saliva and secretions, and the trachea may be extubated.

Posterior fossa surgery for tumors involving the brain stem occasionally lead to injury of one or more cranial nerves or cranial nerve nuclei and vocal cord paralysis. This will be immediately recognized by the anesthesiologist as stridor and partial or complete airway obstruction. The differential diagnosis of airway obstruction in this clinical situation will be much simpler if the patient has been extubated when awake. If oxygenation can be maintained with the administration of supplemental oxygen, the diagnosis can be confirmed by indirect or fiberoptic laryngoscopy. If airway obstruction is severe, anesthesia should be reinduced and the airway should be secured by conventional means.

For patients not meeting the clinical criteria for extubation, adequate levels of sedatives and opiates should be given and the patient should be transported to an intensive care unit with the endotracheal tube secured for postoperative mechanical ventilation.

■ Initial Postoperative Care

Mechanical Ventilation

The goal of mechanical ventilation in the neurosurgical pediatric patient is to ensure optimal exchange of oxygen and carbon dioxide across the alveolar capillary membrane while causing minimal adverse effects on cerebral perfusion.

Several developmental aspects of respiratory mechanics affect the practice of mechanical ventilation of the pediatric patient. The normal respiratory rate of the newborn is 20–60 breaths/min, as opposed to 12–16 breaths/min in the adult. Inspiratory time in the infant is normally 0.4–0.5 seconds, compared to about 1.25 seconds in the adult [26]. Tidal volume, on the other hand, remains relatively constant throughout childhood development at approximately 6–8 ml/kg [27, 28]. Maximum inspiratory flow in the infant is about 20 L/min, compared with 300–600 L/min in the adult [29]. The static and dynamic differences in the developing respiratory system dictate the technical requirements of respiratory support in infants and children.

In the neonate and infant, ventilators that are pressure limited and/ or time limited are most commonly employed. These ventilators offer the advantages of avoiding excessive inflating pressures and, presumably, decreased risk of barotrauma. However, a decrease in the compliance (or conductance) of the patient's respiratory system (or ventilator circuit) will cause a reduction in delivered tidal volume. An increase in either parameter, conversely, will result in an increased tidal volume.

Volume-limited ventilators, on the other hand, deliver a relatively constant volume of gas despite changes in the patient's chest compliance. The presence of high inflating pressures signal decreased compliance or conductance of the breathing circuit (e.g., occluded tracheal tube), chest wall (e.g., offset of neuromuscular blockade), or airway (e.g., bronchospasm). Disadvantages of these ventilators include the potential generation of very high inflating pressures and the possibly increased risk of barotrauma or impairment of cerebral venous drainage. With proper monitoring of inspiratory pressure, including the use of alarms, changes in the patient's pulmonary mechanics can be observed and the risk of barotrauma minimized. Because of technical difficulties in accurately delivering very small tidal volumes (e.g., under 50 ml), volume-limited ventilators are primarily used in patients over 5 kg body weight.

Gas leaks around uncuffed tracheal tubes represent an important source of volume loss. The magnitude of such gas leaks commonly varies with the patient's head position. As a result, there may be a variable discrepancy between inspired and exhaled tidal volumes related to head position. This may result in changes in arterial CO_2 tension and cerebral blood flow. Thus, it is important to monitor both inspired and exhaled tidal volumes closely in pediatric patients with indwelling uncuffed tracheal tubes in order to ensure appropriate alveolar ventilation.

There are many other variations in features offered by different types of pediatric mechanical ventilators, including mechanisms for power drive, modes of initiating inspiration, patterns of inspiratory flow, etc. Of primary importance is that practitioners be familiar with the various types of mechanical ventilators in use at their institution. There is no substitution for bedside observation of the patient. When mechanical ventilation is utilized, for example, the physician should monitor thoracic excursion and ventilatory pattern to ensure that the desired parameters are achieved. The patient should be continuously observed for signs of respiratory distress, indicating the need for ruling out occlusion of the tracheal tube, ventilator malfunction, or a change in chest compliance. Vigilance is essential in order to obviate secondary CNS injury associated with mechanical ventilation mishaps. For example, elevation of mean airway pressure due to inadvertent positive end-expiratory pressure or high inflating pressures can cause untoward elevation of intracranial pressure. Monitors, including ventilator alarms, pulse oximetry, and capnography, should be maintained at all times.

Control of Hemodynamics

After neurosurgical interventions, it is important to ensure that children maintain adequate cerebral perfusion while avoiding high blood pressures that place the child at risk for cerebral hemorrhage.

Inadequately treated pain and activation of the sympathetic nervous system are the most common etiologies for postoperative hypertension in children after neurosurgery. After ensuring that pain and anxiety have been adequately treated, persistent hypertension may then be managed by an infusion of esmolol. The advantage of esmolol over longer-acting beta-antagonists is that its administration may be carefully titrated to a changing cardiovascular condition. Its advantage over direct-acting vasodilators such as sodium nitroprusside is that esmolol causes no cerebral vasodilation and has no deleterious effect upon intracranial pressure.

When intracranial pressure is of lesser concern (e.g., following tumor excision), cerebral swelling is not usually significant; therefore, cerebral compliance is not diminished, and nitroprusside is an excellent option for blood pressure control. The usual starting dose is the same in children as in adults, 0.5 µg/kg/min. Nitroprusside has the advantage, as compared to other agents such as nifedipine or hydralazine, of being more titratable and shorter acting.

Hypotension following neurosurgery in children is seldom of cardiogenic origin; much more common is unrecognized hypovolemia. Monitoring central venous pressure may not always detect significant hypovolemia because activation of the sympathetic nervous system will lead to venoconstriction and movement of volume from peripheral to central compartments. Better indicators are perfusion of the distal extremities, urine output, and acid-base balance. Therefore, it follows that inotropic support is seldom indicated in the immediate period following neurosurgery.

■ References

1. Dawes GS. Fetal and neonatal physiology. Chicago: Yearbook Medical, 1973:191
2. Bucher HU, Fanconi S, Fallenstein F, Duc G. Transcutaneous carbon dioxide tension in newborn infants: reliability and safety of continuous 24-hour measurement at 42°C. Pediatrics 1986;78:631
3. Hess D. Capnometry and capnography: technical aspects, physiologic aspects, and clinical applications. Respir Care 1990;35:557
4. Downing SE. Neural regulation of circulation during hypoxia and acidosis with special reference to the newborn. Fed Proc 1972;31:1209
5. Dawes GS, Mott JC, Shelley HJ. The importance of cardiac glycogen for the maintenance of life in foetal lambs and newborn animals during anoxia. J Physiol 1959; 146:516
6. Friedman WF. The intrinsic physiologic properties of the developing heart. In: Friedman WF, Lesch M, Sonnenblick E, eds. Neonatal heart disease. New York: Grune and Stratton, 1973:21
7. Albin M. The paradox of paradoxic air embolism. Anesthesiology 1984;61:222
8. Venes JL, Linder SL, Elderman RD. Neurologic examination of infants and children. In: Youmans JR, ed. Neurologic surgery. 3rd ed. Philadelphia: Saunders, 1990;Chap 2:37
9. Peacock WJ. The postnatal development of the brain and its coverings. In: Raimondi AJ, Choux M, Rocco CD, eds. Head injuries in the newborn and infant. New York: Springer-Verlag, 1986;Chap 4:53–66
10. Bruce DA. Concepts of intracranial volume and pressure. In: James HE, Anas NG, Perkin RM, eds. Brain insults in infants and children. Orlando, FL: Grune and Stratton, 1985;Chap 2:19
11. Raimondi AJ, Hirschauer J. Clinical criteria—children's coma score and outcome scale for decision making in managing head injured infants and toddlers. In: Raimondi AJ, Choux M, Rocco CD, eds. Head injuries in the newborn and infant. New York: Springer Verlag, 1986;Chap 10:141–150
12. Hollinger IB, Goodrich JT. Pediatric neuroanesthesia. In: Frost EAM, ed. Clinical anesthesia in neurosurgery. 2nd ed. Boston: Butterworth, 1991;Chap 13:287–333
13. Bruce DA. Cerebrovascular dynamics. In: James HE, Anas NG, Perkin RM, eds. Brain insults in infants and children. Orlando, FL: Grune and Stratton, 1985;Chap 5:53–60
14. Shapiro K, Marmarou A. Mechanisms of intracranial hypertension in children. In: McLaurin RL, Schut L, Venes JL, Epstein F, eds. Pediatric Neurosurgery. 2nd ed. Philadelphia: Saunders, 1989;Chap 17:238
15. Bruce DA. Ventilation, hyperventilation, megaventilation and cerebral blood flow. In: James HE, Anas NG, Perkin RM, eds. Brain insults in infants and children. Orlando, FL: Grune and Stratton, 1985;Chap 25:257–262
16. James HE, Trauner DA. The Glasgow coma scale. In: James HE, Anas NG, Perkin RM, eds. Brain insults in infants and children. Orlando, FL: Grune and Stratton, 1985;Chap 16:179–182
17. Menke JA, Miles R, McIlhany M, et al. The fontanelle tonometer: a noninvasive method for measurement of intracranial pressure. J Pediatr 1982;100:960
18. Walsh P, Logan WJ. Continuous and intermittent measurement of intracranial pressure by Ladd monitor. J Pediatr 1983;102:439
19. Bruce D, Berman WA, Schut L. Cerebrospinal fluid pressure monitoring in children: physiology, pathology and clinical usefulness. Adv Pediatr 1977;24:233
20. Moynihan RJ, Brock-Utne JG, Archer JH, et al. The effect of cricoid pressure on preventing gastric insufflation in infants and children. Anesthesiology 1993;78: 652

21. Minton MD, Grosslight K, Stirt JA, et al. Increases in intracranial pressure from succinylcholine: prevention by prior nondepolarizing blockade. Anesthesiology 1986;65:165
22. March ML, Dunlop BJ, Shapiro HM, et al. Succinylcholine intracranial pressure effects in neurosurgical patients. Anesth Analg 1980;59:550
23. Harris MH, Yemen TA, Strafford MA, et al. Venous air embolism during craniectomy in supine infants. Anesthesiology 1987;67:816
24. Harris MH, Strafford MA, Rowe RW, et al. Venous air embolism and cardiac arrest during craniectomy in a supine infant. Anesthesiology 1986;64:643
25. Bunegin L, Albin MS, Helsel PE, et al. Positioning the right atrial catheter—a model for reappraisal. Anesthesiology 1981;55:343
26. Mushin WW. Clinical aspects of controlled respiration. In: Rendell-Baker L, Thompson PW, Mapleson WW, eds. Automatic ventilation of the lungs. Oxford: Blackwell Scientific, 1980:33
27. Nelson NM. Neonatal pulmonary function. Pediatr Clin North Am 1966;13:769
28. Doershuk CF, Fisher BJ, Matthews LW. Pulmonary physiology of the young child. In: Scarpelli EM, ed. Pulmonary physiology of the fetus, newborn, and child. Philadelphia: Lea and Febiger, 1975:166
29. Auld PAM. Pulmonary physiology of the newborn infant. In: Scarpelli EM, ed. Pulmonary physiology of the fetus and newborn child. Philadelphia: Lea and Febiger, 1975:140

Anesthetics and Cerebroprotection: Experimental Aspects

Jeffrey R. Kirsch, MD
Richard J. Traystman, PhD
Patricia D. Hurn, PhD

Early observations in patients under general anesthesia set the stage for the concept that anesthetic agents could also serve to protect the brain from an ischemic or hypoxic insult [1]. Anesthetics may affect ischemic or traumatic brain injury by numerous mechanisms, and their potential for cerebroprotection and brain resuscitation is clinically relevant. In designing the anesthetic plan for patients at high risk of cerebral ischemia (e.g., carotid endarterectomy, open-heart procedures), it is useful to consider the relative degree of protection provided by various agents. Similarly, treating patients with an anesthetic after cardiac arrest or a focal ischemic insult may be a consideration in improving overall neurological outcome. Much of our knowledge surrounding anesthetics and cerebroprotection originates from animal studies in which outcomes following cerebral ischemia have been compared with different anesthetic regimens. Typically, the protective properties of anesthetic agents have been compared as pretreatments in the presence of an accompanying baseline anesthetic. Relatively few data are available that compare outcomes when administering the anesthetic only after the onset of ischemia/reperfusion or comparing outcomes in awake animals who are free of potentially confounding baseline anesthetic agents.

In interpreting cerebroprotection studies, it is important to characterize the experimental model of ischemia by the magnitude, duration, and distribution of cerebral blood flow (CBF) reduction. By definition, global cerebral ischemia affects whole brain, but CBF reduction may be complete (zero blood flow) or incomplete. Studies of incomplete ischemia can be of special interest if they mimic clinically relevant brain insults. However, these findings can also be difficult to evaluate if CBF is not measured, because various models and experimental paradigms produce different levels of residual blood flow and target-cell injury. Rodent models of global forebrain ischemia are commonly employed because of their simplicity and because they preserve brain stem blood flow and respiratory and cardiovascular stability. Global forebrain blood flow (i.e., to cortex, striatum, hippocampus) is severely reduced (0–5 ml/min/100 g) in these models. Finally, focal ischemic models are employed to study stroke (e.g., middle cerebral artery occlusion that produces a spatial blood flow gradient from core to periphery). The period of occlusion is usually several hours in order to produce consistent infarction. In permanent stroke models, the occlusion is not reversed. In contrast, many experimental approaches incorporate transient, or reversible, focal models in which occlusion is followed by reperfusion.

The purpose of this chapter is to evaluate the cerebroprotective or resuscitative potential of commonly used anesthetics from data obtained in experimental systems. Relevant studies that provide clues to the mechanisms of anesthetic action in brain injury are discussed. Lastly, the effect of each agent on CBF and cerebral oxygen consumption ($CMRO_2$) is summarized because these variables may directly impact ischemic outcomes in vivo.

■ Barbiturates

Protective Effects in Cerebral Ischemia

The first studies to evaluate efficacy of barbiturates in the setting of global cerebral ischemia found them to be of great therapeutic value. In these studies, the duration of ischemia required to produce severe alteration in the neurological examination was much greater in animals treated with barbiturates as compared to animals studied under local or very light levels of alpha-chloralose anesthesia [2–4]. However, these studies were flawed in that the control group of animals were subjected to significant surgical intervention and ischemia with minimal anesthesia and were likely to have very high baseline catecholamine levels. These factors may have negatively impacted ischemic tolerance in the control animals [5, 6].

Further optimism about the potential clinical utility of barbiturates as a therapeutic modality in the setting of global cerebral ischemia came from a study in primates [7]. This led one group to design a study of barbiturate efficacy in patients following cardiac arrest [8]. However, other laboratories, with better controlled experimental designs, were unable to confirm any beneficial effects of barbiturates with transient global ischemia in dog [9, 10] or cat [11] models. In addition, subsequent attempts to repeat the initial positive results in a primate model of transient global ischemia were unsuccessful [12]. It was, therefore, not surprising that the randomized clinical trial of thiopental loading in comatose survivors of cardiac arrest did not support the use of thiopental for brain resuscitation [13].

The possible utility of barbiturates in the setting of focal ischemia was first addressed by Yatsu and colleagues [14], and many subsequent studies have demonstrated a therapeutic role for barbiturates [15–20]. However, several issues remain unresolved. First, part of the benefit associated with barbiturate treatment may be related to the drug's ability to decrease brain temperature [21]. Second, it is not clear if barbiturates are as protective in permanent focal ischemia as in transient occlusion [22]. Clinical studies employing barbiturates for brain protection have shown mixed results in acute stroke and cerebrovascular surgery [23–25]. The most convincing evidence for efficacy of barbiturates has been reported in patients with focal brain injury following open-heart surgery and warm cardiopulmonary bypass [26]. Although some concern has been expressed concerning the validity of this study [27], it was the first randomized study in humans that demonstrated improved outcome resulting from barbiturate therapy [28].

Therefore, barbiturates do not provide protection following transient global ischemia but do protect the brain from injury when administered in specific models of focal ischemia. Although the mechanism of protection is unknown, it is likely to be multifactorial.

Potential Mechanisms

Numerous studies document the depressant effect of barbiturates on both CBF and $CMRO_2$ in many species, including man [29, 30]. These agents do not alter CBF autoregulation [31]; however, the response to hypoxia [31] and hypercapnia is attenuated as a function of metabolic depression [32, 33]. The mechanism of metabolic depression is unknown but is thought to be related to enhanced γ-aminobutyric acid (GABA) binding and consequent increased intracellular chloride ion flux [34]. Early studies in cerebroprotection suggested that barbiturate-associated protection is mediated via reduced metabolic demand [35]. Greatest efficacy has been observed in paradigms in which electroencephalographic (EEG) activity remains present during the ischemic period (e.g., focal ischemia), whereas little efficacy is present when the EEG is ablated during ischemia (e.g., complete transient global ischemia). Nevertheless, the metabolism hypothesis has not been substantiated because subsequent findings suggest that reduction of cerebral metabolism does not necessarily result in cerebral protection [36, 37].

Barbiturates may also have direct effects on vascular tone that could affect ischemic outcomes. In isolated cerebral arteries, thiamylal and thiopental, but not pentobarbital, produce dose-related contraction. However, these effects are not consistently observed in pial vessels in situ [32]. Under basal conditions, CBF is lower in animals anesthetized with pentobarbital as compared to halothane or fentanyl [38]. Although blood flow can be similarly reduced during middle cerebral artery occlusion regardless of anesthetic, postischemic hyperemia is much more robust in cats anesthetized with pentobarbital as compared to halothane or fentanyl [38]. The therapeutic implications of accentuated postischemic hyperemia with pentobarbital anesthesia remain unevaluated. Barbiturates also decrease agonist-induced cerebral vasoconstrictor responses [39–41], either by blocking calcium entry into vascular smooth muscle [42] or by inhibiting protein kinase C activation [43, 44]. Although reduction in CBF may be important in the mechanism of brain protection from head trauma with elevated intracranial pressure (ICP), it does not appear important in ischemic mechanisms [45].

Numerous studies have demonstrated that intracellular calcium increases during ischemia, activating phospholipases and liberating free fatty acids such as arachidonic acid [46, 47], with consequent amplification of prostanoid production and brain injury. Barbiturates could be of therapeutic value because these agents decrease the production of free fatty acids during ischemia [48]. However, barbiturates do not attenuate accumulation of prostanoids during reperfusion [49].

Although some barbiturates act as free radical scavengers, this is not a property of all barbiturates purported to have therapeutic efficacy in the setting of ischemia. For example, phenobarbital, pentobarbital, and methohexital do not act as oxygen radical scavengers [50]. Godin and associates [51] hypothesized that barbiturate protection may be related to stabilization of hemocoordinated iron complexes in red blood cells with decreased radical production. Leukocytes are also important as generators of oxygen radicals during reperfusion. Therefore, barbiturates may indirectly reduce oxygen radical production by virtue of depressing leukocyte function [52].

Many insults, including ischemia, hypoxia, hypoglycemia, and head trauma, have been demonstrated to cause accumulation of excitatory amino acids (e.g., glutamate, aspartate) in brain [53–55] that directly mediate neurotoxicity and neuronal loss. Barbiturates have been found to be potent antagonists of excitatory amino acid receptors in vitro [56–58]. This is important because glutamate receptor antagonists reduce neuronal injury and histopathology associated with focal ischemia [59–61].

In summary, barbiturates appear to be protective in the setting of focal and incomplete, but not complete, global cerebral ischemia. It is not clear why barbiturates do not decrease brain injury in subjects exposed to transient complete global ischemia. The mechanism of protection during focal ischemia may be due to decreased production of free fatty acids during ischemia [48] or inhibition of excitotoxic mechanisms [56–58].

■ Inhalational Anesthetics

Neuroprotection During Ischemia/Reperfusion

The first inhalational anesthetic to be considered a neuroprotectart was cyclopropane when used in patients undergoing temporary carotid artery occlusion [1]. Subsequent work compared halothane to pentobarbital. Several authors reported improved neurological outcome after middle cerebral artery occlusion in pentobarbital anesthetized animals as compared to halothane anesthesia [15, 17]. Michenfelder and Milde [17] reported significant species dependence in these outcomes.

As isoflurane was employed commonly in the 1970s and 1980s, its role as a possible cerebral protectant was evaluated. Initial studies indicated that it could prolong survival time in mice subjected to severe hypoxia and slow the development of ischemic metabolic changes in dogs exposed to severe hypotension [62]. In primates exposed to temporary focal ischemia, isoflurane produced a similar degree of neuroprotection as thiopental [63, 64]. Consistent with a neuroprotective role of isoflurane, retrospective analysis of data from the Mayo Clinic indicates that isoflurane-anesthetized patients demonstrated fewer ischemic EEG changes during carotid surgery than patients anesthetized with enflurane or halothane [65]. In addition, the ischemic threshold (the CBF at which ischemic EEG changes occur) was higher in halothane-anesthetized patients as compared to patients anesthetized with isoflurane [66]. Data from animal studies indicate that the ischemic threshold with isoflurane is greater than that of methohexital [67] but not different from halothane [68].

Although initial studies suggested an advantage of isoflurane and barbiturates over halothane as neuroprotectants, subsequent well-controlled animal studies revealed a similar degree of protection for each of these three agents [20, 69–71]. Likewise, the degree of neuroprotection produced by halothane is similar to that produced by a new inhalational anesthetic, sevoflurane [72]. It is now apparent that the protective effects of halothane can be best appreciated in experimental paradigms that allow strict control over brain temperature [73]. This observation is important because the degree of neuroprotection provided by mild hypothermia (temperature reduction of 3° C) is far greater than that provided solely by inhalational anesthetics [36].

In summary, inhalational anesthetics (isoflurane, halothane, and sevoflurane) reduce brain injury in animal models of focal or incomplete ischemia by mechanisms that are not presently understood. In the sections that follow, the vasodilator effects of the inhalational anesthetics are explored to gain clues to their potential neuroprotective mechanisms.

Vasodilator Mechanisms

Inhalational anesthetics cause an increase in CBF in vivo [74–77] and vasodilation of cerebral blood vessels in vitro [78, 79]. The cerebral hyperemic response is only transient in subprimate mammals [80], but we have recently found it to be sustained in primates [81]. Increased CBF is accompanied by a decrease in $CMRO_2$ and consumption of glucose [75, 82], but high-energy phosphate metabolism is maintained [83]. The decrease in $CMRO_2$ is linked to a decrease in EEG activity and plateaus once the EEG becomes isoelectric [84]. Because these agents both increase CBF and decrease brain metabolism, it is unlikely that the vasodilation is metabolically mediated. Desflurane, a new inhalational anesthetic, also produces an increase in CBF and decrease in $CMRO_2$ that is similar in magnitude to the other potent inhalational anesthetics [85]. Many different mechanisms have been suggested for the vasodilation associated with inhalational anesthetics, including nitric oxide production, which is also implicated in the cellular basis of ischemia injury.

Nitric Oxide Under baseline pentobarbital anesthesia, inhibition of nitric oxide synthase (NOS) prevents cerebral hyperemia to halothane, isoflurane, and nitrous oxide in dogs [86]. This effect is reversible by L-arginine administration, further supporting a direct role of NO in the mechanism of isoflurane-induced cerebral hyperemia [87]. Others have found that NO is an important mediator of halothane-induced cerebral vasodilation in pial vessels [88]. The source of NO production may be perivascular nerves [89], astrocytes [90], and/or parenchymal neurons [91]. The role of NO in the mechanism of ischemia-induced brain injury is controversial, and ischemic outcomes are best interpreted by keeping in mind which isoforms of NOS (e.g., endothelial vs neuronal) are inhibited in the experimental paradigm. Several laboratories have demonstrated that NOS inhibition results in improved outcome from focal ischemia [92, 93]. However, others have suggested that inhibition of NO production may increase brain injury because of accentuated CBF reduction and that administering L-arginine (inferentially increasing NO production) may decrease brain injury [94, 95]. Therefore, if inhalational anesthetics alter brain NO, then they could also alter ischemic injury by a NO-mediated mechanism.

Prostanoids Indomethacin prevents aortic vasodilation produced by halothane, enflurane, and isoflurane in vitro, suggesting that prostanoids may be important in the mechanism of inhalational anesthetic-induced vasodilation [96]. In vivo prostanoids clearly play an important role in the mechanism of isoflurane-induced vasodilation [87]. For example, indomethacin markedly attenuates isoflurane induced vasodilation [87]. Whether increased prostanoid production is important in the cerebroprotection associated with inhalational anesthetics is unclear. Increased levels of prostanoids have been implicated as detrimental in ischemia, yet vasodilator prostanoids may facilitate better recovery of CBF during postischemic reperfusion. Further, any effect of prostanoids to increase cyclic adenosine monophosphate (cAMP) levels in brain may be associated with improved recovery from cerebral ischemia [97].

Excitatory Amino Acids Another potential mechanism for inhalational anesthetic–induced cerebral hyperemia and amelioration of ischemic brain injury involves the excitatory neurotransmitter, glutamate. Several inhalational anesthetics have been demonstrated to have important interactions with the N-methyl-D-aspartate (NMDA) class of glutamate receptors. Enflurane inhibits glutamate binding at the NMDA receptor, probably by interacting with the glycine recognition site [98]. Similarly, halothane, isoflurane, and methoxyflurane all disturb glutamate transmission in vitro, both at the glutamate binding site and via receptor-channel activation mechanisms [99]. In addition, isoflurane significantly reduces L-glutamate and NMDA-mediated intracellular calcium fluxes [100]. These actions suggest that the inhalational anesthetics could inhibit ischemic injury mediated via glutamate toxicity. However, not all data support such a role. For example, neither halothane nor isoflurane affect the release of glutamate or glycine during global cerebral ischemia [101]. In fact, halothane and enflurane increase glutamate release from cortical synaptosomes [102].

In summary, under controlled experimental conditions, inhalational anesthetics provide a degree of neuroprotection that is qualitatively similar to that provided by barbiturates in the setting of focal or incomplete ischemia. The mechanism of neuroprotection is unknown but may be related to nitric oxide synthesis, prostanoid production, or disruption of glutamate neurotransmission.

■ Nitrous Oxide

There are inconsistencies among studies regarding the degree of neuroprotection provided by barbiturates in animal models of ischemia. Some authors have speculated that the reason for the discrepancy is the inconsistent use of nitrous oxide. In general, barbiturates have limited efficacy as cerebral protectants in studies that employed nitrous oxide as part of the anesthetic management. However, barbiturates were efficacious in those studies that did not employ nitrous oxide as part of the anesthetic management [103].

The question of whether nitrous oxide is detrimental to neurological outcome following either focal or global ischemia has never been directly evaluated. However, two studies have addressed the effects of nitrous oxide on anesthetic-induced neuroprotection in the setting of transient focal ischemia. Nitrous oxide decreases isoflurane's efficacy as a neuroprotectant [104], but this is not the case for barbiturates [105]. The authors' hypothesize that nitrous oxide attenuates isoflurane-induced neuroprotection by increasing cerebral metabolism [104]. In contrast, metabolism would be maximally reduced with large doses of barbiturates and potentially unresponsive to nitrous oxide administration [105].

Nitrous oxide causes a mild degree of cerebral vasodilation via a mechanism that involves activation of NOS [86]. The effect of nitrous oxide, alone, on neurological ischemic tolerance is not known. When it is administered alone, for surgery, it does not provide adequate anesthesia and is associated with high systemic catecholamines. The high systemic catecholamine state, in turn, would be expected to result in worsening of neurological outcome following cerebral ischemia [69, 104]. Nitrous oxide may attenuate the protective effects of other anesthetics when these other agents are administered at low levels.

■ Ketamine

Ketamine is a noncompetitive NMDA-receptor antagonist [106] that inhibits agonist-induced calcium ion influx. It also attenuates the systemic catecholamine response that normally occurs during incomplete forebrain ischemia [107]. Ketamine has only been evaluated as a neuroprotectant in the setting of focal or incomplete ischemia. In a gerbil model, ketamine increased the incidence of cerebral infarction during carotid ligation relative to pentobarbital [108]. However, lack of control of brain temperature during anesthesia and surgery may have biased these results. In rat, some [107, 109] but not all studies [110, 111] demonstrate that high-dose ketamine can protect the brain following incomplete forebrain ischemia or transient focal ischemia [111]. The mechanism of protection for ketamine may relate to its properties as an NMDA-receptor antagonist or its ability to attenuate systemic catecholamine release.

■ Etomidate

Etomidate (1-(1-phenylethyl)-1H-imidazole-5-carboxylic acid ethyl ester) decreases CBF and $CMRO_2$ without altering blood pressure [112]. Although the mechanism for the reduction in CBF is believed to be due to a reduction in $CMRO_2$, this has not been proved. Etomidate is used widely for neuroprotection [113] because of its low incidence of hemodynamic instability at doses sufficient to depress the EEG [114, 115]. The agent attenuates ischemia-induced dopamine release in the corpus striatum in rat [116]. Pretreatment with etomidate doubles the time to EEG isoelectricity in response to intravenously administered potassium cyanide [117] and decreases brain injury following a transient focal ischemic/anoxic insult (Levine preparation) in rats [118]. In moderate incomplete global ischemia (significant residual EEG activity present during insult), etomidate delays the loss of cerebral high-energy phosphates and accumulation of brain lactate [119]. This effect presumably is due to drug-induced depression of cerebral metabolism [120], thereby decreasing substrate need at a time of decreased substrate availability. At equally potent doses (doses that produced full ablation of EEG), etomidate and thiopental produce similar neuroprotection in a model of severe forebrain ischemia in rat [121].

Therefore, etomidate is an effective therapeutic agent to prevent brain injury in focal or incomplete ischemia (i.e., like barbiturates, it requires residual neuronal activity for efficacy). Although etomidate has a major advantage over thiopental in that etomidate does not cause hemodynamic instability at a dose that causes maximal reduction in EEG activity, it is associated with significant adrenocortical suppression, even when administered as a single injection [122]. The drug's effect on adrenocortical function has greatly limited its utility in routine anesthetic care but not its utility in neurosurgical cases in which patients are routinely administered high doses of steroids.

■ Opiates

At clinically relevant doses, the effect of opiates on CBF is limited and linked to a reduction in $CMRO_2$. However, some agents have indirect effects that independently affect CBF; for example, morphine causes release of histamine [123] with the potential for cerebral vasodilation. Opiates may also alter CBF because they inhibit release of acetylcholine, norepinephrine, substance P, and dopamine [124] and stimulate adenylate cyclase activity [125] in the central nervous system [124]. Many of the varying effects of opiates on CBF and vascular responses are accounted for by these indirect effects, the agent's concentration, and by the distribution of the different opiate receptors within the vasculature. For example, μ-, δ-, and κ-receptor agonists can produce vasodilation, while ε-receptor agonists vasoconstrict [126].

In general, most currently available, clinically relevant opioids have little effect on CBF, $CMRO_2$, and ischemic tolerance. Further, the nonspecific opiate receptor antagonist naloxone does not improve outcomes after focal ischemia in cats [127] or primates [128, 129]. More recently, several investigators have evaluated the potential therapeutic effect of κ-receptor agonists. This follows, in large part, from the finding that brain levels of the κ-receptor agonist dynorphin are markedly reduced in regions previously exposed to ischemia [130]. Clinically, κ-receptor agonists (e.g., nalbuphine) appear to mediate analgesia and sedation. There is also mounting evidence that κ-receptor agonists may be of benefit [131–134] because they attenuate excitotoxic mechanisms presynaptically [135, 136] and decrease intracellular calcium entry [135, 137], not because of blood flow effects [138, 139]. These agents have efficacy even if administered 6 hours after the onset of focal ischemia [134, 140–142]. The $κ_1$ subtype appears to be the specific κ-receptor that is involved in the mechanism of brain injury [139, 143]. Further development and testing of these agents in both neuroprotection and pain management is likely.

■ Propofol

Propofol *(2,6-di-isopropyl phenol)* depresses cerebral metabolism by an unknown mechanism, decreases CBF in a manner linked to decreased $CMRO_2$ [144–146] and reduced cerebral electrical activity [147], and attenuates the increase in extracellular concentration of glycine that ordinarily accompanies ischemia [101]. The mechanism of reduced CBF is not likely to be vascular because in vitro propofol causes vasodilation, not vasoconstriction [148]. Relative to halothane/nitrous oxide anesthesia, propofol improves CBF recovery but not neuropathologic changes following experimental global ischemia [149]. In the setting of transient focal ischemia, propofol's potential neuroprotection has been compared to other anesthetics with conflicting results. Improved neurological outcome and decreased neuronal damage relative to fentanyl/nitrous oxide have been reported [150]. However, others have found no improvement in these parameters with propofol-treated rats as compared to halothane [151]. Although it has not been directly tested against any of the barbiturates, it is unlikely to offer any substantial benefit over these agents. Propofol has a shorter half-life than thiopental, but it produces a similar degree of cardiovascular depression [152] and is currently much more expensive.

■ $α_2$-Adrenoreceptor Agonists

$α_2$-Receptor agonists are becoming more commonly used agents in clinical medicine and are frequently used as baseline anesthetics (e.g., urethane) in animal models of ischemia. The $α_2$-agonist dexmedetomidine produces sedation [153], decreases CBF, and transiently decreases ICP [154] without changing $CMRO_2$ [155, 156]. Binding sites for $α_2$-agonists within brain are most highly concentrated in areas involved with the control of cardiovascular function [157]. Cerebral arteries are rich with post-synaptic α_2-adrenoceptors [158] that, when stimulated, cause vasoconstriction [159]. The effector mechanism for both vasoconstriction and sedation involves a G protein [160] that inhibits adenylate cyclase and decreases cAMP accumulation [161].

Although these agents appear to be cerebroprotectants, the mechanism of protection may not be related to their ability to act at the α_2-receptor. For example, immediate, postischemic administration of idazoxan, an α_2-receptor antagonist, ameliorates brain injury in rats exposed to transient forebrain ischemia [162, 163]. The proposed mechanism of protection is accentuated catecholamine release within brain [162, 164]. However, the α_2-adrenergic agonist dexmedetomidine also improves neurological outcome from transient incomplete and focal ischemia [5, 165, 166] and is hypothesized to act by attenuating ischemia-induced catecholamine release within brain [167]. Because it is unlikely that both increases and decreases in brain catecholamines are protective, some other mechanism must be involved. For example, both idazoxan and dexmedetomidine could act at the imidazole receptor [168]. A supportive finding is that idazoxan (an α_2-receptor antagonist and an agent with activity at the imidazole receptor) is neuroprotective, whereas SKF 86466, a highly selective α_2-receptor antagonist without imidazole receptor activity, is not protective [168].

■ Benzodiazepines

Benzodiazepines decrease cerebral metabolism and blood flow [169–171]. At least a portion of their effect in brain is linked to modulation of postsynaptic responses to GABA and receptor-linked chloride channels [34]. Associated with GABA-induced, increased chloride conductance is a generalized reduction in EEG and brain function [172]. After ischemia, GABAergic neurons are preserved in hippocampus but with a decreased number of postsynaptic GABA$_A$-benzodiazepine binding sites. This suggests that benzodiazepines, by increasing receptor affinity, could be useful in reducing ischemic neuronal death, at least in the hippocampus [173]. Also consistent with this hypothesis is the observation that enhanced GABA neurotransmission after cerebral ischemia reduces loss of hippocampal neurons [174, 175].

Benzodiazepines and barbiturates have been reported to have similar efficacy after incomplete global cerebral ischemia [176], but not following severe hypoxia. Seizure activity during reperfusion accentuates postischemic brain injury in cerebral cortex, thalamus, and brain stem [177], and diazepam has been shown to be particularly effective in ameliorating neocortical injury when there is a relatively high incidence of postischemic seizures [177]. However, midazolam was not effective in ameliorating brain injury in a multiple cerebral embolic model [178].

■ Lidocaine

Lidocaine was originally evaluated as a neuroprotectant because, as a local anesthetic, it was hypothesized to partially preserve transmembrane ion gradients during ischemia. In addition, lidocaine could reduce release of excitatory amino acids during ischemia by blocking intracellular sodium influx. At high doses, lidocaine can reduce cerebral metabolism [179] but appears to have little direct effect on CBF [180].

Intravenous lidocaine can protect the brain from injury associated with cerebral air embolism [181, 182]. After transient focal ischemia, lidocaine as a bolus transiently improves brain electrical activity but does not reduce infarct size [183]. However, continuous intravenous infusion during both ischemia and reperfusion does result in decreased infarct volume and a higher regional cerebral blood flow [180]. The mechanism of protection is probably related to lidocaine's ability to inhibit ischemic depolarization, which occurs in the lesion periphery or penumbra. After global ischemia, lidocaine has provided variable levels of protection that were dependent on the drug dose, the accompanying baseline anesthetic of the study, and the duration of the ischemic insult [184–186].

■ Summary

A number of anesthetic agents have significant cerebroprotective potential and alter ischemic tolerance in vivo, at least within specific experimental conditions such as focal or incomplete, global cerebral ischemia. As compared to the unanesthetized state, each of these agents has some influence on CBF and metabolism, and many have significant effects on vascular responses to dilator stimuli. Relevant studies that provide clues to the mechanisms of anesthetic action in brain injury have been reviewed, and it is likely that these mechanisms are multifactorial and may overlap from one class of agents to another. Lastly, there is a clear need for further studies that specifically evaluate the neuroprotective mechanism of each agent, determine the effect on outcomes when the anesthetic is administered only as a posttreatment at clinically relevant concentrations, and compare anesthetics with the unanesthetized state when possible.

Supported by grants from the National Institutes of Health NR06730, NS33668, NS 20020.

■ References

1. Wells BA, Keats AS, Cooley DA. Increased tolerance to cerebral ischemia produced by general anesthesia during temporary carotid occlusion. Surgery 1963; 54:216–223
2. Wright RL, Ames III A. Measurement of maximal permissible cerebral ischemia and a study of its pharmacologic prolongation. J Neurosurg 1964;567–574
3. Goldstein A Jr, Wells BA, Keats AS. Effect of anesthesia on tolerance of dog brain to anoxia. Anesthesiology 1964;25:98
4. Goldstein A Jr, Wells BA, Keats AS. Increased tolerance to cerebral anoxia by pentobarbital. Arch Int Pharmacodyn Ther 1966;161:138–143
5. Hoffman WE, Baughman VL, Albrecht RF. Interaction of catecholamines and nitrous oxide ventilation during incomplete brain ischemia in rats. Anesth Analg 1993;77:908–912
6. Werner C, Hoffman WE, Thomas C, et al. Ganglionic blockade improves neurologic outcome from incomplete ischemia in rats: partial reversal by exogenous catecholamines. Anesthesiology 1990;73:923–929
7. Bleyaert AL, Nemoto EM, Safar P, et al. Thiopental amelioration of brain damage after global ischemia in monkeys. Anesthesiology 1978;49:390–398
8. Breivik H, Safar P, Sands P, et al. Clinical feasibility trials of barbiturate therapy after cardiac arrest. Crit Care Med 1978;6:228–244
9. Steen PA, Milde JH, Michenfelder JD. No barbiturate protection in a dog model of complete cerebral ischemia. Ann Neurol 1979;5:343–349
10. Snyder BD, Ramirez Lassepas M, Sukhum P, et al. Failure of thiopental to modify global anoxic injury. Stroke 1979;10:135–141
11. Todd MM, Chadwick HS, Shapiro HM, et al. The neurologic effects of thiopental therapy following experimental cardiac arrest in cats. Anesthesiology 1982;57: 76–86
12. Gisvold SE, Safar P, Hendrick HH, et al. Thiopental treatment after global brain ischemia in pigtailed monkeys. Anesthesiology 1984;60:88–96
13. Brain Resuscitation Clinical Trial I Study Group. Randomized clinical study of thiopental loading in comatose survivors of cardiac arrest. N Engl J Med 1986; 314:397–403
14. Yatsu FM, Diamond I, Graziano C, Lindquist P. Experimental brain ischemia: protection from irreversible damage with a rapid-acting barbiturate (methohexital). Stroke 1972;3:726–732
15. Smith AL, Hoff JT, Nielsen SL, Larson CP. Barbiturate protection in acute focal cerebral ischemia. Stroke 1974;5:1–7
16. Hoff JT, Smith AL, Hankinson HL, Nielsen SL. Barbiturate protection from cerebral infarction in primates. Stroke 1975;6:28–33
17. Michenfelder JD, Milde JH. Influence of anesthetics on metabolic, functional and pathological responses to regional cerebral ischemia. Stroke 1975;6:405–410
18. Moseley JI, Laurent JP, Molinari GF. Barbiturate attenuation of the clinical course and pathologic lesions in a primate stroke model. Neurology 1975;25:870–874
19. Michenfelder JD, Milde JH, Sundt TM. Cerebral protection by barbiturate anesthesia. Use after middle cerebral artery occlusion in java monkeys. Arch Neurol 1976;33:345–350
20. Baughman VL, Hoffman WE, Thomas C, et al. Comparison of methohexital and isoflurane on neurologic outcome and histopathology following incomplete ischemia in rats. Anesthesiology 1990;72:85–94
21. Drummond JC. Do barbiturates really protect the brain? Anesthesiology 1993;78: 611–613

22. Selman WR, Spetzler RF, Roessmann UR, et al. Barbiturate-induced coma therapy for focal cerebral ischemia. Effect after temporary and permanent MCA occlusion. J Neurosurg 1981;55:220–226

23. Lawner PM, Simeone FA. Treatment of intraoperative middle cerebral artery occlusion with pentobarbital and extracranial-intracranial bypass. J Neurosurg 1979;51:710–712

24. Agnoli A, Palesse N, Ruggieri S, et al. Barbiturate treatment of acute stroke. Adv Neurol 1979;25:269–274

25. Spetzler RF, Martin N, Hadley MN, et al. Microsurgical endarterectomy under barbiturate protection: a prospective study. J Neurosurg 1986;65:63–73

26. Nussmeier NA, Arlund C, Slogoff S. Neuropsychiatric complications after cardiopulmonary bypass: cerebral protection by a barbiturate. Anesthesiology 1986;64:165–170

27. Stevenson RL, Rogers MC. Con: barbiturates for brain protection during cardiopulmonary bypass: fact or fantasy? J Cardiothoracic Anesth 1988;2:390–392

28. Michenfelder JD. A valid demonstration of barbiturate-induced brain protection in man—at last. Anesthesiology 1986;64:140–142

29. Pierce EC, Lambertsen JG, Deutsch S. Cerebral circulation and metabolism during thiopental anesthesia and hyperventilation in man. J Clin Invest 1962;41:1664–1671

30. Wechsler RL, Dripps RD, Kety SS. Blood flow and oxygen consumption of the human brain during anesthesia produced by thiopental. Anesthesiology 1951;12:308–314

31. Donegan JH, Traystman RJ, Koehler RC, et al. Cerebrovascular hypoxic and autoregulatory responses during reduced brain metabolism. Am J Physiol 1985;249:H421–H429

32. Levasseur JE, Kontos HA. Effects of anesthesia on cerebral arteriolar responses to hypercapnia. Am J Physiol 1989;257:H85–H88

33. Fujishima M, Scheinberg P, Busto R, Reinmuth OM. The relation between cerebral oxygen consumption and cerebral vascular reactivity to carbon dioxide. Stroke 1971;2:251–257

34. Olsen RW. GABA-benzodiazepine-barbiturate receptor interactions. J Neurochem 1981;37:1–13

35. Michenfelder JD, Theye RA. The effects of anesthesia and hypothermia on canine cerebral ATP and lactate during anoxia produced by decapitation. Anesthesiology 1970;33:430–439

36. Sano T, Drummond J, Patel P, et al. A comparison of the cerebral protective effects of isoflurane and mild hypothermia in a model of incomplete forebrain ischemia in the rat. Anesthesiology 1992;76:221–228

37. Todd MM, Warner DS. A comfortable hypothesis reevaluated. Cerebral metabolic depression and brain protection during ischemia. Anesthesiology 1992;76:161–164

38. Helfaer MA, Kirsch JR, Traystman RJ. Anesthetic modulation of cerebral hemodynamic and evoked responses to transient middle cerebral artery occlusion in cats. Stroke 1990;21:795–800

39. Marin J, Rico ML, Salaices M. Interference of pentobarbitone with the contraction of vascular smooth muscle in goat middle cerebral artery. J Pharm Pharmacol 1981;33:357–361

40. Edvinsson L, McCulloch J. Effects of pentobarbital on contractile responses of feline cerebral arteries. J Cereb Blood Flow Metab 1981;1:437–440

41. Taga K, Fukuda S, Nishimura N, et al. Effects of thiopental, pentobarbital, and ketamine on endothelin-induced constriction of porcine cerebral arteries. Anesthesiology 1990;72:939–941

42. Sanchez Ferrer CF, Marin J, Salaices M, et al. Interference of pentobarbital and

thiopental with the vascular contraction and noradrenaline release in human cerebral arteries. Gen Pharmacol 1985;16:469–473

43. Mikawa K, Maekawa N, Hoshina H, et al. Inhibitory effect of barbiturates and local anaesthetics on protein kinase C activation. J Int Med Res 1990;18:153–160

44. Robinson White AJ, Muldoon SM, Robinson FC. Inhibition of inositol phospholipid hydrolysis in endothelial cells by pentobarbital. Eur J Pharmacol 1989;172:291–303

45. Koch KA, Jackson DL, Schmiedl M, et al. Effect of thiopental therapy on cerebral blood flow after total cerebral ischemia. Crit Care Med 1984;12:90–95

46. Wieloch T, Siesjo BK. Ischemic brain injury: the importance of calcium, lipolytic activities, and free fatty acids. Pathol Biol (Paris) 1982;30:269–277

47. Sun GY, Tang W, Huang SF-L, Foudin L. Is phosphatidylinositol involved in the release of fatty acids in cerebral ischemia? In: Bleasdale JE, Eichberg J, Hauser G, eds. Inositol and phosphoinositides: metabolism and biological regulation. Totowa, New Jersey: Humana Press, 1984:511–527

48. Shiu GK, Nemoto EM. Barbiturate attenuation of brain free fatty acid liberation during global ischemia. J Neurochem 1981;37:1448–1456

49. Dorman RV. Effects of cerebral ischemia and reperfusion on prostanoid accumulation in unanesthetized and pentobarbital-treated gerbils. J Cereb Blood Flow Metab 1988;8:609–612

50. Smith DS, Rehncrona S, Siesjo BK. Barbiturates as protective agents in brain ischemia and as free radical scavengers in vitro. Acta Physiol Scand Suppl 1980;492:129–134

51. Godin DV, Mitchell MJ, Saunders BA. Studies on the interaction of barbiturates with reactive oxygen radicals: implications regarding barbiturate protection against cerebral ischaemia. Can Anaesth Soc J 1982;29:203–211

52. Neuwelt EA, Kikuchi K, Hill SA, et al. Barbiturate inhibition of lymphocyte function. Differing effects of various barbiturates used to induce coma. J Neurosurg 1982;56:254–259

53. Schwarcz R, Foster AC, French ED, et al. Excitotoxic models for neurodegenerative disorders. Life Sci 1984;35:19–32

54. Benveniste H, Drejer J, Schousboe A, Diemer NH. Elevation of the extracellular concentrations of glutamate and aspartate in rat hippocampus during transient cerebral ischemia monitored by intracerebral microdialysis. J Neurochem 1984;43:1369–1374

55. Hagberg H, Lehmann A, Sandberg M, et al. Ischemia-induced shift of inhibitory and excitatory amino acids from intra- to extracellular compartments. J Cereb Blood Flow Metab 1985;5:413–419

56. Collins GGS, Anson J. Effects of barbiturates on responses evoked by excitatory amino acids in slices of rat olfactory cortex. Neuropharmacology 1987;26:167–171

57. Horne AL, Simmonds MA. The pharmacology of quisqualate and AMPA in the cerebral cortex of the rat in vitro. Neuropharmacology 1989;28:1113–1118

58. Teichberg VI, Tal N, Goldberg O, Luini A. Barbiturates, alcohols and the CNS excitatory neurotransmission: specific effects on the kainate and quisqualate receptors. Brain Res 1984;291:285–292

59. Sheardown MJ, Nielsen EO, Hansen AJ, et al. 2,3-Dihydroxy-6-nitro-7-sulfamoyl-benzo(F)quinoxaline: a neuroprotectant for cerebral ischemia. Science 1990;247:571–574

60. Park CK, Nehls DG, Graham DI, et al. Focal cerebral ischaemia in the cat: treatment with the glutamate antagonist MK-801 after induction of ischaemia. J Cereb Blood Flow Metab 1988;8:757–762

61. Nishikawa T, Kirsch JR, Koehler RC, et al. Competitive N-methyl-D-aspartate receptor blockade reduces brain injury following transient focal ischemia in cats. Stroke 1994;25:2258–2264

62. Newberg LA, Michenfelder JD. Cerebral protection by isoflurane during hypoxemia or ischemia. Anesthesiology 1983;59:29–35

63. Nehls DG, Todd MM, Spetzler RF, et al. A comparison of the cerebral protective effects of isoflurane and barbiturates during temporary focal ischemia in primates. Anesthesiology 1987;66:453–464

64. Milde LN, Milde JH, Lanier WL, et al. Comparison of the effects of isoflurane and thiopental on neurologic outcome and neuropathology after temporary focal cerebral ischemia in primates. Anesthesiology 1988;69:905–913

65. Michenfelder JD, Sundt TM, Fode N, Sharbrough FW. Isoflurane when compared to enflurane and halothane decreases the frequency of cerebral ischemia during carotid endarterectomy. Anesthesiology 1987;67:336–340

66. Messick JM Jr, Casement B, Sharbrough FW, et al. Correlation of regional cerebral blood flow (rCBF) with EEG changes during isoflurane anesthesia for carotid endarterectomy: critical rCBF. Anesthesiology 1987;66:344–349

67. Warner DS, Zhou J, Ramani R, Todd MM. Reversible focal ischemia in the rat: effect of halothane, isoflurane, and methohexital anesthesia. J Cereb Blood Flow Metab 1991;11:794–802

68. Verhaegen MJ, Todd MM, Warner DS. A comparison of cerebral ischemic flow thresholds during halothane/N2O and isoflurane/N2O anesthesia in rats. Anesthesiology 1992;76:743–754

69. Baughman VL, Hoffman WE, Miletich DJ, et al. Neurologic outcome in rats following incomplete cerebral ischemia during halothane, isoflurane, or N_2O. Anesthesiology 1988;69:192–198

70. Gelb AW, Boisvert DP, Tang C, et al. Primate brain tolerance to temporary focal cerebral ischemia during isoflurane- or sodium nitroprusside-induced hypotension. Anesthesiology 1989;70:678–683

71. Hoffman WE, Thomas C, Albrecht RF. The effect of halothane and isoflurane on neurologic outcome following incomplete cerebral ischemia in the rat. Anesth Analg 1993;76:279–283

72. Warner DS, McFarlane C, Todd MM, et al. Sevoflurane and halothane reduce focal ischemic brain damage in the rat. Anesthesiology 1993;79:985–992

73. Warner DS, Ludwig PS, Pearlstein R, Brinkhous AD. Halothane reduces focal ischemic injury in the rat when brain temperature is controlled. Anesthesiology 1995;82:1237–1245

74. Cucchiara RF, Theye RA, Michenfelder JD. The effects of isoflurane on canine cerebral metabolism and blood flow. Anesthesiology 1974;40:571–574

75. Todd MM, Drummond JC. A comparison of the cerebrovascular and metabolic effects of halothane and isoflurane in the cat. Anesthesiology 1984;60:276–282

76. Gelman S, Fowler KC, Smith LR. Regional blood flow during isoflurane and halothane anesthesia. Anesth Analg 1984;63:557–565

77. Lundeen G, Manohar M, Parks C. Systemic distribution of blood flow in swine while awake and during 1.0 and 1.5 MAC isoflurane anesthesia with or without 50% nitrous oxide. Anesth Analg 1983;62:499–512

78. Jensen NF, Todd MM, Kramer DJ, et al. A comparison of the vasodilating effects of halothane and isoflurane on the isolated rabbit basilar artery with and without intact endothelium. Anesthesiology 1992;76:624–634

79. Flynn NM, Buljubasic N, Bosnjak ZJ, Kampine JP. Isoflurane produces endothelium-independent relaxation in canine middle cerebral arteries. Anesthesiology 1992;76:461–467

80. Brian JE, Traystman RJ, McPherson RW. Changes in cerebral blood flow over time during isoflurane anesthesia in dogs. J Neurosurg Anesth 1990;2:122–130

81. McPherson RW, Kirsch JR, Tobin JR, et al. Cerebral blood flow in primates is increased by isoflurane over time and is decreased by nitric oxide synthase inhibition. Anesthesiology 1994;80:1320–1327

82. Hansen TD, Warner DS, Todd MM, Vust LJ. The role of cerebral metabolism in determining the local cerebral blood flow effects of volatile anesthetics: evidence for persistent flow-metabolism coupling. J Cereb Blood Flow Metab 1989;9: 323–328

83. Kofke WA, Hawkins RA, Davis DW, Biebuyck JF. Comparison of the effects of volatile anesthetics on brain glucose metabolism in rats. Anesthesiology 1987;66: 810–813

84. Newberg LA, Milde JH, Michenfelder JD. The cerebral metabolic effects of iso-flurane at and above concentrations that suppress cortical electrical activity. Anesthesiology 1983;59:23–28

85. Lutz LJ, Milde JH, Milde LN. The cerebral functional, metabolic, and hemodynamic effects of desflurane in dogs. Anesthesiology 1990;73:125–131

86. McPherson RW, Kirsch JR, Traystman RJ. N^w-nitro-L-arginine methyl ester prevents cerebral hyperemia by inhaled anesthetics in dogs. Anesth Analg 1993;77: 891–897

87. Moore LE, Kirsch JR, Helfaer MA, et al. Nitric oxide and prostanoids contribute to isoflurane-induced cerebral hyperemia in pigs. Anesthesiology 1994;80: 1328–1337

88. Koenig HM, Pelligrino DA, Albrecht RF. Halothane vasodilation and nitric oxide in rat pial vessels (Abstract). J Neurosurg Anesthesiology 1992;4:301

89. Toda N, Okamura T. Role of nitric oxide in neurally induced cerebroarterial relaxation. J Pharmacol Exp Ther 1991;258:1027–1032

90. Murphy S, Minor RL Jr, Welk G, Harrison DG. Evidence for an astrocyte-derived vasorelaxing factor with properties similar to nitric oxide. J Neurochem 1990;55: 349–351

91. Bredt DS, Hwang PM, Snyder SH. Localization of nitric oxide synthase indicating a neural role for nitric oxide. Nature 1990;347:768–770

92. Nishikawa T, Kirsch JR, Koehler RC, et al. Nitric oxide synthase inhibition reduces caudate injury following transient focal ischemia in cats. Stroke 1994;25:877–885

93. Nishikawa T, Kirsch JR, Koehler RC, et al. Effect of nitric oxide synthase inhibition on cerebral blood flow and injury volume during focal ischemia in cats. Stroke 1993;24:1717–1724

94. Ashwal S, Cole DJ, Osborne TN, Pearce WJ. Low dose L-NAME reduces infarct volume in the rat MCAO/reperfusion model. J Neurosurg Anesth 1993;5: 241–249

95. Morikawa E, Huang Z, Moskowitz MA. L-arginine decreases infarct size caused by middle cerebral arterial occlusion in SHR. Am J Physiol 1992;263:H1632–H1635

96. Stone DJ, Johns RA. Endothelium-dependent effects of halothane, enflurane, and isoflurane on isolated rat aortic vascular rings. Anesthesiology 1989;71:126–132

97. Toung TJK, Kirsch JR, Traystman RJ. Enhanced recovery of brain electrical activity by cyclic AMP following complete global ischemia in dog. Crit Care Med 1995 (in press)

98. Martin DC, Abraham JE, Plagenhoef M, Aronstam RS. Volatile anesthetics and NMDA receptors. Enflurane inhibition of glutamate-stimulated MK-801 binding and reversal by glycine. Neurosci Lett 1991;132:73–76

99. Martin DC, Plagenhoef M, Abraham J, et al. Volatile anesthetics and glutamate activation of N-methyl-D-aspartate receptors. Biochem Pharmacol 1995;49: 809–817

100. Bickler PE, Buck LT, Hansen BM. Effects of isoflurane and hypothermia on glutamate receptor-mediated calcium influx in brain slices. Anesthesiology 1994; 81:1461–1469

101. Illievich UM, Zornow MH, Choi KT, et al. Effects of hypothermia or anesthetics on hippocampal glutamate and glycine concentrations after repeated transient global cerebral ischemia. Anesthesiology 1994;80:177–186

102. Hirose T, Inoue M, Uchida M, Inagaki C. Enflurane-induced release of an excitatory amino acid, glutamate, from mouse brain synaptosomes. Anesthesiology 1992;77:109–113

103. Hartung J, Cottrell JE. Nitrous oxide reduces thiopental-induced prolongation of survival in hypoxic and anoxic mice. Anesth Analg 1987;66:47–52

104. Baughman VL, Hoffman WE, Thomas C, et al. The interaction of nitrous oxide and isoflurane with incomplete cerebral ischemia in the rat. Anesthesiology 1989; 70:767–774

105. Warner DS, Zhou JG, Ramani R, et al. Nitrous oxide does not alter infarct volume in rats undergoing reversible middle cerebral artery occlusion. Anesthesiology 1990;73:686–693

106. Olney J, Price M, Fuller T, et al. The anti-excitotoxic effects of certain anesthetics, analgesics, and sedative-hypnotics. Neurosci Lett 1986;68:29–34

107. Hoffman WE, Pelligrino D, Werner C, et al. Ketamine decreases plasma catecholamines and improves outcome from incomplete cerebral ischemia in rats. Anesthesiology 1992;76:755–762

108. Lightfoote WE II, Molinari GF, Chase TN. Modification of cerebral ischemic damage by anesthetics. Stroke 1977;8:627–628

109. Church J, Zeman S, Lodge D. The neuroprotective action of ketamine and MK-801 after transient cerebral ischemia in rats. Anesthesiology 1988;69:702–709

110. Jensen ML, Auer RN. Ketamine fails to protect against ischaemic neuronal necrosis in the rat. Br J Anaesth 1988;61:206–210

111. Ridenour TR, Warner DS, Todd MM, McAllister AC. Mild hypothermia reduces infarct size resulting from temporary but not permanent focal ischemia in rats. Stroke 1992;23:733–738

112. Frizzell RT, Fichtel FM, Jordan MB, et al. Effects of etomidate and hypothermia on cerebral metabolism and blood flow in a canine model of hypoperfusion. J Neurosurg Anesthesiol 1993;5:104–110

113. Batjer HH. Cerebral protective effects of etomidate: experimental and clinical aspects. Cerebrovasc Brain Metab Rev 1993;5:17–32

114. Gooding JM, Corssen G. Effect of etomidate on the cardiovascular system. Anesth Analg 1977;56:717–719

115. Criado A, Maseda J, Navarro E, et al. Induction of anaesthesia with etomidate: haemodynamic study of 36 patients. Br J Anaesth 1980;52:803–806

116. Koorn R, Brannan TS, Martinez-Tica J, et al. Effect of etomidate on in vivo ischemia-induced dopamine release in the corpus striatum of the rat: a study using cerebral microdialysis. Anesth Analg 1994;78:73–79

117. Ashton D, Van Reempts J, Wauquier A. Behavioural, electroencephalographic and histological study of the protective effect of etomidate against histotoxic dysoxia produced by cyanide. Arch Int Pharmacodyn Ther 1981;254:196–213

118. Van Reempts J, Borgers M, Van Eyndhoven J, Hermans C. Protective effects of etomidate in hypoxic-ischemic brain damage in the rat. A morphologic assessment. Exp Neurol 1982;76:181–195

119. Milde LN, Milde JH. Preservation of cerebral metabolites by etomidate during incomplete cerebral ischemia in dogs. Anesthesiology 1986;65:272–277

120. Milde LN, Milde JH, Michenfelder JD. Cerebral functional, metabolic, and hemodynamic effects of etomidate in dogs. Anesthesiology 1985;63:371–377

121. Sano T, Patel PM, Drummond JC, Cole DJ. A comparison of the cerebral protective effects of etomidate, thiopental, and isoflurane in a model of forebrain ischemia in the rat. Anesth Analg 1993;76:990–997

122. Preziosi P, Vacca M. Adrenocortical suppression and other endocrine effects of etomidate. Life Sci 1988;42:477–489

123. Thompson WL, Walton RP. Elevation of plasma histamine levels in the dog follow-

ing administration of muscle relaxants, opiates and macromolecular polymers. J Pharmacol Exp Ther 1964;143:131–136

124. Snyder SH. The opiate receptor and morphine-like peptides in the brain. Am J Psychiatry 1978;135:645–652

125. Onali P, Olianas MC. Naturally occurring opioid receptor agonists stimulate adenylate cyclase activity in rat olfactory bulb. Mol Pharmacol 1991;39:436–441

126. Armstead WM, Mirro R, Busija DW, Leffler CW. Prostanoids modulate opioid cerebrovascular responses in newborn pigs. J Pharmacol Exp Ther 1990;255: 1083–1089

127. Hubbard JL, Sundt TM. Failure of naloxone to affect focal incomplete cerebral ischemia and collateral blood flow in cats. J Neurosurg 1983;59:237–244

128. Zabramski JM, Spetzler RF, Selman WR, et al. Naloxone therapy during focal cerebral ischemia evaluation in a primate model. Stroke 1984;15:621–627

129. Gaines C, Nehls DG, Suess DM, et al. Effect of naloxone on experimental stroke in awake monkey. Neurosurgery 1984;14:308–314

130. Fried RL, Nowak TS. Opioid peptide levels in gerbil brain after transient ischemia: lasting depletion of hippocampal dynorphin. Stroke 1987;18:765–770

131. Kusumoto K, Mackay KB, McCulloch J. The effect of the kappa-opioid receptor agonist CI-977 in a rat model of focal cerebral ischaemia. Brain Res 1992;576: 147–151

132. Silvia RC, Slizgi GR, Ludens JH, Tang AH. Protection from ischemia-induced cerebral edema in the rat by U-50488H, a kappa opioid receptor agonist. Brain Res 1987;403:52–57

133. Contreras PC, Raga DM, Bremer ME, et al. Evaluation of U-50,488H analogs for neuroprotective activity in the gerbil. Brain Res 1991;546:79–82

134. Birch PJ, Rogers H, Hayes AG, et al. Neuroprotective actions of GR89696, a highly potent and selective k-opioid receptor agonist. Br J Pharmacol 1991;103: 1819–1823

135. Bradford HF, Crowder JM, White EJ. Inhibitory actions of opioid compounds on calcium fluxes and neurotransmitter release from mammalian cerebral cortical slices. Br J Pharmacol 1986;88:87–93

136. Gannon RL, Terrian DM. U-50,488H inhibits dynorphin and glutamate release from guinea pig hippocampal mossy fiber terminals. Brain Res 1991;548:242–247

137. Macdonald RL, Werz MA. Dynorphin A decreases voltage-dependent calcium conductance of mouse dorsal root ganglion neurones. J Physiol (Lond) 1986;377: 237–249

138. Furui T. Potential protection by a specific kappa-opiate agonist U-50488H against membrane failure in acute ischemic brain. Neurol Med Chir 1993;33:133–138

139. Mackay KB, Kusumoto K, Graham DI, McCulloch J. Effect of the kappa-1 opioid agonist CI-977 on ischemic brain damage and cerebral blood flow after middle cerebral artery occlusion in the rat. Brain Res 1993;629:10–18

140. Baskin DS, Widmayer MA, Browning JL, et al. Evaluation of delayed treatment of focal cerebral ischemia with three selective k-opioid agonists in cats. Stroke 1994;25:2047–2054

141. Baskin DS, Kuroda H, Hosobuchi Y, Lee NM. Treatment of stroke with opiate antagonists—effects of exogenous antagonists and dynorphin 1-13. Neuropeptides 1985;5:307–310

142. Baskin DS, Hosobuchi Y, Loh HH, Lee NM. Dynorphin(1-13) improves survival in cats with focal cerebral ischaemia. Nature 1984;312:551–552

143. Mackay KB, Kusumoto K, Graham DI, McCulloch J. Focal cerebral ischemia in the cat: pretreatment with a kappa-1 opioid receptor agonist, CI-977. Brain Res 1993;618:213–219

144. Van Hemelrijck J, Fitch W, Mattheussen M, et al. Effect of propofol on cerebral circulation and autoregulation in the baboon. Anesth Analg 1990;71:49–54

145. Vandesteene A, Trempont V, Engelman E, et al. Effect of propofol on cerebral blood flow and metabolism in man. Anaesthesia 1988;43(Suppl):42–43
146. Stephan H, Sonntag H, Schenk HD, Kohlhausen S. Effect of Disoprivan (propofol) on the circulation and oxygen consumption of the brain and CO_2 reactivity of brain vessels in the human. Anaesthesist 1987;36:60–65
147. Werner C, Hoffman WE, Kochs E, et al. The effects of propofol on cerebral and spinal cord blood flow in rats. Anesth Analg 1993;76:971–975
148. Park WK, Lynch C, III, Johns RA. Effects of propofol and thiopental in isolated rat aorta and pulmonary artery. Anesthesiology 1992;77:956–963
149. Weir DL, Goodchild CS, Graham DI. Propofol: effects on indices of cerebral ischemia. J Neurosurg Anesth 1989;1:284–289
150. Kochs E, Hoffman WE, Werner C, et al. The effects of propofol on brain electrical activity, neurologic outcome, and neuronal damage following incomplete ischemia in rats. Anesthesiology 1992;76:245–252
151. Ridenour TR, Warner DS, Todd MM, Gionet TX. Comparative effects of propofol and halothane on outcome from temporary middle cerebral artery occlusion in the rat. Anesthesiology 1992;76:807–812
152. Edelist G. A comparison of propofol and tiopentone as induction agents in outpatient surgery. Can J Anaesth 1987;34:110–116
153. Belleville JP, Ward DS, Bloor BC, Maze M. Effects of intravenous dexmedetomidine in humans. 1. Sedation, ventilation, and metabolic rate. Anesthesiology 1992; 77:1125–1133
154. Zornow MH, Scheller MS, Sheehan PB, et al. Intracranial pressure effects of dexmedetomidine in rabbits. Anesth Analg 1992;75:232–237
155. Karlsson BR, Forsman M, Roald OK, et al. Effect of dexmedetomidine, a selective and potent alpha 2-agonist, on cerebral blood flow and oxygen consumption during halothane anesthesia in dogs. Anesth Analg 1990;71:125–129
156. Zornow MH, Fleischer JE, Scheller MS, et al. Dexmedetomidine, an alpha 2-adrenergic agonist, decreases cerebral blood flow in the isoflurane-anesthetized dog. Anesth Analg 1990;70:624–630
157. Unnerstall JR, Kopajtic TA, Kuhar MJ. Distribution of alpha 2 agonist binding sites in the rat and human central nervous system: analysis of some functional, anatomic correlates of the pharmacologic effects of clonidine and related adrenergic agents. Brain Res 1984;319:69–101
158. Tsukahara T, Taniguchi T, Usui H, et al. Sympathetic denervation and alpha adrenoceptors in dog cerebral arteries. Naunyn Schmiedebergs Arch Pharmacol 1986;334:436–443
159. Coughlan MG, Lee JG, Bosnjak ZJ, et al. Direct coronary and cerebral vascular responses to dexmedetomidine. Significance of endogenous nitric oxide synthesis. Anesthesiology 1992;77:998–1006
160. Doze VA, Chen B, Tinkleberg JA, et al. Pertussis toxin and 4-aminopyridine differentially affect the hypnotic-anesthetic action of dexmedetomidine and phenobarbital. Anesthesiology 1990;73:304–307
161. Maze M, Tranquilli W. Alpha-2 adrenoceptor agonists: defining the role in clinical anesthesia. Anesthesiology 1991;74:581–605
162. Gustafson I, Westerberg E, Wieloch T. Protection against ischemia-induced neuronal damage by the alpha 2-adrenoceptor antagonist idazoxan: influence of time of administration and possible mechanisms of action. J Cereb Blood Flow Metab 1990;10:885–894
163. Gustafson I, Miyauchi Y, Wieloch TW. Postischemic administration of idazoxan, an α-2 adrenergic receptor antagonist, decreases neuronal damage in the rat brain. J Cereb Blood Flow Metab 1989;9:171–174
164. Gustafson I, Westerberg EJ, Wieloch T. Extracellular brain cortical levels of noradrenaline in ischemia: effects of desipramine and postischemic administration of idazoxan. Exp Brain Res 1991;86:555–561

165. Hoffman WE, Kochs E, Werner C, et al. Dexmedetomidine improves neurologic outcome from incomplete ischemia in rat. Reversal by the α_2-adrenergic antagonist atipamezole. Anesthesiology 1991;75:328–332
166. Maier C, Steinberg GK, Sun GH, et al. Neuroprotection by the α_2-adrenoreceptor agonist dexmedetomidine in a focal model of cerebral ischemia. Anesthesiology 1993;79:306–312
167. Matsumoto M, Zornow MH, Rabin BC, Maze M. The α_2 adrenergic agonist, dexmedetomidine, selectively attenuates ischemia-induced increases in striatal norepinephrine concentrations. Brain Res 1993;627:325–329
168. Maiese K, Pek L, Berger SB, Reis DJ. Reduction in focal cerebral ischemia by agents acting at imidazole receptors. J Cereb Blood Flow Metab 1992;12:53–63
169. Nugent M, Artru AA, Michenfelder JD. Cerebral metabolic, vascular and protective effects of midazolam maleate: comparison to diazepam. Anesthesiology 1982; 56:172–176
170. Forster A, Juge O, Morel D. Effects of midazolam on cerebral blood flow in human volunteers. Anesthesiology 1982;56:453–455
171. Fleischer JE, Milde JH, Moyer TP, Michenfelder JD. Cerebral effects of high-dose midazolam and subsequent reversal with Ro 15-1788 in dogs. Anesthesiology 1988;68:234–242
172. Forster A, Juge O, Louis M, Nahory A. Effects of a specific benzodiazepine antagonist (RO 15-1788) on cerebral blood flow. Anesth Analg 1987;66:309–313
173. Johansen FF, Christensen T, Jensen MS, et al. Inhibition in postischemic rat hippocampus: GABA receptors, GABA release, and inhibitory postsynaptic potentials. Exp Brain Res 1991;84:529–537
174. Johansen FF, Diemer NH. Enhancement of GABA neurotransmission after cerebral ischemia in the rat reduces loss of hippocampal CA1 pyramidal cells. Acta Neurol Scand 1991;84:1–6
175. Schwartz RD, Yu X, Katzman MR, et al. Diazepam, given postischemia, protects selectively vulnerable neurons in the rat hippocampus and striatum. J Neurosci 1995;15:529–539
176. Siemkowicz E. Improvement of restitution from cerebral ischemia in hyperglycemic rats by pentobarbital or diazepam. Acta Neurol Scand 1980;61:368–376
177. Voll CL, Auer RN. Postischemic seizures and necrotizing ischemic brain damage: neuroprotective effect of postischemic diazepam and insulin. Neurology 1991;41: 423–428
178. Kochhar A, Zivin JA, Mazzarella V. Pharmacologic studies of the neuroprotective actions of a glutamate antagonist in ischemia. J Neurotrauma 1991;8:175–186
179. Astrup J, Srensen PM, Srensen HR. Inhibition of cerebral oxygen and glucose consumption in the dog by hypothermia, pentobarbital, and lidocaine. Anesthesiology 1981;55:263–268
180. Shokunbi MT, Gelb AW, Wu XM, Miller DJ. Continuous lidocaine infusion and focal feline cerebral ischemia. Stroke 1990;21:107–111.
181. Evans DE, Korbine AI, LeGrys DC, Bradley ME. Protective effect of lidocaine in acute cerebral ischemia induced by air embolism. J Neurosurg 1984;60:257–263
182. Evans DE, Catron PW, McDermott JJ, et al. Effect of lidocaine after experimental cerebral ischemia induced by air embolism. J Neurosurg 1989;70:97–102
183. Shokunbi MT, Gelb AW, Peerless SJ, et al. An evaluation of the effect of lidocaine in experimental focal cerebral ischemia. Stroke 1986;17:962–966
184. Sutherland G, Ong BY, Louw D, Sima AAF. Effect of lidocaine on forebrain ischemia in rats. Stroke 1989;20:119–122
185. Warner DS, Godersky JC, Smith M-L. Failure of pre-ischemic lidocaine administration to ameliorate global ischemic brain damage in the rat. Anesthesiology 1988; 68:73–78
186. Rasool N, Faroqui M, Rubinstein EH. Lidocaine accelerates neuroelectrical recovery after incomplete global ischemia in rabbits. Stroke 1990;21:929–935

Hypothermia-associated Protection from Ischemic Brain Injury: Implications for Patient Management

C. Thomas Wass, MD
William L. Lanier, MD

In the history of neuroanesthesia, numerous therapies have been invoked to protect the brain from ischemic injury. Of all the possible protective modalities, perhaps none has been so widely studied nor has undergone such dramatic alterations in its usage as induced hypothermia.

In the following article, we will review the clinical use of hypothermic brain protection, including profound, moderate, and mild hypothermia. We will review the proposed mechanisms responsible for hypothermia-mediated brain protection. We also will discuss technical and physiological factors that have limited the widespread use of hypothermia as a means of providing brain protection. Lastly, we will provide a management plan for using hypothermia in patients at risk for ischemic injury.

For the purposes of this discussion, we will define profound and moderate hypothermia as temperatures of $<20°$ C and $20°$ C–$30°$ C, respectively. Mild alterations in temperature are defined as any that occur at $\geq30°$ C.

■ Cerebral Protection by Profound Hypothermia

The earliest and most striking examples of temperature-mediated cerebral protection were demonstrated in humans subjected to profound hypothermia during cardiopulmonary bypass (CPB)-assisted circulation and circulatory arrest [1–3]. Investigators reported that, when core temperature is reduced to $17°$ C to $20°$ C, the human brain can tolerate circulatory arrest for approximately 1 hour without sustaining permanent injury [1–3]. This duration is in striking contrast to estimates of the duration of complete ischemia tolerated by the normothermic mammalian brain (i.e., 5 to 15 minutes, depending on the species) [4].

The clinical indications for utilizing profound hypothermia as a means of cerebral protection have changed over the years. For example, in the early 1960s, profound hypothermia and circulatory arrest were employed to facilitate intracranial aneurysm clipping [5–7] or arteriovenous malformation resection [7] in many scenarios that today would be viewed as rather routine. In support of this radical therapy of the 1960s, multiple investigators reported a significant improvement in postoperative neurological outcome when compared to patients who were treated with more traditional techniques of that era [1, 3, 5–7]. However, modern improvements in surgical techniques (e.g., the use of microscopic dissection) [8] and the use of pre-emptive or definitive invasive neuroradiological interventions [9, 10] have dramatically lessened the need for cerebral protection via profound hypothermia.

Currently, profound hypothermia and circulatory arrest in neurosurgery are limited to the resection of massive, or relatively inaccessible, aneurysms (e.g., giant basilar artery aneurysms) [11, 12] or arteriovenous malformations [13]. In other disciplines, profound hypothermia and circulatory arrest are used to protect the brain during surgical repairs of complex cardiac or central vascular disorders, particularly in children [14, 15].

■ The Search for Protection by Moderate Reductions in Brain Temperature

Major limitations to the widespread use of profound hypothermia for cerebral protection are the need for CPB-assisted circulation and systemic anticoagulation. Not only is CPB support technically demanding and expensive, it also adds an independent risk of bypass-associated injury to the brain [16].

Perhaps because of these factors, several investigators explored the use of less profound, or moderate, hypothermia for cerebral protection during endogenous (i.e., non-CPB) circulation. Initial studies met with dismal results. For example, Michenfelder and Milde [17] induced focal cerebral ischemia (i.e., middle cerebral artery occlusion) in monkeys whose core temperatures were maintained at 29° C. Hypothermia was begun 30 minutes after permanent middle cerebral artery (MCA) occlusion and continued for 48 hours in an intensive care environment. When compared to normothermic control animals, hypothermia was clearly detrimental to both functional and histological outcome. That is, none of the hypothermic animals survived more than 3 hours following the 48-hour intensive care period. Additionally, all hypothermic animals had massive cerebral edema with underlying infarction. In a subsequent study from the same laboratory, Steen and colleagues [18] studied outcome in monkeys and cats in which temperature management was identical to that in their previous study [17]. Six of 9 normothermic monkeys with MCA occlusion survived 7 days; whereas, all 8 hypothermic monkeys with MCA occlusion died during or shortly after rewarming [18]. In the feline arm of this study, prolonged hypothermia was almost uniformly fatal, regardless of whether cats were exposed to MCA occlusion or not. As noted in their previous study [17], death typically occurred during or shortly after rewarming [18].

These investigators attributed the worsened outcome to systemic factors that would offset any direct benefit of temperature reduction on the ischemic brain [17–19]. Specifically, they demonstrated that hypothermic subjects experienced a temperature-induced reduction in cardiac output to 7% of control while at 29° C and during rewarming [19]. Upon warming, it was theorized that the extracerebral tissues released their sequestered acid metabolites, which in turn depressed the myocardium and led to cardiovascular collapse [19, 20].

The available human data also suggested that during prolonged induced temperature changes to <30° C the adverse systemic effects of hypothermia would overwhelm any beneficial effects on the nervous system. For example, Fay [21] treated cancer victims with total body refrigeration to relieve pain. One hundred twenty-four patients were subjected to temperature reductions to 24° C to 32° C for durations of up to 10 days. Of the 124 patients, 19 died. The majority (i.e., 89%) of deaths occurred either during, or within 24 hours after, rewarming. Of the deaths, 58% resulted from sudden cardiac failure [21]. In another series of patients managed by Fields from the University of Texas at Houston (and reported by Steen and colleagues [18, 19]), 12 acute stroke patients were cooled to 28° C to 30° C for 4 to 7 days. Consistent with the experience of the above-cited investigators, 10 patients died following rewarming.

Perhaps because of this collective experience, almost a decade passed between studies of prolonged, moderate hypothermia and studies of cerebral protection by acute temperature reductions to no lower than 32° C.

■ Effects of Mild Alterations in Temperature on Outcome

Since 1987, numerous investigators have reported that, in animal models, temperature reductions of ≤6° C resulted in an improvement in postischemic neurological function [22–26] and histopathology [23–29]. In contrast, temperature increases have been reported to worsen outcome [27, 30–33]. Taken together, these temperature effects have been observed in models of either global [22–28, 31–33] or focal [29, 30] ischemia. Perhaps the most striking examples of temperature-related alterations in postischemic outcome have come from Warner and associates [30] (Fig 1), who used a model of focal cerebral ischemia in rats, and Wass and coworkers [31], who used a model of complete ischemia in dogs (Fig 2). These authors

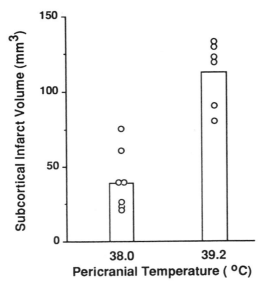

Fig 1. *Cerebral subcortical infarct volumes at 96 hours following 90 minutes of middle cerebral artery occlusion in normothermic (n = 6) or hyperthermic (n = 7) halothane-anesthetized rats. In the subcortex, a significant difference between groups was demonstrated (P = 0.007). Bars represent the mean value for each group. There also was a tendency for cortical infarct volumes to differ in this study (P = 0.067) (cortical data not presented). (From Warner and associates [30]. With permission.)*

reported that temperature changes of a mere 1.2° C [30] and 1.0° C [31], respectively, altered both functional and histological outcome.

Although mild hypothermia is commonly employed clinically for cerebral protection, there currently are no studies in humans demonstrating improved outcome following cerebral ischemia. However, in patients suffering from severe (i.e., Glasgow Coma Scale score of <7) closed head injury (CHI), Clifton and colleagues [34] and Marion and associates [35] reported that inducing systemic hypothermia (i.e., 32° C to 33° C) within 6 and 10 hours, respectively, of the traumatic event resulted in a tendency for improved neurological outcome (p = 0.29 and 0.24, respectively). Other investigators have published complementary studies of statistically significant improvements in postischemic neurological function in animals exposed to hypothermia following CHI [36, 37].

Thus, the available human studies of hypothermia-mediated improvement of outcome following CHI [34, 35] appear promising. However, further investigation is needed to determine if mild hypothermia will improve outcome following atraumatic brain injury (e.g., ischemia) in humans.

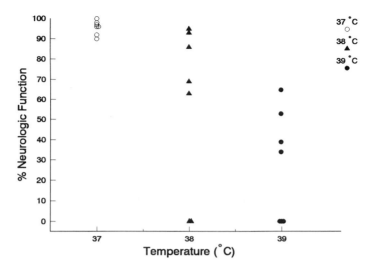

Fig 2. *Percent neurologic function scores at 72 hours following complete cerebral ischemia in dogs. A score of 100 denotes normalcy; a score of 0 denotes brain death. Compared with reference group dogs (maintained at 37° C), neurological function was significantly worse in dogs maintained at 38° C (P < 0.01) or 39° C (P < 0.001). (From Wass and coworkers [31]. With permission.)*

■ Timing of Hypothermia

Cerebral protection by hypothermia is consistently demonstrated when temperature reduction is initiated prior to the insult and is present during the insult [1–7, 22, 24–29]. Other studies have demonstrated improved outcome when hypothermia is initiated after the acute insult [23–25, 38–40].

Using two differing canine models of complete ischemia, researchers from the University of Pittsburgh reported that mild hypothermia, induced immediately upon recirculation, resulted in an improvement in postischemic neurological function and histology [23–25, 40]. However, when the onset of hypothermia was delayed for 15 minutes, improvement was attenuated [23]. Consistent with these results, moderate hypothermia in a rat model of incomplete global ischemia improved histology if induced within 5 minutes of recirculation; however, benefit was not observed when hypothermia was initiated 30 minutes following ischemia [38].

Taken together, the above-cited studies suggest that benefit from hypothermia is achieved when initiated before or perhaps within the first few minutes following an ischemic insult. Delays in the initiation of hypothermia will lessen the likelihood of benefit. The existence of conflicting reports [39, 41] in the literature suggest that more research is needed before it will be possible to determine the time of onset of hypothermia, extent of temperature reduction, and duration of the exposure, which are critical for improving outcome.

■ Mechanism of Protection by Hypothermia

As recently reviewed by Lanier [42], protection by hypothermia has long been assumed to result from a simple depression of cerebral metabolism. According to this theory, during an ischemic insult, the hypothermic brain consumes fewer critical substrates and accumulates fewer toxic metabolites. In support of this theory, there is experimental evidence demonstrating that progressive reductions in temperature are accompanied by progressive reductions in cerebral metabolic rate for oxygen consumption ($CMRO_2$) [43–45]. Additionally, when the brain is subjected to ischemia during profound hypothermia, there is better intraischemic preservation of high-energy phosphates and less accumulation of lactate [46].

However, the evaluation of cerebral metabolism during mild hypothermia suggests that factors other than alterations in basal metabolism are responsible for protection. For example, Busto and coworkers [28] used a rat model of global ischemia (i.e., four-vessel occlusion) to study cerebral metabolites at the completion of ischemia and outcome at 3 days postischemia. Groups of rats were maintained at either 39° C, 36° C, 34° C, or 33° C during ischemia. Reduction in temperature attenuated histological injury. However, this improved outcome did not correlate with alterations in the depletion of brain adenosine triphosphate, phosphocreatine, glucose, and glycogen nor in the accumulation of lactate [28]. Similarly, Natale and D'Alecy [22] evaluated neurological function in dogs exposed to 10 minutes of cardiac arrest. Brain temperature was maintained at either 39° C or 33° C during ischemia. All dogs in the hypothermic group survived for 24 hours; however, all dogs maintained at 39° C died. Under these experimental conditions, there were no differences between the two groups in cortical lactate concentrations during and following ischemia.

In further support of a mechanism of protection other than simple alterations in the supply and demand characteristics of the brain, there are reports demonstrating that hypothermia initiated after an ischemic insult also may improve outcome [23–25, 38–40]. These effects obviously did not originate from alterations in intraischemic metabolism.

Other possible explanations for hypothermia-related improvement in outcome include: (1) alterations in ion homeostasis (including calcium and potassium fluxes), (2) increased membrane stability (including the blood-brain barrier), (3) altered enzyme function (e.g., phospholipase, xanthine oxidase, nitric oxide synthase activity), (4) alterations in neurotransmitter release or reuptake (e.g., glutamate or aspartate), and (5) changes in free radical production or scavenging [4, 22, 28, 31, 47–51]. Although there is mounting experimental evidence that temperature alterations affect these processes, it is not clear which factors are critical in modulating outcome.

■ Developing an Approach to Clinical Management

Despite a lack of evidence that mild hypothermia is of benefit in humans experiencing cerebral ischemia and limited evidence of benefit in the setting of CHI [34, 35], the practice of inducing hypothermia—or permitting passive hypothermia to develop—has become commonplace in high-risk neurosurgical patients [52]. For example, in a recent survey of 41 major teaching hospitals, Craen and coworkers [52] queried neuro-anesthesiologists regarding their use of cerebral protective therapies during cerebral aneurysm clipping (i.e., a patient population in which 26% of those admitted neurologically intact to the hospital will acquire a persistent, postoperative neurological deficit [53]). They discovered that 60% of the respondent anesthesiologists used specific brain protective measures in this setting [52]. Of this subset of respondents, 71% used some level of induced hypothermia, and 23% felt it was unethical to continue to use normothermia. In this survey, the use of induced hypothermia was second only to barbiturate administration as a cerebroprotective therapy.

If one assumes that the use of induced hypothermia is appropriate and that convincing evidence of protection in humans will follow, it then is incumbent that clinicians develop a rational approach to temperature management. We next will discuss experimental observations that influence patient management, including studies addressing difficulties in monitoring brain temperature, the side effects of hypothermia, and the control of brain temperature.

Monitoring Brain Temperature

Traditionally, clinicians have not directly monitored brain temperature in patients at risk for ischemic neurological injury but instead have assumed that brain temperature parallels core and pericranial temperatures. As we will see later, such a practice may result in clinically relevant errors.

In order to develop more effective monitoring, it is useful to review the origins of brain temperature. Brain temperature results from three major factors: cerebral blood flow (CBF), cerebral metabolism, and the extracerebral environment.

Cerebral Blood Flow   The quantities of blood flowing to the brain and the temperature gradient between the brain and blood flow emanating from the core will determine the magnitude and direction of heat exchange [54, 55]. For example, if the brain is warmer than the core, CBF will tend to cool the brain. If the brain is cooler than the core, CBF will tend to warm the brain. Experimental studies suggest that the temperature of blood perfusing the brain (i.e., CBF) is the primary determinant of brain temperature [54]. Thus, the core and brain temperatures are generally in good agreement in the normal, nonischemic brain [54–59].

Brain Heat Production The brain has one of the highest metabolic rates in the entire body, and, as a result of this metabolism, heat is produced [58]. This probably explains why the temperature of the resting brain is reported to be 0.1° C to 0.9° C warmer than core temperature [11, 55–58].

Heat Exchange with the Environment The third determinant of brain temperature is heat exchange with the environment [54, 59]. In the normal, intact animal, the temperature of the environment immediately surrounding the brain (i.e., bone, muscle, and skin) will approximate—or be slightly less than—core temperature. However, if the temperature of these surrounding tissues is lowered further, the temperature of the brain should decrease, beginning with the outermost layers [11, 22, 57, 60].

Based on the above factors, it follows that, during anesthesia, if the cranium remains intact and the background anesthetic minimally affects baseline CBF and $CMRO_2$, then there should be good agreement between core and brain temperatures. Such a scenario was studied by Lanier and associates [56], who evaluated core and brain temperature in normocapnic dogs anesthetized with 1.0 minimal alveolar concentration isoflurane. Core temperature was manipulated over a 4° C range (i.e., 33.0° C to 37.0° C) using convective cooling and rewarming of the body, exclusive of the head. During this experiment, there was always good agreement (i.e., $r \geq 0.97$) between brain temperature and core temperature measured from a variety of extracerebral sites (e.g., pulmonary artery, tympanic membrane, esophagus, rectum). Specifically, brain temperature remained consistently 0.1° C to 0.6° C warmer than core, throughout the study. Using subjects having intact calvaria and nonischemic brains, other investigators have reported similar findings when evaluating temperature gradients within the brain and between the brain and core [54, 55].

In contrast, when anesthetic management, the surgical intervention, or the subject's pathology alter the above-mentioned determinants of brain temperature, large brain-to-core gradients can develop. Previous reports [11, 57] in which brain temperature was measured during craniotomy have discovered that the temperatures of superficial brain layers were cooler than in deeper brain structures. This probably reflected cerebral heat loss to the environment (i.e., cold operating room and irrigation fluids). Specifically, in the report of Stone and coworkers [11], temperature at a depth of 4 cm beneath the cortical surface was 36.9° C ± 0.2° C (mean ± standard deviation) in 4 patients having systemic normothermia. However, as

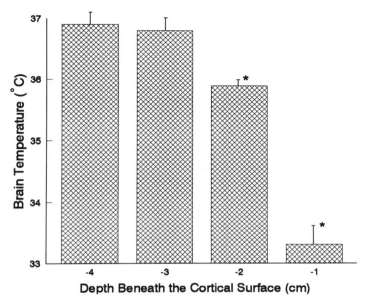

Fig 3. *Regional brain temperature in patients undergoing resection of an epileptogenic focus during general anesthesia. The bars represent brain temperature, as a needle thermistor was withdrawn from a maximal depth of 4 cm beneath the cortical surface. Temperature at a depth of 4 cm beneath the cortical surface was 36.9° C ± 0.2° C (mean ± standard deviation) in 4 patients having systemic normothermia. However, as the needle thermistor was withdrawn, temperature steadily declined to 33.3° C ± 0.3° C (i.e., a reduction of 3.6° C). *P < 0.05 when compared to the preceding value. (Constructed from the data of Stone and coworkers [11].)*

the needle thermistor was withdrawn, temperature steadily declined to 33.3° C ± 0.3° C (i.e., a reduction of 3.6° C) in the more superficial brain (Fig 3).

Brain ischemia also may affect brain-to-core temperature gradients, as demonstrated in several animal studies [28, 33, 54, 59, 61]. Specifically, while simultaneously monitoring the temperature of the core and multiple brain sites, Hayward and Baker [54] demonstrated that an abrupt cessation of CBF resulted in immediate cooling of the scalp and superficial brain structures relative to the core and deeper brain monitoring sites. Additionally, after 10 minutes of brain ischemia, deeper brain structures also began to cool at the same rates as scalp and superficial brain sites [54]. Brain cooling in this scenario was thought to be due to cerebral heat loss to the surrounding environment.

In addition to the above-mentioned factors, changes in arterial carbon dioxide tension [54], vasoconstricting anesthetics (e.g., barbiturates) [54], and external cooling devices [22, 60] all can affect the brain-to-core temperature gradient and our ability to indirectly assess brain temperature. These factors most probably act by interfering with more than one determinant of brain temperature. Thus, it follows that other complex alterations in cerebral physiology (e.g., as may accompany ischemia-related convulsions) also have the potential to confound the indirect assessment of brain temperature.

Collectively, the above data suggest that core temperature measurement provides the single best estimate of global brain temperature [56, 57]. However, the potential error in these estimates—particularly as they relate to regional brain temperatures in neurosurgical or neurologically impaired patients—may approximate or exceed the 1° C to 2° C previously reported to affect outcome.

Effects of Induced Hypothermia on Systemic Physiology

The use of core temperature to alter brain temperature may be limited by a variety of adverse systemic effects. In extreme examples (i.e., as seen in the above mentioned studies of Michenfelder and Milde [17], Steen and colleagues [18], and Fay [21]), the systemic effects of hypothermia may be life threatening. Some of the more critical effects of induced hypothermia and rewarming during endogenous (i.e., non-CPB) circulation are outlined below.

Hypothermia will result in a progressive slowing of cardiac conduction (manifested as prolongation of the PR, QRS, and QT intervals, and sinus bradycardia), atrial and ventricular ectopy [56, 62, 63], and decreases in myocardial contractility [63, 64]. Hypothermia also produces shifts of potassium intracellularly, resulting in hypokalemia [23, 63, 65]. If potassium-containing solutions are administered in an attempt to restore normokalemia during hypothermia, hyperkalemic-mediated cardiac arrhythmias may occur during rewarming (i.e., as intracellularly sequestered potassium is being released) [65]. In addition to altering cardiac conduction and contractility, hypothermia causes a shift of the oxyhemoglobin dissociation curve to the left [63, 66, 67]. Taken together, these effects on cardiac conduction, cardiac output, and the oxyhemoglobin dissociation curve could potentially decrease oxygen and nutrient delivery to the brain. However, barring any catastrophic effect on systemic physiology (e.g., malignant cardiac arrhythmias, systemic shock), any alterations in brain oxygen delivery during mild hypothermia should be offset by a direct beneficial effect of hypothermia on the brain.

Hypothermia may precipitate myocardial ischemia in elderly patients. For example, when compared to normothermic patients (i.e., defined as having a sublingual temperature ≥35° C), Frank and colleagues [68] reported that hypothermic patients (i.e., defined as having a sublingual temperature <35° C) had a threefold increase in the incidence of myocardial ischemia but no difference in the incidence of shivering or myocardial infarction. Although cold-induced myocardial ischemia is often attributed to increases in total body oxygen consumption associated with shivering, there are no data to support this assumption [68, 69].

Since their original study found no correlation between shivering and myocardial ischemia, Frank and associates [70] performed a separate study to evaluate the origins of cold-induced myocardial ischemia. They reported that patients having mild hypothermia (i.e., core temperature 35.3° C ± 0.9° C) experienced significant increases in plasma norepinephrine concentrations, greater peripheral vasoconstriction, and higher blood pressures than normothermic patients (i.e., core temperature 36.7° C ± 0.9° C). In a subsequent study, Frank and coworkers [71] demonstrated that shivering in the elderly (i.e., age ≥ 60 years) resulted in a 38% increase in total body oxygen consumption rather than the 300%–400% often quoted. Taken together, cold-induced myocardial ischemia is likely due to a physiological stress response and, secondarily, to increases in total body oxygen consumption associated with shivering. Additionally, despite an association between myocardial ischemia and hypothermia, to our knowledge, there have been no reports linking myocardial infarction to mild hypothermia [68, 69].

Other systemic effects of hypothermia include, but are not limited to, platelet sequestration and dysfunction, enhanced fibrinolytic activity, slowing of enzymatic activity required for clotting, attenuation of hypoxic pulmonary vasoconstriction, increased systemic and pulmonary vascular resistance, increased blood viscosity, decreased hepatic and renal blood flow, slowed metabolism and anesthetics and muscle relaxants, and impaired leukocyte motility and phagocytosis [4, 63, 66, 72].

Hypothermia also may interfere with monitoring of neurological function. For example, hypothermia prolongs the latency of somatosensory evoked potentials and motor evoked potentials and produces slowing of the electroencephalogram [56, 63]. These alterations in baseline nervous system electrical activity may make it more difficult to detect new-onset changes related to ischemia.

Despite the multiple systemic effects of hypothermia, to date there is no convincing evidence that concern for systemic side effects should preclude the use of controlled temperature reductions in most patients at high risk for ischemic brain injury. Human studies have demonstrated that most individuals will tolerate the effects of a 2° C to 5° C reduction in temperature [34, 35, 68, 69]. Slightly larger reductions in core temperature (i.e., >5° C) may be well tolerated in healthier individuals. As noted earlier, these temperature reductions should be sufficient to confer cerebral protection.

Clinical Control of Brain Temperature

From the above analysis, it is apparent that the most expedient and most effective method to control brain temperature is by controlling systemic temperature [54–59]. With profound hypothermia, this is accomplished by placing the patient on CPB [1–3].

However, when managing core temperature independent of CPB, there are several factors that must be considered. First, temperature should be maintained at a beneficial target value during and shortly after the ischemic insult. Thus, in patients suffering from—or at risk for—ischemia, temperature increases (e.g., fever) should be avoided at all times [27, 30–33]. Induced hypothermia, when used, should be conducted employing techniques that allow brisk reductions of temperature prior to the period of greatest risk. In the surgical suite, this can be accomplished by a variety of techniques, including lowering room temperature, ventilating the lungs with high flows of unwarmed gases through the anesthesia machine, and enhancing body exposure to facilitate heat exchange with the environment [34, 35, 56, 69]. The latter will include the removal of insulating coverings on the patients and the use of surface convective [56, 69] or conductive cooling devices [34, 35, 69]. Using simultaneous convective and conductive cooling techniques, Baker and colleagues [69] were able to cool their patients at an average rate of $1.0° C \pm 0.4° C/hr$.

Ironically, one of the major concerns in managing patient cooling is the ability to provide patient warming as well. It is critical to halt temperature reductions at the desired target, thus, avoiding morbidity associated with excessive hypothermia. Achieving and maintaining a desired target temperature is often challenging [56, 63, 69]. For example, using a canine model, Lanier and associates [56] reported that the core temperature (i.e., pulmonary artery) passively decreased to $32.4° C \pm 0.3° C$ following discontinuation of active cooling at a target temperature of $33.0° C$. Similarly, in humans, Baker and colleagues [69] reported a temperature afterdrop to $34.3° C$ despite the cessation of active cooling at a target of $35° C$ and initiating active rewarming at $34.5° C$. Fortunately, thermoregulatory vasoconstriction will typically limit passive, mild hypothermia to approximately $34° C$ [63]. Further, the adverse systemic effects of hypothermia are largely reversed upon completion of rewarming [56, 62, 69, 72].

Effective methods for limiting afterdrop beyond the target temperature and subsequent rewarming include increasing the ambient temperature [63], humidification of inspired gases [63, 73], and conductive [63, 74], convective [56, 63, 74], and radiant [63, 75] (e.g., heat lamps) techniques. These rewarming modalities may vary dramatically in their efficacy and potential side effects. This is evident in a recent study by Hynson and Sessler [76] in which the efficacies of three commonly used intraoperative warming devices were compared (Fig 4).

■ Summary

There is a large amount of experimental evidence that mild hypothermia in laboratory animals will protect the brain from ischemic injury. Con-

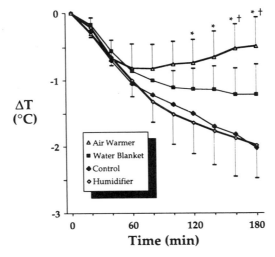

Fig 4. *Tympanic membrane temperature from 20 adult patients decreased uniformly during the first hour after induction of anesthesia. During the subsequent 2 hours, temperature increased in patients treated with a forced-air warming device but remained nearly constant in those lying on a warmed circulating-water mattress. Patients in the control and heated-humidifier groups continued to become more hypothermic throughout the operation. Differences between the forced-air warmer and the control and heated-humidifier groups were significant (*) after 100 minutes. Differences between the forced-air and circulating-water mattress groups were significant (†) at ≥160 minutes. $p < 0.05$. (From Hynson and Sessler [76]. With permission.)*

versely, mild hyperthermia will exacerbate injury. Supporting data in humans are limited. However, cerebral protection has consistently been demonstrated in humans subjected to complete circulatory arrest during profound hypothermia.

Induced and passive mild hypothermia have become common in the management of patients at risk for ischemic neurological injury. Currently, brain temperature is managed largely by altering core temperature. Limitations of this approach are that gradients can develop between brain and core temperatures as a result of the surgical intervention, anesthetic interventions, or the patient's pathology. Further, large reductions in systemic temperature may place an undue burden on systemic physiology and, in extreme examples, systemic factors may adversely affect neurological well-being.

Obviously, proper temperature management in humans at high risk for neurological injury will benefit from the following factors: First, greater evidence is needed that small changes in temperature modulate outcome in humans, commensurate with demonstrations of benefit in animals. Second, better methods are needed to monitor brain temperature during periods of risk for ischemic injury. And third, management techniques should be identified that will use brain-to-core temperature gradients to the patient's advantage, thus producing optimal alterations in brain temperature while minimally affecting systemic temperature and physiology. Before these goals can be accomplished, more research is needed, both in laboratory animals and in humans.

■ References

1. Silverberg GD, Reitz BA, Ream AK. Hypothermia and cardiac arrest in the treatment of giant aneurysms of the cerebral circulation and hemangioblastoma of the medulla. J Neurosurgery 1981;55:337–346
2. Greeley WJ, Kern FH, Ungerleider RM, et al. The effect of hypothermic cardiopulmonary bypass and total circulatory arrest on cerebral metabolism in neonates, infants, and children. J Thorac Cardiovasc Surg 1991;101:783–794
3. Spetzler RF, Hadley MN, Rigamonti D, et al. Aneurysms of the basilar artery treated with circulatory arrest, hypothermia, and barbiturate cerebral protection. J Neurosurg 1988;68:868–879
4. Wass CT, Lanier WL. Improving neurologic outcome following cardiac arrest. Anesthesiology Clin North Am 1995;13:869–903
5. Uihlein A, MacCarty CS, Michenfelder JD, et al. Deep hypothermia and surgical treatment of intracranial aneurysms: a five-year survey. JAMA 1966;195:639–641
6. Michenfelder JD, Kirklin JW, Uihlein A, et al. Clinical experience with a closed-chest method of producing profound hypothermia and total circulatory arrest in neurosurgery. Ann Surg 1964;159:125–131
7. MacCarty CS, Michenfelder JD, Uihlein A. Treatment of intracranial vascular disorders with the aid of profound hypothermia and total circulatory arrest: three years' experience. J Neurosurg 1964;5:372–377
8. Yasargil MG. Clinical considerations in operability. In: Yasargil MG, ed. Microsurgery. New York: Thieme, 1994:317–386
9. Meyer FB, Morita A, Puumala MR, Nichols DA. Medical and surgical management of intracranial aneurysms. Mayo Clin Proc 1995;70:153–172
10. Halbach VV, Higashida RT, Dowd CF, et al. The efficacy of endovascular aneurysm occlusion in alleviating neurological deficits produced by mass effect. J Neurosurg 1994;80:659–666
11. Stone JG, Young WL, Smith CR, et al. Do standard monitoring sites reflect true brain temperature when profound hypothermia is rapidly induced and reversed? Anesthesiology 1995;82:344–351
12. Solomon RA, Smith CR, Raps EC, et al. Deep hypothermic circulatory arrest for the management of complex anterior and posterior circulation aneurysms. Neurosurgery 1991;29:732–738
13. Williams MD, Rainer WG, Fieger HG, et al. Cardiopulmonary bypass, profound hypothermia, and circulatory arrest for neurosurgery. Ann Thorac Surg 1991;52:1069–1074

14. Jonas RA. Hypothermia, circulatory arrest, and the pediatric brain. J Cardiothorac Vasc Anesth 1996;10:66–74
15. Greeley WJ, Kern FH, Undergleider RM, et al. The effect of hypothermic cardiopulmonary bypass and total circulatory arrest on cerebral metabolism in neonates, infants, and children. J Thorac Cardiovasc Surg 1991;101:783–794
16. Slogoff S, Girgis KZ, Keats AS. Etiologic factors in neuropsychiatric complications associated with cardiopulmonary bypass. Anesth Analg 1982;61:903–911
17. Michenfelder JD, Milde JH. Failure of prolonged hypocapnia, hypothermia, or hypertension to favorably alter acute stroke in primates. Stroke 1977;8:87–91
18. Steen PA, Soule EH, Michenfelder JD. Detrimental effect of prolonged hypothermia in cats and monkeys with and without regional cerebral ischemia. Stroke 1979; 10:522–529
19. Steen PA, Milde JH, Michenfelder JD. The detrimental effects of prolonged hypothermia and rewarming in the dog. Anesthesiology 1980;52:224–230
20. Michenfelder JD. Anesthesia and the brain: clinical, functional, metabolic, and vascular correlates. New York: Churchill Livingstone, 1988:23–34
21. Fay T. Early experiences with local and generalized refrigeration of the human brain. J Neurosurg 1959;16:239–260
22. Natale JE, D'Alecy LG. Protection from cerebral ischemia by brain cooling without reduced lactate accumulation in dogs. Stroke 1989;20:770–777
23. Kuboyama K, Safar P, Radovsky A, et al. Delay in cooling negates the beneficial effect of mild resuscitative cerebral hypothermia after cardiac arrest in dogs: a prospective, randomized study. Crit Care Med 1993;21:1348–1358
24. Weinrauch V, Safar P, Tisherman S, et al. Beneficial effect of mild hypothermia and detrimental effect of deep hypothermia after cardiac arrest in dogs. Stroke 1992;23:1454–1462
25. Leonov Y, Sterz F, Safar P, et al. Mild cerebral hypothermia during and after cardiac arrest improves neurologic outcome in dogs. J Cereb Blood Flow Metab 1990;10:57–70
26. Nurse S, Corbett D. Direct measurement of brain temperature during and after intraischemic hypothermia: correlation with behavioral, physiological, and histological endpoints. J Neurosci 1994;14:7726–7734
27. Minamisawa H, Smith ML, Siesjo BK. The effect of mild hyperthermia and hypothermia on brain damage following 5, 10, and 15 minutes of forebrain ischemia. Ann Neurol 1990;28:26–33
28. Busto R, Dietrich WD, Globus MY-T, et al. Small differences in intraischemic brain temperature critically determine the extent of ischemic neuronal injury. J Cereb Blood Flow Metab 1987;7:729–738
29. Ridenour TR, Warner DS, Todd MM, McAllister AC. Mild hypothermia reduces infarct size resulting from temporary but not permanent focal ischemia in rats. Stroke 1992;23:733–738
30. Warner DS, McFarlane C, Todd MM, et al. Sevoflurane and halothane reduce focal ischemic brain damage in the rat: possible influence on thermoregulation. Anesthesiology 1993;79:985–992
31. Wass CT, Lanier WL, Hofer RE, et al. Temperature changes of $\geq 1°$ C alter functional neurologic outcome and histopathology in a canine model of complete cerebral ischemia. Anesthesiology 1995;83:325–335
32. Dietrich WD, Busto R, Valdes I, Loor Y. Effects of normothermic versus mild hyperthermic forebrain ischemia in rats. Stroke 1990;21:1318–1325
33. Kuroiwa T, Bonnekoh P, Hossmann K-A. Prevention of postischemic hyperthermia prevents ischemic injury of CA1 neurons in gerbils. J Cereb Blood Flow Metab 1990;10:550–556
34. Clifton GL, Allen S, Barrodale P, et al. A phase II study of moderate hypothermia in severe brain injury. J Neurotrauma 1993;10:263–271

35. Marion DW, Obrist WD, Carlier PM, et al. The use of moderate therapeutic hypothermia for patients with severe head injuries: a preliminary report. J Neurosurg 1993;79:354–362

36. Clifton GL, Jiang JY, Lyeth BG, et al. Marked protection by moderate hypothermia after experimental traumatic brain injury. J Cereb Blood Flow Metab 1991;11:114–121

37. Lyeth BG, Jiang JY, Liu S. Behavioral protection by moderate hypothermia initiated after experimental traumatic brain injury. J Neurotrauma 1993;10:57–64

38. Busto R, Dietrich WD, Globus MY-T, Ginsberg MD. Postischemic moderate hypothermia inhibits CA1 hippocampal ischemic neuronal injury. Neurosci Lett 1989;101:299–304

39. Coimbra C, Wieloch T. Moderate hypothermia mitigates neuronal damage in the rat brain when initiated several hours following transient cerebral ischemia. Acta Neuropathol 1994;87:325–331

40. Sterz F, Safar P, Tisherman S, et al. Mild hypothermic cardiopulmonary resuscitation improves outcome after prolonged cardiac arrest in dogs. Crit Care Med 1991;19:379–389

41. Chen H, Chopp M, Vande Linde AM, et al. The effects of post-ischemic hypothermia on the neuronal injury and brain metabolism after forebrain ischemia in the rat. J Neurol Sci 1992;107:191–198

42. Lanier WL. Cerebral metabolic rate and hypothermia: their relationship with ischemic neurologic injury. J Neurosurg Anesth 1995;7:216–221

43. Michenfelder JD, Milde JH. The relationship among canine brain temperature, metabolism, and function during hypothermia. Anesthesiology 1991;75:130–136

44. Michenfelder JD, Milde JH. The effect of profound levels of hypothermia (below 14°C) on canine cerebral metabolism. J Cereb Blood Flow Metab 1992;12:877–880

45. Nakashima K, Todd MM, Warner DS. The relation between cerebral metabolic rate and ischemic depolarization. A comparison of the effects of hypothermia, pentobarbital, and isoflurane. Anesthesiology 1995;82:1199–1208

46. Michenfelder JD, Theye RA. The effects of anesthesia and hypothermia on canine cerebral ATP and lactate during anoxia produced by decapitation. Anesthesiology 1970;33:430–439

47. Busto R, Globus MY-T, Dietrich WD, et al. Effect of mild hypothermia on ischemia-induced release of neurotransmitters and free fatty acids in rat brain. Stroke 1989;20:904–910

48. Milde LN, Weglinski MR. Pathophysiology of metabolic brain injury. In: Cottrell JE, Smith DS, eds. Anesthesia and Neurosurgery. St. Louis: Mosby, 1994:59–92

49. Karibe H, Chen SF, Zarow GJ, et al. Mild intraischemic hypothermia suppresses consumption of endogenous antioxidants after temporary focal ischemia in rats. Brain Res 1994;649:12–18

50. Kader A, Frazzini VI, Baker CJ, et al. Effect of mild hypothermia on nitric oxide synthesis during focal cerebral ischemia. Neurosurgery 1994;35:272–277

51. Zornow MH. Inhibition of glutamate release: a possible mechanism of hypothermic neuroprotection. J Neurosurg Anesth 1995;7:148–151

52. Craen RA, Gelb AW, Eliasziw M, Lok P. Current anesthetic practices and use of brain protective therapies for cerebral aneurysm surgery at 41 North American centers. J Neurosurg Anesth 1994;6:303

53. Kassell NF, Torner JC, Haley EC Jr, et al. The international cooperative study on the timing of aneurysm surgery. Part 1: overall management results. J Neurosurg 1990;73:18–36

54. Hayward JN, Baker MA. Role of cerebral arterial blood in the regulation of brain temperature in the monkey. Am J Physiol 1968;215:389–403

55. Baker MA, Stocking RA, Meehan JP. Thermal relationship between tympanic mem-

brane and hypothalamus in conscious cat and monkey. J Appl Physiol 1972;32: 739–742

56. Lanier WL, Iaizzo PA, Murray MJ. The effects of convective cooling and rewarming on systemic and central nervous system physiology in isoflurane-anesthetized dogs. Resuscitation 1992;23:121–136

57. Whitby JD, Dunkin LJ. Cerebral, oesophageal and nasopharyngeal temperatures. Br J Anaesth 1971;43:673–676

58. Shiraki K, Sagawa S, Tajima F, et al. Independence of brain and tympanic temperatures in an unanesthetized human. J Appl Physiol 1988;65:482–486

59. Minamisawa H, Mellergård P, Smith ML, et al. Preservation of brain temperature during ischemia in rats. Stroke 1990;21:758–764

60. Mellergård P. Changes in human intracerebral temperature in response to different methods of brain cooling. Neurosurgery 1992;31:671–677

61. Moyer DJ, Welsh FA, Zager EL. Spontaneous cerebral hypothermia diminishes focal infarction in rat brain. Stroke 1992;23:1812–1816

62. Solomon A, Barish RA, Browne B, Tso E. The electrocardiographic features of hypothermia. J Emerg Med 1989;7:169–173

63. Schubert A. Side effects of mild hypothermia. J Neurosurg Anesth 1995;7:139–147

64. Tveita T, Mortensen E, Hevrøy O, et al. Experimental hypothermia: effects of core cooling and rewarming on hemodynamics, coronary blood flow, and myocardial metabolism in dogs. Anesth Analg 1994;79:212–218

65. Koht A, Cane R, Cerullo LJ. Serum potassium levels during prolonged hypothermia. Intensive Care Med 1983;9:275–277

66. Danzl DF, Pozos RS. Accidental hypothermia. N Engl J Med 1994;331:1756–1760

67. Gutierrez G, Warley AR, Dantzker DR. Oxygen delivery and utilization in hypothermic dogs. J Appl Physiol 1986;60:751–757

68. Frank SM, Beattie C, Christopherson R, et al. Unintentional hypothermia is associated with postoperative myocardial ischemia. The perioperative ischemia randomized anesthesia trial study group. Anesthesiology 1993;78:468–476

69. Baker KZ, Young WL, Stone G, et al. Deliberate mild intraoperative hypothermia for craniotomy. Anesthesiology 1994;81:361–367

70. Frank SM, Higgins MS, Breslow MJ, et al. The catecholamine, cortisol, and hemodynamic responses to mild perioperative hypothermia: a randomized clinical trial. Anesthesiology 1995;82:83–93

71. Frank SM, Fleisher LA, Olson KF, et al. Multivariate determinants of early postoperative oxygen consumption in elderly patients: effects of shivering, body temperature, and gender. Anesthesiology 1995;83:241–249

72. Valeri CR, Feingold H, Cassidy G, et al. Hypothermia-induced reversible platelet dysfunction. Ann Surg 1987;205:175–181

73. Stone DR, Downs JB, Paul WL, Perkins HM. Adult body temperature and heated humidification of anesthetic gases during general anesthesia. Anesth Analg 1981; 60:736–741

74. Kurz A, Kurz M, Poeschl G, et al. Forced-air warming maintains intraoperative normothermia better than circulating-water mattresses. Anesth Analg 1993;77: 89–95

75. Giuffre M, Finnie J, Lynam DA, Smith D. Rewarming postoperative patients: lights, blankets, or forced warm air. J Post Operative Nursing 1991;6:387–393

76. Hynson JM, Sessler DI. Intraoperative warming therapies: a comparison of three devices. J Clin Anesth 1992;4:194–199

Nitric Oxide and the Brain

Dale A. Pelligrino, PhD
Verna L. Baughman, MD
Heidi M. Koenig, MD

Nitric oxide (NO) is a simple molecule that exerts an extensive and complex influence within the central nervous system (CNS). Who would have ever imagined that nitric oxide, which had been studied for a number of years as a constituent of cigarette smoke and a common air pollutant, is now recognized as the first member of a new class of biologic messengers. As a neurotransmitter, NO functions completely differently from the classic transmitters, which are enzymatically synthesized and stored in vesicles in the presynaptic neuron, released by exocytosis into the synaptic cleft, and act on postsynaptic membranes by binding to receptors on those membranes. In the brain under normal conditions, modest amounts of NO are continually produced in vascular endothelial cells and selected neurons. Nitric oxide does not appear to be stored in these cells, but its synthesis can be rapidly increased in the presence of specific stimuli. The NO diffuses into neighboring cells and exerts its effect primarily by stimulating guanylate cyclase (GC), although GC-independent effects have been identified (e.g., inhibition of aconitase, K^+ channel stimulation, ribosylation/nitrosylation reactions, oxidation/reduction modulation [1–5]). The capacity for NO to influence its targets, GC included, derives from its strong affinity for heme and nonheme iron, sulfhydryls, and specific amino acid residues on proteins. Some of the more important actions attributed to NO are vasodilation, antiplatelet aggregation, blocking platelet and leukocyte adhesion, neurotransmission, neuromodulation, a microbicidal action, and cytostatic and cytotoxic actions [3].

Nitric oxide is formed by NO synthase (NOS) [6, 7]. This enzyme catalyzes the conversion of the semiessential amino acid L-arginine, com-

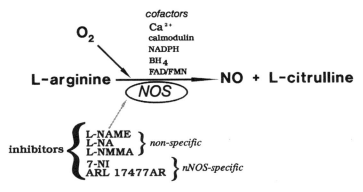

Fig 1. *Nitric oxide (NO) formation via constitutive nitric oxide synthase (NOS). L-arginine, in the presence of oxygen and specific cofactors, is converted to NO and L-citrulline by NOS. Both constitutive isoforms of this enzyme (i.e., neuronal [nNOS] and endothelial) can be competitively, but nonspecifically, blocked by the L-arginine analogues nitro-L-arginine (L-NA), nitro-L-arginine-methyl-ester (L-NAME), and N-monomethyl-L-arginine (L-NMMA). The nNOS isoform can be inhibited by the aqueous-insoluble agent 7-nitroindazole (7-NI) or ARL 17477AR (a newly developed water-soluble agent showing experimental promise as a specific nNOS inhibitor). Ca^{2+} = calcium; NADPH = reduced nicotinamide adenine dinucleotide phosphate; BH_4 = tetrahydrobiopterin; FAD = flavin adenine dinucleotide; FMN = flavin mononucleotide.*

bined with oxygen, into L-citrulline and NO (Fig 1). There are three known isoforms of the NOS enzyme: two of which are constitutive (cNOS) and one inducible (iNOS). Each isoform is encoded by its own gene. The two constitutive isoforms, neuronal NOS (nNOS) and endothelial NOS (eNOS), require cofactors including calcium (Ca^{2+}), calmodulin, reduced nicotinamide adenine dinucleotide phosphate, flavin adenine dinucleotide, flavin mononucleotide, and tetrahydrobiopterin (BH_4). The iNOS does not require calcium or calmodulin.

Neuronal NOS and eNOS are called constitutive because their activation does not require new protein synthesis. Conversely, iNOS must be synthesized before production of any NO. That process requires hours for DNA transcription and subsequent protein synthesis. The iNOS has been identified in many tissues and cell types including endothelial cells, vascular smooth muscle, cerebral astroglia and microglia, and macrophages. It is activated by a number of immunological stimuli such as bacterial endotoxins, lipopolysaccharides, and a variety of cytokines [8]. The induction process can be blocked by protein synthesis inhibitors and anti-inflammatory agents such as dexamethasone. Once iNOS is stimulated, massive amounts of NO are produced over prolonged periods. Inducible NOS–derived NO can attack bacteria, tumor cells, and unfortunately, at times, normal tissue. It is currently thought that NO produced by iNOS may account for the intensive vasodilation accompanying septic shock. Thus, a molecule with the function of destroying invading pathogens may also produce a vascular response that often is untreatable (i.e., terminal septic shock).

Nitric oxide was originally thought to have a very short half-life—less than 1 second. Recently, that concept has been challenged, to the extent that the half-life of NO in vivo may actually be on the order of many seconds or longer [9]—a half-life that is much more in keeping with NO's multiple roles in the brain as a physiological messenger, neurotransmitter, and neuromodulator. This longer half-life may be due to the formation of more chemically stable substances, like nitrosothiols. Such substances may even serve as NO reservoirs. The initial supposition of a short NO half-life stems from a general overestimation of NO reactivity, and, in particular, the rate of NO reaction with O_2. In aqueous solutions, the reaction leads to formation of NO_2, with immediate conversion to NO_2^- and NO_3^-. At NO concentrations normally occurring in vivo, the rate of that reaction has been reported to be far too slow to be of physiological relevance [1, 9]. The most likely mechanism of NO removal in the brain is through diffusion to capillaries and deactivation by binding to hemoglobin. Another potentially important pathway for NO removal in vivo is via reaction with superoxide anion to form peroxynitrite—a highly reactive and potent oxidant [9]. This route may become increasingly active under conditions of cerebral ischemia (see below).

Most laboratory research on NO involves the use of NOS inhibitors, generally, L-arginine analogues, that affect all NOS isoforms [7, 10–12]. The most commonly used include: nitro-L-arginine-methyl-ester (L-NAME), nitro-L-arginine (L-NA), and N-monomethyl-L-arginine. These substances block the production of NO but do not affect the cyclic guanosine monophosphate (cGMP) response produced by NO donors such as sodium nitroprusside. Studies employing agents that selectively inhibit nNOS or iNOS but do not affect the remaining isoforms are beginning to appear in the literature [13–16]. An even more elegant research tool in delineating the function of NO derived from specific NOS isoforms is the gene knockout mouse model. These animals can be bred lacking the gene necessary for synthesis of nNOS, eNOS, or iNOS. One caveat in interpreting results from studies in which such animals are used is that one cannot eliminate the possibility that other factors may become expressed during the course of development that may compensate for the absence of the specific NOS enzyme. Nevertheless, the use of such NOS isoform–specific inhibitors and gene knockout models will be quite helpful in identifying specific functions for nNOS, eNOS, and iNOS.

In the material presented below, a number of general areas regarding the role of NO in the brain are discussed. The major focus of this discussion will be cerebral ischemia. Additionally, some attention will be given to seizure, physiological regulation of the cerebral circulation, pain perception, and anesthetic potency.

■ Nitric Oxide and Cerebral Ischemia

Defining the role for NO in cerebral ischemia is a difficult task. Although NO has been studied extensively in this regard, considerable controversy remains, with some reports suggesting a neuroprotective role and others a neurotoxic role. There are a number of factors that probably contribute to this conflict. First, NO's involvement in cerebral physiology and pathophysiology is quite complex and not completely understood. Second, NO's effects may depend on the NOS isoform from which the NO is derived. Third, experimental outcome may depend on the specific ischemia models used. The rodent models most frequently used in studying the role of NO in brain ischemia can be divided into two general categories—focal ischemia and forebrain ischemia. Focal ischemia most often involves middle cerebral artery occlusion (MCAO) simulating embolic or thrombotic stroke. Forebrain ischemia generally employs occlusion of the carotid arteries (and sometimes the vertebrals as well) and is often combined with hypotension, simulating hypoperfusion ischemia (i.e., cardiac arrest/insufficiency). With the introduction of better methodologies (e.g., NOS isoform–specific inhibitors, NOS knockout models) some patterns are emerging. The aim of this section is to identify those patterns, with the understanding that other interpretations are certainly possible. We will review the literature and discuss the implications, understanding that tomorrow it is quite possible that we will look at this literature in a completely different way. As with any new topic, data appear to be conflicting, and only after significant research effort is expended in this field will the real activities of NO during ischemia become verified.

Focal Ischemia

Nitric oxide production increases during focal cerebral ischemia in rats [17], with NOS inhibition reported both to protect and to worsen outcomes [3, 7, 18]. The dose and timing of NOS inhibition may determine the postischemic outcome. Furthermore, whether the MCAO is permanent or transient will impact on the effects of NOS inhibition. High dose NOS inhibition potentiates brain damage when applied near the onset of permanent MCAO, presumably by preventing NO-mediated vasodilation and reducing perfusion in the penumbral zone surrounding the area of infarction. Conversely, long-term repeated low-dose injections of these agents following MCAO are accompanied by significant reductions in infarct volumes [19–21]. Similarly, in transient focal ischemia high-dose NOS inhibition increases infarct volume [22] while low-dose treatment with a NOS inhibitor can be protective [23, 24]. Thus, NOS inhibitors appear to be neuroprotective at low doses and neurotoxic at high doses.

Focal Ischemia and iNOS   It is possible that NO-related neurotoxicity is a function of iNOS activation, resulting in an excessive NO production following MCAO. What causes this activation is not clear, but one possibility is that it is cytokine induced [25]. The increase in brain cytokine levels may derive from post-MCAO infiltration of ischemic border zone tissue with leukocytes or macrophages [26]. Recent findings have indicated that leukocytes may not only be the trigger for iNOS activation, but are actually the repository for iNOS. Iadecola and coworkers [27, 28] reported that, starting at 24 hours following the onset of a permanent MCAO, iNOS expression increases significantly in the infarcted hemisphere and is localized to infiltrating polymorphonucleocytes. In another study from the same laboratory [16], it was shown that treatment with the putative iNOS inhibitor, aminoguanidine (given 24 hours after the onset of MCAO), reduced the amount of brain damage. These findings might indeed explain why low-dose, repeated administration of nonspecific NOS inhibitors following MCAO provides neuroprotection. However, we cannot dismiss the possibility that part of that protective action may relate to suppressing the activity of constitutive NOS isoforms (eNOS, nNOS), the expression of which has also been shown to increase following MCAO [29, 30].

Focal Ischemia and cNOS   The literature also provides evidence for the possibility that NO derived from constitutive NOS (nNOS in particular) may contribute to MCAO-induced neuropathology. Moskowitz and coworkers, in rats treated with the nNOS-specific inhibitor 7-nitro-indazole (7-NI) [15] and in transgenic mice lacking the nNOS gene [31], reported reduced infarct volumes following MCAO when compared to controls. Findings from our laboratory also support a neuroprotective role for 7-NI in association with MCAO, but only within a narrow dose range (Fig 2). A transient (i.e., 30 minutes) MCAO was imposed in these rats. Neurological function assessments [32] were made daily over a 3-day period, at the end of which the rats were sacrificed and the brains processed for infarct volume measurement. The neurological outcome results (see Fig 2, left) were somewhat surprising in that $5 \text{ mg} \cdot \text{kg}^{-1}$ 7-NI showed no effect, whereas $10 \text{ mg} \cdot \text{kg}^{-1}$ was protective. The $20 \text{ mg} \cdot \text{kg}^{-1}$ 7-NI dose produced variable results, but trended toward being associated with worsened outcomes. Higher doses (not shown) were often fatal. The infarct volume assessments (see Fig 2, right) followed a similar pattern as the neurological outcome evaluations.

Endothelial NOS-derived NO does not appear to contribute to the neurotoxicity accompanying focal ischemia and in fact may be neuroprotective. Treatment of nNOS knockout mice with the nonspecific NOS inhibitor L-NA actually worsened outcome following MCAO [31]. Since the only constitutive NOS isoform remaining in these mice was eNOS, these results support a neuroprotective function for eNOS-derived NO. Furthermore, it was recently reported that eNOS knockout mice exhibit larger infarct volumes than in their wild-type counterparts [33]. The suggested eNOS-related neuroprotection may be in keeping with the antiaggregatory

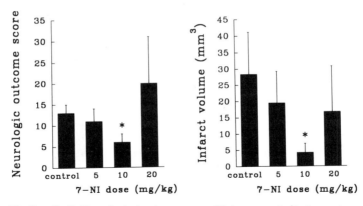

Fig 2. (Left) Neurological outcome scores (higher scores indicate greater neurological deficits) and (right) infarct volumes following transient middle cerebral artery occlusion in rats treated with 7-nitro-indazole (7-NI) or vehicle (corn oil). Use of this specific neuronal nitric oxide synthase (nNOS) inhibitor showed a narrow window of protection (only the 10 mg/kg dose was effective) as evidenced by better neurological outcome scores and smaller infarct volumes. *P < 0.05 vs control.

and antiadhesion effects of NO. Indeed, an endothelial site of NO formation would be likely for this purpose.

Free Radicals

A large increase in NO generation can lead to overproduction of free radicals. Although NO itself is considered to be a free radical, its damaging influence may result from the conversion of NO to far more reactive and cytotoxic free radicals [9]. For example, NO can react with superoxide anion to form peroxynitrite, which in turn can promote lipid peroxidation, leading to cell membrane damage in addition to inducing nitration of proteins, thus altering their function. In an acid environment, peroxynitrite can rapidly convert to the highly reactive free radical hydroxyl ($^{\cdot}$OH). The neurotoxicity accompanying NO-related enhancement of the production of toxic oxidants and free radicals may, in fact, override the beneficial effects of NO (i.e., those related to improved perfusion and reduced blood cell adhesion). Excessive NO production can also promote neurotoxicity via mechanisms not directly related to free radicals. These include adenosine diphosphate (ADP) ribosylation-related actions [34, 35], impairment of protein synthesis and oxidative metabolism [8], and promoting the release of large amounts of excitatory amino acids [36], potentiating neuronal Ca^{2+} influx and excitotoxicity [37]. The release of other potentially damaging neurotransmitters may be enhanced as well [36, 38].

Free radicals have been proposed as primary mediators of reperfusion injury [39]. That free radicals play a much greater role in promoting brain damage in transient MCAO versus permanent MCAO is supported by experimental findings. For example, transgenic mice overexpressing superoxide dismutase showed reduced infarct volumes when exposed to transient but not permanent MCAO [40, 41]. Free radical production may be greater following transient MCAO because of the greater availability of O_2 and other blood-borne, free radical–promoting elements. Of particular significance in this regard is leukocyte or macrophage infiltration. These cells not only generate free radicals, but, as stated earlier, release iNOS-activating cytokines, and can synthesize NO as well. In support of this, neutrophil depletion [42] or inhibition of cytokine production [43] reduced infarct volumes in rats exposed to transient MCAO.

Transient Forebrain Ischemia

Transient forebrain ischemia (TFI) is also associated with increased NO formation [44]. Some studies have shown a limited benefit accompanying NOS inhibition [45, 46], while the majority of TFI studies have shown that administration of NOS inhibitors is not protective [47–51]. Indeed, in gerbils subjected to 5–10 minutes bilateral carotid occlusion, pretreatment with the NOS inhibitor L-NA [49] or L-NAME [48] worsened outcome. In rats, L-NA or L-NAME pretreatment did not improve outcome following a four-vessel occlusion [47, 50]. We hypothesize that NO release may play an important and protective role by acting to attenuate cerebral blood flow (CBF) reductions in moderate TFI models. That is, in the four-vessel occlusion model, in which intraischemic blood flow is virtually undetectable, NOS inhibition does not alter neuropathology. In our TFI model, CBF is reduced ~75% in the ischemic tissue. Thus, there is a substantially greater potential for exacerbating ischemic severity and neuropathology following NOS inhibition. In fact, experimental findings have confirmed that supposition. Results obtained with our unilateral carotid occlusion plus hypotension (mean arterial pressure 30 mm Hg) model are summarized in Figure 3. The data show that during ischemia inhibition of NOS produces a 95% decrease in CBF (see Fig 3, left). In contrast, the control group showed only a 74% CBF reduction. Neurological deficits were considerably more pronounced in the NOS-inhibited rats compared to controls (see Fig 3, right). In additional experiments, in which blood withdrawal in NOS-inhibited rats was used to achieve a CBF reduction identical to that seen in controls, neurological outcomes in the 2 groups were the same (data not shown). Thus, the enhanced neurological deficit in NOS-inhibited animals appears to be almost entirely related to a diminished vasodilatory reserve. Also, the observation that NOS inhibitors may worsen outcome associated with TFI may be a reflection of the importance of NO in modulating blood flow or blood cell adhesion when the occlusion is removed.

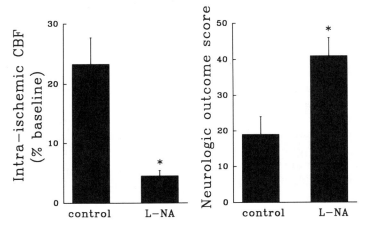

Fig 3. *(Left) Intraischemic cerebral blood flow (CBF) and (right) neuro-logical outcome with transient forebrain ischemia produced by unilateral carotid occlusion plus hypotension. Rats treated with the nonspecific nitric oxide synthase inhibitor nitro-L-arginine (L-NA) had a significantly lower intraischemic CBF and worse (higher) neurological deficit scores. *P < 0.05 vs control.*

Summary of Ischemia

Results to date suggest a double edged role for nitric oxide during and following cerebral ischemia (Table). In permanent MCAO models, NO appears to be neuroprotective acutely, but after some hours (possibly once iNOS is activated), NO becomes neurotoxic. Current evidence generally supports an enhancement of ischemic border tissue perfusion as being the most likely neuroprotective action of NO, but one cannot dismiss the potential benefits associated with the antiaggregatory and antiadhesion actions of NO. Nitric oxide may have other beneficial effects such as limiting N-methyl-D-aspartate (NMDA)-linked Ca^{2+} influx [52], reducing lipid peroxidation [53, 54], blocking xanthine oxidase (a potential major source for superoxide radicals in ischemia) [55], and suppression of metabolic acid production [3]. On the negative side, excessive NO production, which can result from an increase in iNOS activity, may promote substantial oxidant and free radical activity and may potentiate cytotoxicity related to excitatory amino acids by virtue of a capacity to enhance glutamate release. In focal ischemic models involving reperfusion, NO-related neurotoxicity may be a function of free radical and oxidant-induced effects.

Clinical Correlation

Assuming that rodent data hold true for humans, what can we extract from the above discussion? Protection of brain from ischemic insults can be produced in two ways. First, acute production of NO by nNOS and

Nitric Oxide and Its Actions in Ischemia

Neuroprotective
  Decrease Ca^{2+} influx via NMDA receptor
  Improve CBF
  Inhibit lipid peroxidation
  Decrease platelet aggregation
  Decrease leukocyte adhesion
Neurotoxic
  Increase $ONOO^-$ (peroxynitrite)
    Increase toxic free radical formation
    Enhance protein nitration
  Increase excitatory amino acid release
  DNA fragmentation
    Poly-ADP-ribose synthase activation
    Decrease NAD^+
    Impaired energy production
  Inhibit mitochondrial enzymes

See text for discussion and references.
Ca^{2+} = calcium; NMDA = N-methyl-D-aspartate; CBF = cerebral blood flow; ADP = adenosine diphosphate; NAD^+ = nicotinamide adenine dinucleotide (oxidized form).

eNOS stimulation will provide enhancement of CBF to ischemic brain tissue surrounding the focal infarct and decrease platelet aggregation and leukocyte adhesion, again maintaining and enhancing blood flow to neurons at risk. This may be achieved by administration of NO donors (e.g., nitroprusside); however, these drugs also decrease systemic blood pressure, and it is well known that a reduction in cerebral perfusion pressure during ischemia is detrimental [56]. Other techniques used to increase NO levels include administration of arginine, the substrate for NO production. Care must be taken, however, because increasing L-arginine levels may also accelerate the formation of potentially neurotoxic substances via other metabolic pathways, like ornithine decarboxylase (which is turned on during cerebral ischemia [57]). The resulting enhanced synthesis of polyamines may have detrimental effects [57, 58].

The second strategy involves inhibition of iNOS, which would prevent the delayed production of large amounts of NO. This could limit the damage attributed to NO-associated production of highly reactive oxidants and free radicals [9], as well as NO-induced DNA fragmentation, ADP polyribosylation, and suppression of energy production [59]. Dexamethasone has been shown to block induction of iNOS [60]. However, in clinical trials [61] and in adult rodent cerebral ischemia models [62], dexamethasone has not proved to be consistently efficacious. Inducible NOS appears to be more dependent on tetrahydrobiopterin than does eNOS or nNOS. Inhibition of the rate limiting enzyme for BH_4 synthesis, guanosine triphosphate cyclohydrolase I, substantially attenuated macrophage NO synthesis, and when given with dexamethasone, it totally eliminated macrophage NO production [60]. A simpler strategy would be to administer an iNOS-specific inhibitor like aminoguanidine. That approach has proved to be effective in rats subjected to MCAO. A third approach would be to treat with inhibitors specific for nNOS. However, nNOS inhibitors appear to display a rather narrow effective dose range for brain protection, making such agents less than ideal for use in the clinical setting. Nevertheless, there are some exciting possible methods of brain protection related to NO on the horizon; hopefully some of them will be useful in the clinical arena.

■ Nitric Oxide and Seizures

Recent evidence would indicate that NO plays an important modulatory role in experimentally induced seizures. It appears that NO acts as an endogenous anticonvulsant, because when NOS is inhibited, seizures last longer than when NO is present [63]. The anticonvulsant action of NO may be due to its ability to act as a negative feedback modulator of the N-methyl-D-aspartate subclass of excitatory amino acid receptors. As such, it may suppress to some degree the hyperexcitable state associated with introduction of seizurogenic agents such as NMDA [64, 65], kainate [66], or bicuculline [63, 67]. It is thought that excitatory amino acid receptor activation during seizure enhances calcium influx, which activates NOS. The NO so produced diffuses out of the cell and can interact with the NMDA receptor, both in the originating cell and in neighboring cells, thereby reducing receptor activity [52]. This brake on excitatory activity may [4] or may not [68] involve a redox (i.e., sulfhydryl-containing) modulatory site.

It has been suggested that NO may have an indirect effect on seizures via its ability to modulate glutamate release. NO has been reported both to increase [36] and to suppress [69] glutamate release in the brain. Which action predominates may depend on the brain region or the amount of NO released. That, in turn, may determine whether NO suppresses or activates seizures [70]. Low doses of NOS inhibitors (which only partially suppress NO production) can have an anticonvulsant effect, whereas almost total suppression of NOS may promote seizure activity by blocking all NO production, thereby preventing the negative feedback inhibitory action on NMDA receptors [63, 64].

■ Nitric Oxide and Cerebrovascular Reactivity

NO and Resting CBF

The administration of nonspecific NOS inhibitors is accompanied by reductions in resting CBF in the range of 20%–50% [7]. Because NOS inhibitors do not decrease cerebral metabolism, their vasoconstrictive effect cannot be attributed to a depression in brain function [71]. The extent to which NO contributes to cerebral vasomotor tone varies among brain regions and species [7]. Recent findings would suggest that nNOS and eNOS contribute roughly equally to the resting vasomotor tone in the brain [14].

Mechanisms of NO-related Cerebrovasodilation

The classical concept of NO-mediated cerebrovasodilation holds that NO is generated in cNOS-containing cells (e.g., endothelium, perivascular neurons) and then diffuses to the vascular smooth muscle, where it stimulates production of cGMP. The cGMP, in turn, promotes vasodilation, to a large extent, by reducing smooth muscle Ca^{2+} levels and the sensitivity of the contractile proteins to Ca^{2+}. Recent findings would suggest that, in the presence of a number of vasodilating stimuli, the capacity of NOS inhibitors to suppress vascular relaxation occurs not by preventing increased synthesis of cGMP, but rather by reducing basal vascular smooth muscle cGMP levels below a critical threshold. This particular NO/cGMP effect has been labeled as "permissive." Put another way, a certain level of cGMP may need to be present for optimal function of one or more key components in the signal transduction pathways triggered by various vasodilating agents. A permissive function for NO and cGMP in cerebrovasodilation has been indicated for a number of stimuli, including alpha$_2$ adrenoceptor agonists [72], hypercapnia [73], increased extracellular K^+ [74], and cerebral activation (U. Dirnagl, personal communication, 1996). That list will probably continue to grow. It is also quite possible that under a number of circumstances both permissive and classic elements may contribute to the vasodilating response. The specific mechanisms involved in the permissive functions of cGMP are virtually unknown, but as interest continues to grow in this area, some answers are likely to emerge.

Hypercapnia

A large number of studies have shown that NOS inhibitors, in a dose-dependent manner, attenuate the vasodilation induced by hypercapnia [7]. Hypercapnic vasodilation is most effectively blocked by NOS inhibition at partial pressure of CO_2 (pCO_2) levels of 50–80 mm Hg [75, 76]. Because NOS inhibition partially attenuates hypercapnic vasodilation, and only within a specific pCO_2 range, other factors or mechanisms must also participate. Among those, the leading candidate would be vasodilator prostanoids [76]. It should be emphasized, based on studies using NOS and prostanoid-synthesis inhibitors, that NO and prostanoid effects overlap to a considerable degree, which raises the possibility of "cross-talk" among their second-messenger pathways. The vasodilating actions of NO and the prostanoids relate to cGMP and cyclic adenosine monophosphate (cAMP), respectively. Because cGMP is known to modulate cAMP breakdown [77], it is possible that NO, via cGMP, exerts its action in hypercapnia (even if that action is permissive—see discussion above) by potentiating prostanoid-induced cAMP-mediated vasodilation [78].

The nNOS inhibitor 7-NI attenuates the hypercapnic response to the same degree as the nonspecific inhibitors L-NA and L-NAME. Furthermore, endothelial injury does not blunt the hypercapnic response. Based on those observations, it is believed that nNOS, but not eNOS, contributes to hypercapnic cerebrovasodilation [14, 79].

We recently found that hypercapnia-induced CBF increases were less attenuated by chronic administration of L-NA than by acute L-NA treatment [76], even though the former treatment protocol produces a much greater level of brain NOS inhibition. A similar picture appears to be emerging in studies using the nNOS knockout mouse models. Thus, whereas acute NOS inhibitor treatment in normal wild-type mice revealed a significant role for NO in the cerebrovasodilation accompanying hypercapnia [80], those functions appear to be normal in the knockout mice. The emergence of alternative factors to modulate a specific activity is not unique to hypercapnic vasodilation. It has also been observed in conjunction with the vascular relaxation elicited by cerebral activation and in association with the ability of NO to modulate pain perception and anesthetic potency (see below).

Cerebral Activation

The role of NO in the CBF increases associated with seizure activity is controversial. Inhibition of NOS, either acutely [63] or chronically [67], does not alter the cerebral hyperemic response associated with systemic administration of the seizure-promoting gamma-aminobutyric acid antagonist bicuculline. However, evidence from a recent report in which acute NOS inhibition was used in association with focal bicuculline-induced seizures did support a role for NO in the CBF increase [81]. The NMDA subtype of excitatory amino acid receptors can play a key role in the genesis and maintenance of seizure states. The cerebrovasodilation that accompanies NMDA administration can be blocked by acute NOS inhibition [64, 82]. However, in rats in which NOS was chronically inhibited, the magnitude of the peak CBF increase associated with NMDA administration was found to be normal [64].

Vibrissal stimulation (whisker stroking) is a commonly used model for cerebral activation in rodents. The cortical areas representing the whiskers are extensive in these animals, making it an excellent method for studying the coupling of blood flow and metabolism. Whisker stimulation produces a characteristic elevation of CBF in the contralateral cerebral cortex. Although some contrary evidence has been published [83], the majority of reports indicate that the CBF increase accompanying vibrissal stimulation is significantly dependent on NO, presumably derived from nNOS [84–86]. Mice lacking the nNOS gene showed a normal but NO-independent CBF increase during whisker stroking [86]. This suggests that, similar to the situation with hypercapnia-induced and NMDA-induced cerebrovasodilation, the release of other vasodilating substances may be enhanced in association with chronic loss of brain NOS activity. The specific vasodilating factors involved remain to be established. It will be interesting, in future studies, to examine whether other NO-dependent vasodilators, especially those dependent on eNOS (e.g., acetylcholine), are affected similarly.

Hypoxia

The mechanism of hypoxia-induced cerebrovasodilation is different from that of hypercapnia [87]. It appears to be partly NO-dependent, but only if the hypoxia is of sufficient severity (arterial oxygen tension < 40 mm Hg). Furthermore, hypoxia-induced cerebrovasodilation appears to be dependent on neuronal activation. That activation, in turn, promotes the additive release of both NO and the vasodilating substance adenosine. The NO-dependent portion of the hypoxic response appears to derive primarily from NMDA-receptor activation.

■ Nitric Oxide, Pain Sensation, and Anesthetic Potency

Nitric oxide has been shown to play a role in pain sensation [88]. Introduction of NOS inhibitors at the spinal level provides substantial analgesia in rodent hyperalgesia models [89]. However, under normal (nonhyperalgesic) conditions, intrathecal administration of NOS inhibitors may [90] or may not [91, 92] affect pain sensation. At supraspinal sites, the role of NO is unclear. This includes findings indicating no role for NO [92], a nociceptive function for NO [90, 93, 94], and an antinociceptive role for NO [95–99]. There are a number of reports in the literature, in rodent models, regarding NO-related effects on morphine-induced analgesia. In general, these studies indicate that NOS inhibitors can potentiate morphine-induced analgesia by actions at peripheral (presumably spinal) sites. In other words, NO acts to oppose the analgesic effects of morphine [100]. Whether NO has a similar effect on morphine-induced analgesia mediated at supraspinal sites in rodents is less clear [90, 97, 101].

In studies from our laboratory, using fourth cerebroventricular administration of L-NA and morphine in awake dogs, it was found that NOS inhibition alone was analgesic and that NOS inhibition augmented the

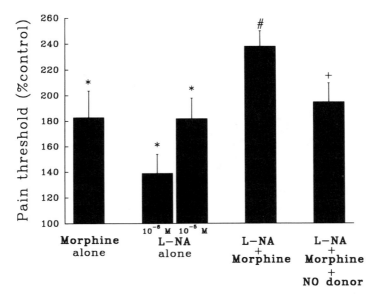

Fig 4. *The analgesic effects of morphine and the nitric oxide (NO) syn-thase inhibitor nitro-L-arginine (L-NA) on the response to pain elicited by electric shock to the hindpaw in the dog. The pain threshold is defined as the current strength (in mA) at which the dog raises the stimulated paw. Morphine (1 μg/ml), infused into the fourth cerebral ventricle, significantly elevated the pain threshold by 80%. NOS inhibition (L-NA) alone in-creased the pain threshold in a dose-dependent manner. The combined infu-sion of L-NA (10⁻⁵ M) and morphine (1 μg/ml) significantly increased analgesia compared to morphine alone. The addition of nitric oxide (by cere-bral ventricular infusion of the NO donor, S-nitroso-acetylpenicillamine [SNAP, 10⁻⁴ M]) reduced the combined analgesic effect of morphine plus L-NA, returning analgesia to the level seen with morphine alone. That finding provides further evidence that the enhanced analgesia elicited by L-NA specifically related to a reduction in endogenous NO production. *P < 0.05 vs control; #P < 0.05 vs morphine alone; +P < 0.05 vs L-NA + morphine.*

analgesia that accompanies morphine administration (Fig 4). The observed effects clearly represent actions at supraspinal sites. An additional benefit of combining L-NA and morphine, in these experiments, was a reduction in the ventilatory depression one sees when morphine is given by itself. The clinical implication of the latter observation is that combining NOS inhibition with morphine may permit the use of safer (with respect to respiratory depression) yet more effective (with respect to analgesia) doses of morphine.

Several reports have shown that NOS inhibition can produce sedation and reduce the anesthetic thresholds for halothane and isoflurane [102, 103]. Specifically how NO acts to promote wakefulness and oppose anesthesia is unclear but may involve effects on excitatory amino acid systems [104]. It is interesting to note that in nNOS knockout mice, volatile anesthetic potency is normal and unaffected by acute administration of a NOS inhibitor [103]. Related to this, it was recently reported that the knockout mice developed hyperalgesia identical to that seen in controls and were unresponsive to acute NOS inhibition [105]. Thus, similar to certain NO-dependent vasodilating responses (see above), NO does appear to play an important, but not an essential, role in nociceptive processing and anesthetic actions, since other factors compensate when NO is not available.

In summary, based on the reports of NOS inhibitors enhancing the potency of analgesic (opioid) drugs and volatile anesthetics, the possibility arises that NOS inhibitors may become useful agents in anesthetic practice. However, it is clear that much more experimental evidence is needed before such combinations are clinically applicable.

■ Conclusion

From the time it was identified as EDRF (endothelium-derived relaxing factor) in 1981, many laboratories have been active in studies related to NO. In 1992, NO was honored as "Molecule of the Year" by the editorial board of *Science*. Since its identification as an important vasodilator molecule, NO has been found to be involved in many other physiological and pathophysiological processes, too numerous to list here. It is not surprising that this simple gas influences many activities of the CNS. Nitric oxide modulates CBF and brain activity; it is involved in learning and memory [106]; it acts as a modulator of pain; and it influences the state of wakefulness. Nitric oxide can be cytotoxic or protective during cerebral ischemia. Which of those actions predominates appears to depend on temporal factors and the specific NOS isoform involved.

■ References

1. Butler AR, Flitney FW, Williams DLH. NO, nitrosonium ions, nitroxide ions, nitrosothiols and iron-nitrosyls in biology: a chemist's perspective. Trends Pharmacol Sci 1995;16:18–22
2. Bolotina VM, Najibi S, Palacino JJ, et al. Nitric oxide directly activates calcium-dependent potassium channels in vascular smooth muscle. Nature 1994;368:850–853
3. Pelligrino DA. Saying NO to cerebral ischemia. J Neurosurg Anesth 1993;5:221–231
4. Lipton SA, Choi YB, Pan ZH, et al. A redox-based mechanism for the neuroprotective and neurodestructive effects of nitric oxide and related nitroso-compounds. Nature 1993;364:626–632
5. Wood PL. Nitric oxide and excitatory amino acid-coupled signal transduction in

the cerebellum and hippocampus. In: Nitric oxide in the nervous system. London: Academic Press, 1995:103–123

6. Forstermann U, Kleinert H. Nitric oxide synthase: expression and expressional control of the three isoforms. Naunyn-Schmied Arch Pharmacol 1995;352: 351–364

7. Iadecola C, Pelligrino DA, Moskowitz MA, Lassen NA. Nitric oxide synthase inhibition and cerebrovascular regulation. J Cereb Blood Flow Metab 1994;14: 175–192

8. Hibbs JB. Synthesis of nitric oxide from L-arginine: a recently discovered pathway induced by cytokines with antitumour and antimicrobial activity. Res Immunol 1991;142:565–569

9. Varner PD, Beckman JS. Nitric oxide toxicity in neuronal injury and degeneration. In: Nitric oxide in the nervous system. New York: Academic Press, 1995:191–206

10. Nathan C. Nitric oxide as a secretory product of mammalian cells. FASEB J 1992; 6:3051–3064

11. Moncada S, Palmer RM, Higgs EA. Nitric oxide: physiology, pathophysiology, and pharmacology. Pharmacol Rev 1991;43:109–142

12. Archer S. Measurement of nitric oxide in biological models. FASEB J 1993;7: 349–360

13. Moore PK, Wallace P, Gaffen Z, et al. Characterization of the novel nitric oxide synthase inhibitor 7-nitro indazole and related indazoles—antinociceptive and cardiovascular effects. Br J Pharmacol 1993;110:219–224

14. Wang Q, Pelligrino DA, Baughman VL, et al. The role of neuronal nitric oxide synthase in regulation of cerebral blood flow in normocapnia and hypercapnia in rats. J Cereb Blood Flow Metab 1995;15:774–778

15. Yoshida T, Limmroth V, Irikura K, et al. The NOS inhibitor, 7-nitroindazole, decreases focal infarct volume but not the response to topical acetylcholine in pial vessels. J Cereb Blood Flow Metab 1994;14:924–929

16. Iadecola C, Zhang FY, Xu XH. Inhibition of inducible nitric oxide synthase ameliorates cerebral ischemic damage. Am J Physiol 1995;37:R286–R292

17. Malinski T, Bailey F, Zhang ZG, et al. Nitric oxide measured by a porphyrinic microsensor in rat brain after transient middle cerebral artery occlusion. J Cereb Blood Flow Metab 1993;13:355–358

18. Dawson DA. Nitric oxide and focal cerebral ischemia: multiplicity of actions and diverse outcome. Cerebrovasc Brain Metab Rev 1994;6:299–324

19. Buisson A, Plotkine M, Boulu RG. The neuroprotective effect of a nitric oxide inhibitor in a rat model of focal cerebral ischaemia. Br J Pharmacol 1992;106: 766–767

20. Nagafuji T, Matsui T, Koide T, et al. Blockade of nitric oxide formation by N omega-nitro-L-arginine mitigates ischemic brain edema and subsequent cerebral infarction in rats. Neurosci Lett 1992;147:159–162

21. Nowicki JP, Duval D, Poignet H, et al. Nitric oxide mediates neuronal death after focal cerebral ischemia in the mouse. Eur J Pharmacol 1991;204:339–340

22. Kuluz JW, Prado RJ, Dietrich WD, et al. The effect of nitric oxide synthase inhibition on infarct volume after reversible focal cerebral ischemia in conscious rats. Stroke 1993;24:2023–2029

23. Ashwal S, Cole DJ, Osborne TN, et al. Low dose L-NAME reduces infarct volume in the rat MCAO/reperfusion model. J Neurosurg Anesth 1993;5:241–249

24. Ashwal S, Cole DJ, Osborne TN, et al. Dual effects of l-NAME during transient focal cerebral ischemia in spontaneously hypertensive rats. Am J Physiol 1994; 267:H276–H284

25. Feuerstein G, Liu T, Clark R, et al. Inflammatory reaction in brain ischemia—the role of leukocytes and interleukin-1β. J Cereb Blood Flow Metab 1993;13 (Suppl 1):S26

26. Lees GJ. The possible contribution of microglia and macrophages to delayed neuronal death after ischemia. J Neurol Sci 1993;114:119–122
27. Iadecola C, Xu XH, Zhang FY, et al. Marked induction of calcium-independent nitric oxide synthase activity after focal cerebral ischemia. J Cereb Blood Flow Metab 1995;15:52–59
28. Iadecola C, Zhang FG, Xu S, et al. Inducible nitric oxide synthase gene expression in brain following cerebral ischemia. J Cereb Blood Flow Metab 1995;15:378–384
29. Zhang ZG, Chopp M, Zaloga C, et al. Cerebral endothelial nitric oxide synthase expression after focal cerebral ischemia in rats. Stroke 1993;24:2016–2021
30. Zhang ZG, Chopp M, Gautam S, et al. Upregulation of neuronal nitric oxide synthase and mRNA, and selective sparing of nitric oxide synthase-containing neurons after focal cerebral ischemia in rat. Brain Res 1994;654:85–95
31. Huang ZH, Huang PL, Panahian N, et al. Effects of cerebral ischemia in mice deficient in neuronal nitric oxide synthase. Science 1994;265:1883–1885
32. Hoffman WE, Braucher E, Pelligrino DA, et al. Brain lactate and neurologic outcome following incomplete ischemia in fasted, nonfasted, and glucose-loaded rats. Anesthesiology 1990;72:1045–1050
33. Huang Z, Huang PL, Fishman MC, et al. Focal cerebral ischemia in mice deficient in either endothelial (eNOS) or neuronal nitric oxide (nNOS) synthase. Stroke 1996;27:173
34. Lee HC. A signaling pathway involving cyclic ADP-ribose, cGMP, and nitric oxide. News Physiol Sci 1994;9:134–137
35. Zhang J, Dawson VL, Dawson TM, et al. Nitric oxide activation of poly(ADP-ribose) synthetase in neurotoxicity. Science 1994;263:687–689
36. Lonart G, Wang J, Johnson KM. Nitric oxide induces neurotransmitter release from hippocampal slices. Eur J Pharmacol 1992;220:271–272
37. Siesjo BK, Memezawa H, Smith ML. Neurocytotoxicity: pharmacological implications. Fundam Clin Pharmacol 1991;5:755–767
38. Lonart G, Cassels KL, Johnson KM. Nitric oxide induces calcium-dependent [h-3]-dopamine release from striatal slices. J Neurosci Res 1993;35:192–198
39. Hallenbeck JM, Dutka AJ. Background review and current concepts of reperfusion injury. Arch Neurol 1990;47:1245–1254
40. Chan PH, Kamii H, Yang G, et al. Brain infarction is not reduced in SOD-1 transgenic mice after a permanent focal cerebral ischemia. NeuroReport 1993;5:293–296
41. Yang GY, Chan PH, Chen J, et al. Human copper-zinc superoxide dismutase transgenic mice are highly resistant to reperfusion injury after focal cerebral ischemia. Stroke 1994;25:165–170
42. Shiga Y, Onodera H, Kogure K, et al. Effect of depletion of neutrophils on infarct size following transient focal brain ischemia. J Cereb Blood Flow Metab 1993;13(Suppl 1):S117
43. Shiga Y, Onodera H, Matsuo Y, et al. Cyclosporin A protects against ischemia-reperfusion injury in the brain. J Cereb Blood Flow Metab 1993;13(Suppl 1):S118
44. Sato S, Tominaga T, Ohnishi T, et al. EPR spin-trapping study of nitric oxide formation during bilateral carotid occlusion in the rat. Biochem Biophys Acta 1993;1181:195–197
45. Caldwell M, Oneill M, Earley B, et al. N-g-nitro-l-arginine protects against ischaemia-induced increases in nitric oxide and hippocampal neuro-degeneration in the gerbil. Eur J Pharmacol 1994;260:191–200
46. Nagafuji T, Sugiyama M, Matsui T, et al. A narrow therapeutical window of a nitric oxide synthase inhibitor against transient ischemic brain injury. Eur J Pharmacol 1993;248:325–328
47. Moncada C, Lekieffre D, Arvin B, et al. Effect of NO synthase inhibition on

NMDA- and ischaemia-induced hippocampal lesions. NeuroReport 1992;3: 530–532

48. Sancesario G, Iannone M, DAngelo V, et al. N omega-nitro-L-arginine-methyl ester inhibits electrocortical recovery subsequent to transient global brain ischemia in Mongolian gerbil. Funct Neurol 1992;7:123–127

49. Weissman BA, Kadar T, Brandeis R, et al. NG-nitro-L-arginine enhances neuronal death following transient forebrain ischemia in gerbils. Neurosci Lett 1992;146: 139–142

50. Buchan AM, Gertler SZ, Huang ZG, et al. Failure to prevent selective CA1 neuronal death and reduce cortical infarction following cerebral ischemia with inhibition of nitric oxide synthase. Neuroscience 1994;61:1–11

51. Shapira S, Kadar T, Weissman BA. Dose-dependent effect of nitric oxide synthase inhibition following transient forebrain ischemia in gerbils. Brain Res 1994;668: 80–84

52. Manzoni O, Prezeau L, Marin P, et al. Nitric oxide-induced blockade of NMDA receptors. Neuron 1992;8:653–662

53. Rubbo H, Radi R, Trujillo M, et al. Nitric oxide regulation of superoxide and peroxynitrite-dependent lipid peroxidation—formation of novel nitrogen-containing oxidized lipid derivatives. J Biol Chem 1994;269:26066–26075

54. Wink DA, Cook JA, Krishna MC, et al. Nitric oxide protects against alkyl peroxide-mediated cytotoxicity: further insights into the role nitric oxide plays in oxidative stress. Arch Biochem Biophys 1995;319:402–407

55. Fukahori M, Ichimori K, Ishida H, et al. Nitric oxide reversibly suppresses xanthine oxidase activity. Free Radical Res 1994;21:203–212

56. Cole DJ, Drummond JC, Osborne TN, et al. Hypertension and hemodilution during cerebral ischemia reduce brain injury and edema. Am J Physiol 1990;259: H211–H217

57. Kindy MS, Hu YG, Dempsey RJ. Blockade of ornithine decarboxylase enzyme protects against ischemic brain damage. J Cereb Blood Flow Metab 1994;14: 1040–1045

58. Otsuki M, Davidson M, Goodenough S, et al. In vivo pharmacological study of spermine-induced neurotoxicity. Neurosci Lett 1995;196:81–84

59. Dawson VL. Nitric oxide: role in neurotoxicity. Clin Exp Pharmacol Physiol 1995; 22:305–308

60. Schoedon G, Schneemann M, Hofer S, et al. Regulation of the l-arginine-dependent and tetrahydrobiopterin-dependent biosynthesis of nitric oxide in murine macrophages. Eur J Biochem 1993;213:833–839

61. Chumas PD, Del Bigio MR, Drake JM, et al. A comparison of the protective effect of dexamethasone to other potential prophylactic agents in a neonatal rat model of cerebral hypoxia-ischemia. J Neurosurg 1993;79:414–420

62. Shimauchi M, Yamamoto YL. Effects of retrograde perfusion of the brain with combined drug therapy after focal ischemia in rat brain. Stroke 1992;23: 1805–1810

63. Theard MA, Baughman VL, Wang Q, et al. The role of nitric oxide in modulating brain activity and blood flow during seizure. NeuroReport 1995;6:921–924

64. Pelligrino DA, Gay RL, Baughman VL, et al. Nitric oxide synthase inhibition modulates N-methyl-D-aspartate-induced changes in cerebral blood flow and EEG activity. Am J Physiol 1996 (in press)

65. Buisson A, Lakhmeche N, Verrecchia C, et al. Nitric oxide: an endogenous anticonvulsant substance. NeuroReport 1993;4:444–446

66. Rondouin G, Bockaert J, Lernernatoli M. L-nitroarginine, an inhibitor of NO synthase, dramatically worsens limbic epilepsy in rats. NeuroReport 1993;4: 1187–1190

67. Wang Q, Theard A, Pelligrino DA, et al. Nitric oxide as an endogenous anticonvul-

sant but not a mediator of the cerebral hyperemia accompanying bicuculline treatment in rats. Brain Res 1994;658:192–198

68. Fagni L, Olivier M, Lafoncazal M, et al. Involvement of divalent ions in the nitric oxide-induced blockade of n-methyl-d-aspartate receptors in cerebellar granule cells. Mol Pharmacol 1995;47:1239–1247

69. Kamisaki Y, Wada K, Nakamoto K, et al. Nitric oxide inhibition of the depolarization-evoked glutamate release from synaptosomes of rat cerebellum. Neurosci Lett 1995;194:5–8

70. Rundfeldt C, Koch R, Richter A, et al. Dose-dependent anticonvulsant and proconvulsant effects of nitric oxide synthase inhibitors on seizure threshold in a cortical stimulation model in rats. Eur J Pharmacol 1995;274:73–81

71. Macrae IM, Dawson DA, Norrie JD, et al. Inhibition of nitric oxide synthesis—effects on cerebral blood flow and glucose utilisation in the rat. J Cereb Blood Flow Metab 1993;13:985–992

72. Bryan RM, Steenberg ML, Eichler MY, et al. Permissive role of NO in alpha(2)-adrenoceptor-mediated dilations in rat cerebral arteries (rapid communication). Am J Physiol 1995;38:H1171–H1174

73. Iadecola C, Zhang FY, Xu XH. SIN-1 reverses attenuation of hypercapnic cerebrovasodilation by nitric oxide synthase inhibitors. Am J Physiol 1994;267:R228–R235

74. Dreier JP, Korner K, Gorner A, et al. Nitric oxide modulates the CBF response to increased extracellular potassium. J Cereb Blood Flow Metab 1995;15:914–919

75. Iadecola C, Zhang F. Nitric oxide-dependent and independent components of cerebrovasodilation elicited by hypercapnia. Am J Physiol 1994;266:R546–R552

76. Wang Q, Pelligrino DA, Paulson OB, et al. Comparison of the effects of N^G-nitro-L-arginine and indomethacin on the hypercapnic cerebral blood flow increase in rats. Brain Res 1994;641:257–264

77. Eckly AE, Lugnier C. Role of phosphodiesterases III and IV in the modulation of vascular cyclic AMP content by the NO/cyclic GMP pathway. Br J Pharmacol 1994;113:445–450

78. Wagerle LC, Degiulio PA. Indomethacin-sensitive CO2 reactivity of cerebral arterioles is restored by vasodilator prostaglandin. Am J Physiol 1994;266:H1332–H1338

79. Wang Q, Pelligrino DA, Koenig HM, Albrecht RF. The role of endothelium and nitric oxide in rat pial arteriolar dilatory responses to CO2 in vivo. J Cereb Blood Flow Metab 1994;14:944–951

80. Irikura K, Huang PL, Ma JY, et al. Cerebrovascular alterations in mice lacking neuronal nitric oxide synthase gene expression. Proc Natl Acad Sci USA 1995;92:6823–6827

81. Devasconcelos AP, Baldwin RA, Wasterlain CG. Nitric oxide mediates the increase in local cerebral blood flow during focal seizures. Proc Natl Acad Sci USA 1995;92:3175–3179

82. Faraci FM, Breese KR. Nitric oxide mediates vasodilatation in response to activation of N-methyl-D-aspartate receptors in brain. Circ Res 1993;72:476–480

83. Wang Q, Kjaer T, Jorgensen MB, et al. Nitric oxide does not act as a mediator coupling cerebral blood flow to neural activity following somatosensory stimuli in rats. Neurol Res 1993;15:33–36

84. Dirnagl U, Niwa K, Lindauer U, et al. Coupling of cerebral blood flow to neuronal activation: role of adenosine and nitric oxide. Am J Physiol 1994;267:H296–H301

85. Irikura K, Maynard KI, Moskowitz MA. Importance of nitric oxide synthase inhibition to the attenuated vascular responses induced by topical L-nitroarginine during vibrissal stimulation. J Cereb Blood Flow Metab 1994;14:45–48

86. Ma J, Ayata C, Meng W, et al. Regional CBF response to vibrissal stimulation in

mice lacking neuronal or endothelial NOS gene expression. Soc Neurosci Abstr 1995;21:434

87. Pelligrino DA, Wang Q, Koenig HM, Albrecht RF. Role of nitric oxide, adenosine, N-methyl-D-aspartate receptors, and neuronal activation in hypoxia-induced pial arteriolar dilation in rats. Brain Res 1995;704:61–70

88. Meller ST, Lewis SJ, Bates JN, et al. Is there a role for an endothelium-derived relaxing factor in nociception? Brain Res 1990;531:342–345

89. Semos ML, Headley PM. The role of nitric oxide in spinal nociceptive reflexes in rats with neurogenic and non-neurogenic peripheral inflammation. Neuropharmacology 1994;33:1487–1497

90. Przewlocki R, Machelska H, Przewlocka B. Modulation of morphine and cocaine effects by inhibition of nitric oxide synthase. Regul Pept 1994;54:233–235

91. Meller ST, Cummings CP, Traub RJ, et al. The role of nitric oxide in the development and maintenance of the hyperalgesia produced by intraplantar injection of carrageenan in the rat. Neuroscience 1994;60:367–374

92. Iwamoto ET, Marion L. Pharmacologic evidence that spinal muscarinic analgesia is mediated by an l-arginine/nitric oxide/cyclic GMP cascade in rats. J Pharmacol Exp Ther 1994;271:601–608

93. Moore PK, Oluyomi AO, Babbedge RC, et al. L-N^G-nitro arginine methyl ester exhibits antinociceptive activity in the mouse. Br J Pharmacol 1991;102:198–202

94. Kawabata A, Umeda N, Takagi H. L-arginine exerts a dual role in nociceptive processing in the brain—involvement of the kyotorphin-met-enkephalin pathway and NO-cyclic GMP pathway. Br J Pharmacol 1993;109:73–79

95. Kumar A, Raghubir R, Srimal RC, et al. Evidence for involvement of nitric oxide in pretectal analgesia in rat. NeuroReport 1993;4:706–708

96. Ji XQ, Zhu XZ. Possible involvement of nitric oxide in arginine-induced analgesia. Acta Pharmacol Sin 1993;14:289–291

97. Xu JY, Tseng LF. Increase of nitric oxide by L-arginine potentiates beta-endorphin- but not mu-, delta- or kappa-opioid agonist-induced antinociception in the mouse. Eur J Pharmacol 1993;236:137–142

98. Hara S, Kuhns ER, Ellenberger EA, et al. Involvement of nitric oxide in intra-cerebroventricular beta-endorphin-induced neuronal release of methionine-enkephalin. Brain Res 1995;675:190–194

99. Kumar A, Raghubir R, Dhawan BN. Possible involvement of nitric oxide in red nucleus stimulation-induced analgesia in the rat. Eur J Pharmacol 1995;279:1–5

100. Przewocki R, Machelska H, Przewocka B. Inhibition of nitric oxide synthase enhances morphine antinociception in the rat spinal cord. Life Sci 1993;53:PL1–PL5

101. Brignola G, Calignano A, Dirosa M. Modulation of morphine antinociception in the mouse by endogenous nitric oxide. Br J Pharmacol 1994;113:1372–1376

102. Johns RA, Moscicki JC, DiFazio CA. Nitric oxide synthase inhibitor dose-dependently and reversibly reduces the threshold for halothane anesthesia. Anesthesiology 1992;77:779–784

103. Ichinose F, Huang PL, Zapol WM. Effects of targeted neuronal nitric oxide synthase gene disruption and nitro(g)-l-arginine methylester on threshold for isoflurane anesthesia. Anesthesiology 1995;83:101–108

104. Johns RA. Nitric oxide and minimum alveolar concentration: TKO or knockout? Anesthesiology 1995;83:6–7

105. Crosby G, Marota JJA, Huang PL. Intact nociception-induced neuroplasticity in transgenic mice deficient in neuronal nitric oxide synthase. Neuroscience 1995; 69:1013–1017

106. Schuman EM, Madison DV. Nitric oxide and synaptic function. Ann Rev Neurosci 1994;17:153–183

Surgical Intervention and Anesthetic Management of the Patient with Parkinson's Disease

Linda J. Mason, MD

Traian T. Cojocaru, MD

Daniel J. Cole, MD

In 1817, James Parkinson described the syndrome he termed "the shaking palsy." The salient features of this syndrome, which would bear his name, include tremor, akinesia, rigidity, and postural instability. Although the association between the substantia nigra and Parkinson's disease was discovered in 1893, it was not until the last half of this century that the distinctive neurochemical alterations associated with Parkinson's disease—regional variation in the concentration of monoamines and dopamine deficiency in the central nervous system (CNS)—were discovered [1]. The discovery pointed to the first successful treatment for Parkinson's disease and suggested ways of devising new and effective therapies.

Because of the characteristic stooped posture and Chaplinesque shuffling, Parkinson's disease has been called "the happy disease." However, Parkinson's disease is a growing problem, with estimates ranging up to 1 million victims in the United States [2]. Indeed, more people suffer from Parkinson's disease than multiple sclerosis, muscular dystrophy, and amyotrophic lateral sclerosis combined. The overall prevalence rate is 180/100,000 and is age dependent (347/100,000 in the population >40 years of age, and 1600/100,000 in the population >80 years of age), with an annual incidence of 20/100,000 [3, 4]. It has been estimated that there is a cumulative lifetime risk of 1 in 40 for developing Parkinson's disease [5].

Although the etiology of Parkinson's disease is unknown, scientists have long hypothesized that neurodegeneration is induced by genetic, environmental, or infectious factors [6]. The drug 1-methyl-4-phenyl-1236-tetrahydropyridine reliably produces parkinsonian symptoms in humans and experimental animals [7], supporting the hypothesis that under certain conditions the brain might produce a neurotoxic substance, resulting in Parkinson's disease.

■ Pathophysiology of Parkinson's Disease

Classically, a loss of pigmented cells in the substantia nigra is the most consistent finding in Parkinson's disease. Nigral cells contain neuromelanin, a pigment similar to melanin. These cells synapse with dopamine receptors in the striatum (caudate nucleus and putamen) that control movement and balance. Normally, the quantity of nigral cells diminishes with age from 425,000 to 200,000 at 80 years of age. With Parkinson's disease, the substantia nigra shows a marked additional depletion of cells (<100,000) with replacement gliosis. In addition, tyrosine beta-hydroxylase, the rate-limiting enzyme for dopamine synthesis, also diminishes with age, suggesting that aging may increase the vulnerability to Parkinson's disease. The remaining cells in the pigmented structures contain eosinophilic cytoplasmic inclusion bodies, called Lewy bodies, that are pathognomonic for Parkinson's disease [8, 9].

The brain adjusts to the loss of pigmented cells in the substantia nigra by increasing activity in the remaining pigmented cells and by upregulation of striatal dopamine receptors. Additional dopamine may also be produced by cells in the striatum that do not ordinarily produce dopamine. Although these compensatory mechanisms delay the manifestation of Parkinson's disease, eventually clinical symptoms appear. Dopamine is also deficient in other areas of the brain, which may account for secondary symptoms [4, 8, 9].

In Parkinson's disease, acetylcholine is present in normal concentrations in the striatum. However, as a balance between dopamine and acetylcholine is necessary for optimal function, a deficiency of dopamine results in a dopamine/acetylcholine imbalance—thus aggravating the symptoms of Parkinson's disease. This is the rationale for the use of anticholinergic medications that block the actions of acetylcholine and drugs such as levodopa that increase dopamine levels. There may also be a deficiency of cerebral norepinephrine, which acts to govern autonomic function, and other neurotransmitters such as serotonin and gamma aminobutyric acid (GABA) that accounts for secondary symptoms [4, 8].

A free radical hypothesis has been proposed for the genesis of Parkinson's disease [10]. Hydrogen peroxide, a by-product of dopamine metabolism, is catabolized by catalase and peroxidase enzymes. Activity of these enzymes is reduced in nigral regions of parkinsonian patients [4, 10], resulting in neurotoxicity by hydroxy and superoxide free radicals and lipid peroxide.

■ Diagnosis

Currently, there are no laboratory tests that diagnose Parkinson's disease. The diagnosis is based on clinical signs and symptoms that are diffi-

Table 1. *Primary and Secondary Symptoms of Parkinson's Disease*

Primary Symptoms
Tremor
Brady- or akinesia
Difficulty with balance
Difficulty in walking

Secondary Symptoms	
Dementia	Speech difficulty
Sialorrhea	Dependent edema
Dysphagia	Constipation
Shortness of breath	Difficulty voiding
Orthostatic hypotension	Simian posture
Weight loss	Blepharospasm
Depression	Impotence
Sleep disruption	Decreased libido

cult for even the most experienced neurologist to discern. The salient findings of Parkinson's disease are rigidity, tremor, brady- or akinesia, and postural instability, with many secondary symptoms that can be extremely disabling (Table 1). If the symptomatology suggests Parkinson's disease, a trial of antiparkinson drugs such as levodopa may be employed to confirm the diagnosis [4, 5, 8, 9]. The core and disabling features of Parkinson's disease consist of: (1) bradykinesia, (2) poverty of movement, (3) difficulty initiating movement, (4) fatigue, (5) diminished amplitude of repetitive alternating movements, and/or (6) inordinate difficulty in performing simultaneous or sequential motor tasks. The simian posture results from increased muscle tone with predominant involvement of the flexor muscles. Postural instability is usually a late symptom of Parkinson's disease, and on initial presentation, a resting tremor is present in 70% of patients [4, 5, 9].

A common classification of Parkinson's disease is the Hoehn and Yahr Scale, in which the disease is divided into five stages (Table 2) [11]. Often

Table 2. *The Hoehn and Yahr Scale for Staging Parkinson's Disease*

Stage 0	No visible disease
Stage I	Disease that involves only one side of the body
Stage II	Disease that involves both sides of the body but does not impair balance
Stage III	Disease that impairs balance or walking
Stage IV	Disease that markedly impairs balance or walking
Stage V	Disease that results in complete immobility

patients with Parkinson's disease are misdiagnosed or diagnosed with other neurological afflictions when they suffer from Parkinson's disease. The differential diagnosis also includes other hypokinetic disorders (parkinsonism-plus syndromes, drug-induced parkinsonism), repeated head trauma, prolonged use of tranquilizing drugs (e.g., phenothiazines, butyrophenones, reserpine), metaclopramide, and manganese and carbon monoxide poisoning [8, 12, 13].

■ Medical Therapy

The therapeutic management of Parkinson's disease includes pharmacological and nonpharmacological treatments. Optimal results will be achieved by addressing all of the patient's needs with a multidisciplinary team and a variety of therapeutic interventions. Treatment is often symptomatic, with a goal of establishing a proper balance between cholinergic activity and dopaminergic functions [14, 15]. Pharmacotherapy for Parkinson's disease utilizes three treatment strategies (Table 3).

Agents That Replenish the CNS Supply of Dopamine

As Parkinson's disease is a disorder of dopamine metabolism, it seems logical to simply administer exogenous dopamine. However, dopamine does not cross the blood-brain barrier, and cerebral delivery of dopamine is problematic. This impediment is circumvented by administering the precursor of dopamine, levodopa, which does cross the blood-brain barrier and is converted to dopamine by surviving neurons. The decarboxylating enzyme responsible for converting levodopa to dopamine is present in the brain and periphery [16, 17]. Thus, levodopa is given in combination with a peripheral decarboxylase inhibitor such as carbidopa, thereby reducing the levodopa requirement and dose-related side effects of the drug. With the advent of levodopa therapy, mortality in patients with Parkinson's disease has declined substantially [8, 18].

Although levodopa was a major breakthrough in the treatment of Parkinson's disease, there were significant associated problems. Patients receiving levodopa frequently experience severe nausea and vomiting. This problem was partially solved by adding carbidopa to levodopa, resulting in increased efficacy of levodopa, permitting lower doses of levodopa with amelioration of nausea and vomiting. Dopaminergic therapy can predispose the myocardium to arrhythmias, and norepinephrine stores may be depleted and renin release reduced. Dyskinesia, which invariably occurs, is the limiting factor in the use of levodopa ($\approx80\%$ of patients will exhibit dyskinesia after 1 year of levodopa therapy) [19]. In addition, dopamine increases renal blood flow, glomerular filtration rate, and sodium excretion. Thus, intravascular fluid volume will be decreased and renin-

Table 3. *Pharmacotherapy for Parkinson's Disease*

Drugs That Replenish the Supply of Dopamine		
	Actions	Side Effects
Levodopa Larodopa	Converted to dopamine in the brain	Choreiform and dystonic movement, mental changes, orthostatic hypotension
Levodopa/carbidopa Sinemet Atamet	Enhances conversion of levodopa to dopamine inside the brain while blocking its conversion peripherally	Choreiform and dystonic movement, mental changes, orthostatic hypotension
Amantadine HCl Symmetrel	Releases dopamine	Spotting of skin, edema, confusion, hallucinations
Selegiline HCl Eldepryl	Blocks the activity of MAO-B	Dizziness, nausea, insomnia
Drugs That Act Like Dopamine		
Pergolide mesylate Permax Bromocriptine mesylate Parlodel	Stimulates dopamine receptors	Nausea, orthostatic hypotension, mental changes
Drugs That Affect the Biochemical Balance of Cerebral Dopamine		
Amantadine HCl Symmetrel Artane Akineton Cogentin Kemadrin Hyoscyamine sulfate Levbid Levsin Levsinex	Blocks acetylcholine	Dry mouth, blurred vision, mental changes, urinary retention, confusion, constipation, dependent edema, hallucinations

angiotensin-aldosterone activity will be attenuated, resulting in orthostatic hypotension as a common finding in patients taking levodopa [20]. The CNS side effects of levodopa include confusion, depression, agitation, and overt psychosis. In addition, the "on-off syndrome" in which patients may change rapidly from a state of relative mobility to one of nearly complete immobility may occur.

Agents That Affect the Biochemical Balance of CNS Dopamine

Until recently, treatment of Parkinson's disease was directed at symptomatic relief, with few options available for reversing or slowing disease progression. After its production and release from the nerve terminal, dopamine is metabolized primarily by monoamine oxidase-B (MAO-B). Several animal and clinical studies have suggested that the MAO-B inhibitor selegiline may be neuroprotective in the treatment of Parkinson's disease [21–25]. A multicenter study of over 800 newly diagnosed patients with Parkinson's disease (DATATOP study) evaluated treatment with selegiline, vitamin E, or placebo [22]. The data demonstrated a significant delay in the need to start levodopa therapy in the selegiline-treated group. Other recent studies have confirmed these findings [24, 25], reporting both an improvement in symptomatology and a delay in the progression of Parkinson's disease in selegiline-treated patients. Moreover, a retrospective postmortem study demonstrated greater preservation of dopaminergic neurons in selegiline-treated patients [26]. Finally, several studies have suggested that selegiline may rescue dopaminergic neurons through a trophic effect, independent of MAO-B inhibition [27, 28]. An alternative free radical hypothesis has been proposed [10]. In the normal process of dopamine degradation by MAO, free radicals are formed, a process that is enhanced in parkinsonian patients. As selegiline reduces the metabolism of dopamine, it thereby reduces production of free-radical compounds. Selegiline has minimal effect on epinephrine or norepinephrine and is not associated with the changes in sympathetic activity characteristic of previous MAO inhibitors.

Anticholinergic medication is often the initial pharmacological treatment, with the goal of restoring the balance between dopamine and acetylcholine activity. Anticholinergics are more effective against tremor than other parkinsonian symptoms [20, 29]. Side effects include mydriasis, dry mouth, constipation, and urinary retention. The most serious side effects are neuropsychiatric and include a loss of memory and concentration, confusion, and visual hallucinations. A cholinergic crisis can be precipitated if long term anticholinergic treatment is rapidly withdrawn [30]. Although some anticholinergic drugs might augment the dopamine effect by inhibiting striatal presynaptic reuptake of dopamine, it is uncertain whether this contributes to their mechanism of action.

Amantadine is an antiviral agent discovered to have antiparkinson activity [15, 31]. Although not fully elucidated, its mechanisms of action are thought to include an increase in dopamine release, blockade of dopamine reuptake, stimulation of dopamine receptors, and anticholinergic properties. Amantadine appears to be more effective than anticholinergic drugs against akinesia and rigidity but is less effective against tremor. Amantadine should be discontinued gradually to avoid acute exacerbation of parkinsonism.

Dopamine-receptor Agonists

Dopamine agonist monotherapy is typically transient and suboptimal [32–35]. Accordingly, the rationale for dopamine agonists is to reduce cumulative exposure to levodopa and thereby reduce side effects. Dopamine agonists offer the theoretic advantage of exerting a direct action on striatal dopamine receptors, which do not require the function of degenerating dopaminergic nerve terminals. Traditionally, dopamine agonists have been used for patients with a declining response to levodopa or adverse effects of levodopa therapy. Bromocriptine and pergolide are the only dopamine agonists currently available for use in the United States. Bromocriptine has both presynaptic and postsynaptic effects and stimulates D_2-receptors. Side effects include hypotension, nausea, vomiting, hallucinations, peripheral vasoconstriction, and erythromelalgia. Pergolide does not have presynaptic effects and stimulates both D_1- and D_2-receptors. Although pergolide's therapeutic efficacy is similar to bromocriptine, pergolide does not elicit the range of side effects observed with bromocriptine. Domperidone is a dopamine-receptor antagonist that does not cross the blood-brain barrier and effectively prevents the peripheral side effects of the dopamine agonists.

Investigational Drugs

At the time of this writing, there are several drugs in different phases of study for Parkinson's disease, and several are "just around the corner" for clinical use.

■ Surgical Treatment

Surgical attempts to control movement disorders have a long history. In 1890, Sir Victor Horsley resected parts of the precentral cortex in the treatment of athetosis. Over 50 years ago, Russell Meyers performed surgical interventions in the caudate nucleus, basal ganglia, and ansa lenticularis for the treatment of Parkinson's disease [36–39]. The introduction of stereotactic surgery in 1947 was quickly followed by its application for the treatment of Parkinson's disease [40]. However, the results of stereotactic pallidotomy were not as beneficial and prolonged as hoped. In 1954, Hassler and Riechert [41] began to treat Parkinson's disease with surgical lesions in the ventrolateral thalamus. The effect of thalamotomy on tremor was dramatic, and most neurosurgeons abandonded pallidotomy in favor of thalamotomy [37, 38]. With the introduction of levodopa therapy, surgical treatments for Parkinson's disease declined. However, posteroventral pallidotomy has recently been reintroduced for several reasons: (1) the technologic advancements in brain imaging and surgical techniques, (2) the failures of medical therapy, (3) the scientific advances in the understanding of the basal ganglia and pathophysiology of Parkinson's disease, and (4) the recent confirmation of efficacy of pallidotomy for Parkinson's disease [42–44]. Despite the apparent success of the pallidotomy procedure, questions remain concerning the indications, optimal surgical parameters, long term results, and therapeutic mechanism of this stereotactic procedure.

Neuroaugmentation procedures (grafting and stimulation) still have an experimental status [45, 46]. Autotransplantation of adrenal gland tissue to the striatum was performed in over 300 patients in the 1980s; however, few patients demonstrated long term improvement. Fetal tissue transplantation for Parkinson's disease has had better success [44]. Although dopaminergic activity in the brain can be augmented by tissue transplantation, the techniques are complex and limited to a few centers, and ethical issues are still unresolved [45, 47]. The application of stimulation procedures for Parkinson's disease resulted from the observation that stimulation for target confirmation before thalamotomy transiently suppressed the tremor. The high rate of success, low morbidity, reversibility, and adaptability of chronic stimulation make the procedure safer than the thalamotomy, especially when a bilateral procedure is needed. Chronic thalamic stimulation is also therapeutically utilized for levodopa-induced dyskinesias [48].

Surgical Lesions

Thalamotomy has been the most frequently performed procedure for Parkinson's disease. Simplistically, the current concept of surgical interventions for Parkinson's disease is based on the functional connectivity within the basal ganglia–thalamocortical circuit [49]. In this model, the substantia nigra provides dopaminergic innervation to the putamen, which in turn innervates the medial pallidum either directly or by way of an indirect pathway through the external pallidum and the subthalamic nucleus. When a dopamine deficiency exists, there is increased inhibitory activity in the globus pallidus (possibly GABAergic) that results in increased inhibitory output to the thalamus and motor cortex [9]. Levodopa therapy abolishes the inhibition and normalizes motor activity [17].

A cholinergic mechanism has been considered for rigidity, but rigidity may also originate from GABAergic inhibitory hyperactivity in the striopallidal pathways. The rigidity is mediated via the pallidothalamic pathways to the thalamus, which projects to the cortical premotor area. Accordingly, selective lesions in the globus pallidus or thalamus can abolish tremor, bradykinesia and rigidity, or levodopa-induced dyskinesia [37, 42].

Pallidotomy Pallidotomy is primarily considered for bradykinesia and rigidity, although the effect on tremor is reported to be excellent [36, 37, 42]. For the initial target, stereotactic atlases are incorporated into computed tomography (CT) or magnetic resonance imaging (MRI) guidance of lesion placement. There are, however, discrepancies and inaccuracies in many of the atlases, and physiological confirmation of the target is considered mandatory [50]. Evoked potential readings are often used to

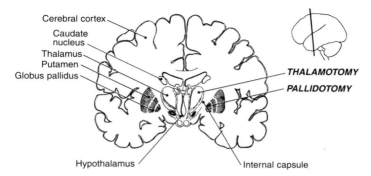

Anatomical locations for the therapeutic lesions (thalamotomy and pallidotomy) for the surgical treatment of Parkinson's disease. The inset shows the plane of the coronal section through the diencephalon, identifying the lesions.

localize the lesion, but for more discrete localization, microelectrode recordings are preferable [50]. The target is 2–3 mm in front of the midcommissural point, 18–21 mm lateral to the midline of the third ventricle, and 6 mm below the plane of the midcommissural line (Fig). The procedure is typically performed through a frontal burr hole. When the stereotactic probe is introduced into the pallidum, the tremor dissipates as the ventral most area of the posterolateral pallidum is lesioned. Complete tremor relief usually requires a relatively large lesion, 100–150 mm³, and it must include the ventral most part of the lateral pallidum. The final lesion site is based on the patient's reaction to electrical stimulation, carried out with a monopolar electrode [38, 42]. The lesion site is in intimate proximity to the optic tract and internal capsule, and side effects include a central homonymous visual field defect, facial weakness, dysphasia, or stroke. Other side effects occur very rarely [38, 42, 43].

Thalamotomy   If the disabling symptom for the Parkinson's disease patient is tremor, the preferred surgical treatment remains stereotactic thalamotomy. Medical management still takes priority in patients with rigidity or bradykinesia. However, it is recognized that medications can lose their effectiveness, and intolerable dyskinesias often occur. Thus, patients who initially are candidates for medical treatment may present later for surgery, or the best management may be a combination of medication plus surgery [51]. The resurgence of thalamotomy resulted from the observation that many patients deteriorated after long term administration of levodopa, or developed dyskinesias that sometimes were more disabling than the disease itself [51].

There are two thalamic targets for Parkinson's disease. For tremor, lesions are made 5 mm anterior to the posterior commissure on the intercommissural line and 13.5–15.0 mm in the parasagittal plane. For rigidity, the target is more anterior. Test lesions can be made at lower temperatures and for short durations or with microinjections of lidocaine to prevent untoward neurological deficits [52, 53]. Morbidity is 3.2% for unilateral procedures. Confusion (10%), facial weakness (8%), numbness (5%), or paresthesias (1%–2%) may be seen. The highest incidence of morbidity is associated with bilateral lesions [54].

■ Anesthetic Considerations

Patients with Parkinson's disease most commonly present for urologic, ophthalmologic, and orthopedic procedures. Alternatively, anesthetic management may be required for pallidotomy or thalamotomy or neuroaugmentive procedures. It is a prevalent opinion in the parkinsonian community that anesthesiologists do not understand the unique problems of Parkinson's disease. There are anecdotal reports of death due to drug interactions, and several patients describe stories of a simple surgery turning into "10 days in hell." Aside from the routine history and physical examination that is performed on all presurgical patients, Table 4 summarizes the systems to focus on for the patient with Parkinson's disease.

When considering anesthesia, potential anesthetic drug interactions must be considered. Table 5 summarizes drugs that may alter parkinsonian symptoms and are ideally avoided or given in consultation with the physician managing the patient's disease. Patients on MAO inhibitors have long been a specific concern for anesthesiologists. However, with the widespread use of selegiline (a MAO-B type inhibitor), the likelihood of having to anesthetize a patient receiving a MAO-A inhibitor is decreased, and anecdotal reports have not shown problems with general anesthesia and the tyramine crisis with selegiline [55]. However, there are reports of agitation, muscle rigidity, hyperthermia, and death in patients receiving meperidine and selegiline, so avoid this combination [56]!

The patient's parkinsonian drug regimen should be administered as close to the beginning of anesthesia as possible. Levodopa's half life is short (1–3 hours), and even brief periods of interruption can result in severe skeletal muscle rigidity that may interfere with ventilation. Unfortunately, all medications currently used for the treatment of Parkinson's disease are only available in an oral preparation. Drugs that cause or exacerbate extrapyramidal symptoms such as phenothiazines, butyrophenone derivatives (droperidol), and metoclopramide are contraindicated (see Table 5). A recent report stated that metoclopramide has side effects so similar to the symptoms of Parkinson's disease that it has resulted in the misdiagnosis of Parkinson's disease and unwarranted use of levodopa in patients with drug-induced parkinsonism [57].

Inhalational anesthetics may exert a dual effect on the disease process,

Table 4. *Recommended Assessment of the Patient with Parkinson's Disease*

System	Assessment by History	Tests
Head and neck	Dysfunction of pharyngeal muscles Dysphagia Sialorrhea Blepharospasm	
Cardiovascular	Orthostatic hypotension Cardiac dysrhythmias Hypertension Hypovolemia Autonomic dysfunction	Electrocardiogram
Respiratory	Respiratory impairment from rigidity, bradykinesia, or uncoordinated involuntary movement of the respiratory muscles	Chest roentgenogram Pulmonary function tests Arterial blood gas
Gastrointestinal	Weight loss Poor nutrition Susceptible to reflux	Serum albumin/transferrin Skin test anergy
Urologic	Difficulty voiding	
Endocrine	Abnormal glucose metabolism (selegiline)	Serum glucose
Musculoskeletal	Muscle rigidity	
Central nervous system	Akinesia Muscle rigidity Tremor Confusion Depression Hallucinations Speech impairment	

either by increasing brain extracellular dopamine concentrations or by decreasing dopaminergic transmission due to simultaneous dopaminergic receptor blockade with depressed neuronal release and reuptake of dopamine [58–60]. A recent case report questioned whether an inhalational anesthetic combined with intercostal nerve blocks (0.5% bupivacaine with 1 : 200,000 epinephrine) unmasked a previously undiagnosed parkinsonian patient. Upon awakening from anesthesia, the patient exhibited a dystonic parkinsonian-type phenomenon that resolved spontaneously. After 18 months, the same patient was diagnosed with Parkinson's disease [61].

For patients taking levodopa, anesthetic agents (e.g., halothane) that sensitize the heart to catecholamines should be avoided due to the potential for dysrhythmias. Hypotension is likely, since there may be relative hypovolemia, norepinephrine depletion, and autonomic dysfunction. Moreover, patients on bromocriptine or pergolide may vasodilate, further

Table 5. *Drugs That May Adversely Interact with Parkinson's Disease or Parkinsonian Symptoms*

Analgesics	Antidepressants	Antihypertensives	Antipsychotics	Gastrointestinal	Miscellaneous
Meperidine (Demerol)	Amoxapine (Asendin)	Clonidine (Catapres)	Acetophenazine (Tindal)	Droperidol (Inapsine)	Alpha-methyldopa (Aldomet)
Fentanyl (Sublimaze)	Phenelzine (Nardil)	Propranolol (Inderal)	Chlorpromazine (Thorazine)	Prochlorperazine (Compazine)	Buspirone (Buspar)
Sufentanil (Sufenta)	Tranylcypromine (Parnate)	Rauwolfia serpentina (Raudixin)	Chlorprothixene (Taractan)	Metoclopramide (Reglan)	Deserpine (Harmonyl)
Alfentanil (Alfenta)	Venlafaxine (Effexor)	Reserpine (Serpasil)	Clozapine (Clozaril)	Thiethylperazine (Torecan)	Lithium (Lithobid)
			Fluphenazine (Prolixin, Permitil)		Rescinnamine (Moderil)
			Haloperidol (Haldol)		
			Loxapine (Loxitane)		
			Mesoridazine (Serentil)		
			Molindone (Moban)		
			Perphenazine (Trilafon)		
			Pimozide (Orap)		
			Thioridazine (Mellaril)		
			Thiothixene (Navane)		
			Trifluoperazine (Stelazine)		
			Triflupromazine (Verprin)		

compounding the hypotension. If vasopressors are needed, a direct-acting agent such as phenylephrine hydrochloride is indicated. A case report of profound hypotension immediately following the insertion of methyl methacrylate during a bipolar endoprosthesis insertion in a patient on long term levodopa therapy illustrates the respect one should have for hemodynamic changes [62].

There is no specific advantage to regional anesthesia, except for the fact that patients may be able to continue the oral antiparkinson regimen. A case report of intraoperative exacerbation of Parkinson's disease underscores the fact that medication can be given while the patient is undergoing surgery [63]. During spinal anesthesia, the patient began having fine tremor, which progressed to an intense form along with a feeling of discomfort. Levodopa/carbidopa was given orally while surgery continued, and the motor activity and the feeling of discomfort resolved. During regional anesthesia, the best sedative seems to be diphenhydramine (H_1-blocker) with central anticholinergic activity. It is particularly good for sedation in patients undergoing ophthalmologic surgery [64].

Upper airway dysfunction may occur in Parkinson's disease patients, especially on withdrawal of antiparkinson medication, which can lead to laryngospasm and respiratory failure [65, 66]. These cases reinforce the need to restart antiparkinsonian drugs before their half life has expired. Ketamine has been given to patients on levodopa, but its use has been questioned because it can exaggerate a sympathetic nervous system response to a stimulus, with resulting tachycardia and hypertension [67]. The choice of muscle relaxants does not seem to be influenced by the presence of Parkinson's disease. Although there has been one case report of hyperkalemia after the administration of succinylcholine [68], a recent evaluation of 7 parkinsonian patients revealed minimal changes in serum potassium after succinylcholine [69]. Opioids are known to produce rigidity, possibly due to the inhibition of dopamine release [70, 71], and may be a theoretical concern. Alfentanil has been reported to produce acute dystonic reactions in untreated patients with Parkinson's disease [72].

Gastrointestinal dysfunction is common in patients with Parkinson's disease and usually presents with dysphagia and sialorrhea. Accordingly, the patients must be considered at risk for aspiration pneumonitis [73]. Postoperatively, patients with Parkinson's disease are more likely to develop confusion and hallucinations [74].

Anesthetic Management for Stereotactic Pallidotomy and Thalamotomy

Classically, local anesthesia with minimal or no sedation has been used for patients undergoing stereotactic pallidotomy or thalamotomy. This allows for patient participation in target localization and immediate observation of the effects of the test and lesion. Antiparkinson medications are withheld for 12–24 hours prior to surgery.

In our experience of over 200 cases [43], patients are brought to the operating room after having the stereotactic frame applied in the MRI suite with local anesthesia. On arrival to the operative room, the standard monitors are placed. Because antiparkinson medications have been withheld, patients may exhibit exaggerated tremors that can interfere with monitoring. Local anesthesia is again used for the burr hole, and if during this time the patient becomes agitated, midazolam can be titrated to the desired effect. It is important that the level of sedation does not impair cooperation or interfere with communication between the patient and surgeon. Age, varying levels of dementia, fatigue, and the cumulative effect of medications make it necessary to titrate the drugs slowly to achieve the desired effect. It is important that drugs not be administered that will decrease the tremor as they will interfere with lesion testing. Although propofol has been recommended by some authors [49], a recent report has suggested that propofol may decrease tremor [75].

Occasionally, the tremor has been so uncontrolled that the patient could not lay flat during the surgical procedure. A small dose of levodopa can be administered by mouth to decrease the intensity of the tremor. Extra padding and rolls to protect the extremities can make the patients more comfortable and allow them to remain still. Typically, these patients are very motivated to cooperate, unless there is dementia present.

A major concern is hypertension and the potential for intracranial hemorrhage. Blood pressure control should not include centrally active β-blockers (e.g., propranolol), as these drugs may decrease tremor intensity. If β-blocker treatment is necessary, agents with limited ability to penetrate the blood-brain barrier (e.g., labetolol) should be considered. Occasionally, a patient with concurrent disease may have a worsening of his or her condition that can be difficult to treat in the stereotactic frame. This was our experience in a patient who inadvertently withheld his asthma medications, as well as the antiparkinsonian medications, on the day of surgery. Instruction to patients with concurrent diseases must ensure that only the antiparkinsonian medications are withheld before surgery and that therapy for concurrent disease is continued.

Complications of pallidotomy and thalamotomy include intracerebral bleeding, motor deficit, visual field deficit, aphasia, and infection. The most serious complication is intracerebral bleeding, which can be manifested by a rapid decrease in consciousness with hemiparesis. Emergency intubation may be required. Prior to surgery, a plan should be agreed on between the surgeon and anesthesiologist for endotracheal intubation. Ideally, this should be done without removing the stereotactic frame, as stereotactic guidance may assist the surgeon in hematoma evacuation. Some stereotactic frames have components shaped in a way to allow easy intubation. Alternatively, a fiberoptic bronchoscope or light wand may be helpful in this situation. If the situation becomes life threatening and intubation with the frame in place is not successful, the frame may need to be removed to facilitate intubation. The patient is then taken for a CT scan to define the exact location of the bleeding, and, subsequently, a craniotomy may be done to remove the hematoma.

■ Summary

With estimates as high as 1 million patients in the United States, Parkinson's disease is a relatively common neurological disorder. It has long been thought that the primary biochemical disturbance in Parkinson's disease is dopamine related. Accordingly, many drugs have been developed that increase the supply of dopamine, affect the biochemical balance of dopamine, or act as a dopamine substitute. These drugs may have significant interactions with anesthetic agents. In addition, there are several disease and drug-induced physiological aberrancies that can have profound anesthetic implications in the patient with Parkinson's disease (e.g., aspiration pneumonitis, myocardial irritability, hypotension, hypertension, and respiratory impairment).

Although surgical therapy for Parkinson's disease has a long history, with the advent of advanced neuroimaging techniques there has been a resurgence of these procedures (e.g., pallidotomy and thalamotomy) for advanced stages of Parkinson's disease. It is likely that these surgical procedures will become more commonplace, possibly prolonging the lifespan of patients with Parkinson's disease. Even though these cases are typically performed with local anesthesia, there are several important caveats to consider in the management of these patients (e.g., airway access with CNS changes, hypertension, and tremor). It's incumbent on anesthesiologists to become familiar with the special needs of patients with Parkinson's disease and alter the "days in hell" attitude among these patients toward surgery and anesthesia.

■ References

1. Redfern RM. History of stereotactic neurosurgery for Parkinson's disease. Br J Neurosurg 1989;3:271–304
2. Kelly PJ. Pallidotomy in Parkinson's disease. Neurosurgery 1995;36:1154–1157
3. Tasker RR. Tremor of parkinsonism and stereotactic thalamotomy. Mayo Clin Proc 1987;62:736–739
4. Yahr MD. Parkinsonism. In: Rowland LP, ed. Merritt's textbook of neurology. Philadelphia: Lea & Febiger, 1989:658–671
5. Quinn N. Parkinsonism—recognition and differential diagnosis. Brit Med J 1995; 310:145–150
6. Harris ZL, Takahashi Y, Miyajima H, et al. Aceruloplasminemia: molecular charac-

terization of this disorder of iron metabolism. Proc Natl Acad Sci USA 1995;92: 2539–2543

7. Heikkila RE, Manzino L, Cabbat FS. Protection against the dopaminergic neurotoxicity of 1-methyl-4-phenyl-1,2,3,6-tetrahydropyridine by monoamine oxidase inhibitors. Nature 1984;311:467–469

8. McDowell F, Cedarbaum J. The extrapyramidal system and disorders of movement. In: Joynt R, ed. Clinical neurology. Philadelphia: J.B. Lippincott, 1991:19–48

9. Wichmann T, DeLong MR. Pathophysiology of parkinsonian motor abnormalities. Adv Neurol 1993;60:53–61

10. Olanow CW. A radical hypothesis for neurodegeneration. Trends Neurosci 1993; 16:439–444

11. Hoehn MM, Yahr MD. Parkinsonism: onset, progression, and mortality. Neurology 1967;17:427–442

12. Koller WC. How accurately can Parkinson's disease be diagnosed. Neurology 1992; 42(Suppl):6–16

13. Stacy M, Jankovic J. Differential diagnosis of Parkinson's disease and the parkinsonian plus syndrome. Neurol Clin 1992;10(Suppl):341–359

14. Quinn N. Drug treatment of Parkinson's disease. Brit Med J 1995;310:575–579

15. Koller W, Silver D, Lieberman A. An algorithm for the management of Parkinson's disease, a supplement of the American Academy of Neurology. Neurology 1994; 44(Suppl 10):S1–S52

16. Markham CH, Diamond SG. Evidence to support early levodopa therapy in Parkinson's disease. Neurology 1981;31:125–131

17. Rajput AN, Rozdilsky B, Rajput A. Levodopa efficacy and pathological basis of parkinson syndrome. Clin Neuropharmacol 1990;13:553–558

18. Hoehn NM. The natural history of Parkinson's disease in the pre-levodopa and post-levodopa eras. Neurol Clin 1992;10(Suppl 2):331–339

19. Martz DG, Schreibmen DI, Matjasko MJ. Neurological diseases. In: Katz J, Benumof JL, Kadis LB, ed. Anesthesia in uncommon disorders. Philadelphia: W.B. Saunders, 1990:563–564

20. Stoelting RK, Dierdorf SF. Diseases of the nervous system. In: Stoelting RK, ed. Anesthesia and coexisting disease. New York: Churchill-Livingstone, 1993:209–211

21. Birkmayer W, Knoll J, Riederer P. Improvement of life expectancy due to L-deprenyl in Parkinson's disease: a long-term study. J Neural Transm 1985;65:113–127

22. The Parkinson Study Group. Effects of tocopherol and deprenyl on the progression of disability in early Parkinson's disease. N Engl J Med 1993;328:176–183

23. The Parkinson Study Group. Effect of deprenyl on the progression of disability in early Parkinson's disease. N Engl J Med 1989;321:1364–1371

24. Myllyla VV, Sotaniemi KA, Vuorinen JA. Selegiline as initial treatment in de novo parkinsonian patients. Neurology 1992;42:339–343

25. Olanow CW, Calne D. Does selegiline monotherapy in Parkinson's disease act by symptomatic or protective mechanisms? Neurology 1992;42(Suppl 4):13–26

26. Rinne JO. Nigral degeneration in Parkinson's disease in relation to clinical features. Acta Neurol 1991;316(Suppl):87–90

27. Salo PT, Tatton WG. Deprenyl reduced the death of motor neurons caused by axotoms. J Neurosci Res 1992;31:394–400

28. Tatton WG, Greenwood CE. Rescue of dying neurons: a new action for deprenyl in MPTP parkinsonism. J Neurosci Res 1991;30:666–672

29. Duvoisin RC. Cholinergic-anticholinergic antagonism in parkinsonism. Arch Neurol 1967;17:124–136

30. Horrocks PM, Vicary DJ, Rees JD, et al. Anticholinergic withdrawal and benzhexol treatment in Parkinson's disease. J Neurol Neurosurg Psychiatry 1973;36:936–941

31. Schwab RS, Poskanzer DC, England AC, et al. Amantadine in Parkinson's disease. JAMA 1972;222:792–795

32. Kurlan R. International symposium on early dopamine agonist therapy of Parkinson's disease. Arch Neurol 1988;45:204–208

33. Goetz CG. Dopaminergic agonists in the treatment of Parkinson's disease. Neurology 1990;40(Suppl 3):50–54

34. Rinne UK. Early combination of bromocriptine and levodopa in the treatment of Parkinson's disease: a five-year follow-up. Neurology 1987;37:826–828

35. Lieberman A. Combination therapy of Parkinson's disease. Neurology 1993;443: 2725–2726

36. Dogali M, Fazzini E, Kolodny E, et al. Stereotactic ventral pallidotomy for Parkinson's disease. Neurology 1995;45:753–761

37. Leitinen LV, Bergenheim AT, Hariz MI. Ventroposterolateral pallidotomy can abolish all parkinsonian symptoms. Stereotact Funct Neurosurg 1992;58(1–4):14–21

38. Leitinen LV. Pallidotomy for Parkinson's disease. Neurosurg Clin North Am 1995; 6:113–125

39. Meyers R. Surgical interruption of the pallidofungal fibers. Its effects on the syndrome of paralysis agitans and technical considerations in its applications. NY State J Med 1942;42:317–325

40. Cooper IS. The neurosurgical alleviation of Parkinsonism. Springfield: Charles C Thomas, 1956

41. Hassler R, Riechert T. Indikationen and lokalisations-methode der gezielten Hirnoperationen. Nervenarzt 1954;25:441–447

42. Leitinen LV, Bergenheim AT, Hariz MI. Leksell's posteroventral pallidotomy in the treatment of Parkinson's disease. J Neurosurgery 1992;76:53–61

43. Iacono RP, Shima F, Lonser RR, et al. The results, indications, and physiology of posteroventral pallidotomy for patients with Parkinson's disease. Neurosurgery 1995;36:1118–1127

44. Iacono RP, Lonser RR, Mandybur G, et al. Stereotactic pallidotomy results for Parkinson's disease exceed those of fetal graft. Am Surg 1994;60:777–782

45. Bakay RAE. Central nervous system grafting: animal and clinical results. Stereotact Funct Neurosurg 1992;58:67–78

46. Benabid AL, Pollak P, Gao D, et al. Chronic electrical stimulation of the ventralis intermedius nucleus of the thalamus as a treatment of movement disorders. J Neurosurg 1996;84:203–214

47. Boyer KL, Bakay RAE. The history, theory, and present status of brain transplantation. Neurosurg Clin North Am 1995;6:113–125

48. Caparros-Lefebvre D, Blond S, Vermersch, et al. Chronic thalamic stimulation improves tremor and levodopa induced dyskinesias in Parkinson's disease. J Neurol Neurosurg Psychiatry 1993;56:268–273

49. Burchiel KJ. Thalamotomy for movement disorders. Neurosurg Clin North Am 1995;6:55–71

50. Lozano A, Hutchison W, Kiss Z, et al. Methods for microelectrode-guided posteroventral pallidotomy. J Neurosurg 1996;84:194–202

51. Gildenberg PP. Management of movement disorders—an overview. Neurosurg Clin North Am 1995;6:43–53

52. Parent AG, Tasker RR, Dostrovski JO. Tremor reduction by microinjection of lidocaine during stereotactic neurosurgery. Acta Neurochir (Wien) 1993;58(Suppl): 45–47

53. Dostrovski JO, Sher GD, Davis KD, et al. Microinjection of lidocaine in human thalamus: a useful tool in stereotactic surgery. Stereotactic Funct Neurosurgery 1993;60:168–174

54. Burchiel KJ. Thalamotomy for movement disorders. Neurosurg Clin North Am 1995;6:55–71

55. Golbe LI, Langston GW, Shoulsten I. Selegiline in Parkinson's disease. Drugs 1990; 39:646

56. Zornberg GI, Bodkin JA, Colon BM. Severe adverse interaction between pethidine and selegiline. Lancet 1991;337:246
57. Avorn J, Gurwictz JH, Bohrn RL, et al. Increased incidence of levodopa therapy following metoclopramide use. JAMA 1995;274:1780–1782
58. Stahle L, Collin AK, Ungerstedt U. Effects of halothane anaesthesia on extracellular levels of dopamine, dihydroxyphenylacetic acid, homovanillic acid, and 5-hydroxyindoleacetic acid in rat striatum: a microdialysis study. Naunyn-Schmied Arch Pharmacol 1990;342:136–140
59. El-Maghrabi EA, Eckenhoff RG. Inhibition of dopamine transport in rat brain synaptosomes by volatile anesthetics. Anesthesiology 1993;78:750–756
60. Mantz TJ, Varlet C, Lecharny J-B, et al. Effects of volatile anesthetics, thiopental, and ketamine on spontaneous and depolarization-evoked dopamine release from striatal synaptosomes in rat. Anesthesiology 1994;80:352–364
61. Muravchick S, Smith DS. Parkinsonian symptoms during emergence from general anesthesia. Anesthesiology 1995;82:305–307
62. Kim YC, Cho MS, Kim SS, et al. Profound hypotension immediately following insertion of methyl methacrylate during bipolar endoprosthesis in a patient with long-term levodopa-treated paralysis agitans. J Korean Med Sci 1995;10:31–35
63. Reed AP, Han DG. Intraoperative exacerbation of Parkinson's disease. Anesth Analg 1992;75:850–853
64. Stone DJ, Difazio CA. Sedation for patients with Parkinson's disease undergoing ophthalmology surgery. Anesthesiology 1988;68:821
65. Eastdown JL, Tessler M, Jeffrey M. Upper airway involvement in Parkinson's disease resulting in postoperative respiratory failure. Can J Anesth 1995;42:344–347
66. Backus WW, Ward RR, Vitkun SA, et al. Postextubation laryngeal spasm in an unanesthetized patient with Parkinson's disease. J Clin Anesth 1991;3:314–316
67. Ngai SH. Parkinsonism, levodopa and anesthesia. Anesthesiology 1972;3:340–344
68. Gravelee GP. Succinylcholine induced hyperkalemia in a patient with Parkinson's disease. Anesth Analg 1980;59:444–446
69. Munzi DA, Black S, Cucchiara RF. The lack of effect of succinylcholine on serum potassium in patients with Parkinson's disease. Anesthesiology 1989;71:322
70. Weinger MS, Smith NT, Blasco TA, Koob GF. Brain sites mediating opiate-induced muscle rigidity in the rat: methylnaloxonium mapping study. Brain Res 1991;544:181–190
71. Loh HH, Brase DA, Sampath-Khan S, et al. β-Endorphin in vitro inhibition of striatal dopamine release. Nature 1976;264:567–568
72. Mets B. Acute dystonia after alfentanil in untreated Parkinson's disease. Anesth Analg 1991;72:557–558
73. Korczyn AB. Autonomic nervous system disturbances in Parkinson's disease. Adv Neurol 1990;53:463
74. Golden WE, Lavender RC, Metzen WS. Acute postoperative confusion and hallucinations in Parkinson's disease. Ann Intern Med 1989;111:218
75. Anderson BJ, Marks PV, Futter ME. Propofol-contrasting effects in movement disorders. Br J Neurosurg 1994;8:387–388

Anesthetic Management for Surgical Ablation of Giant Cerebral Aneurysms

C. Philip Larson Jr, MD

Because of the very great risks of permanent neurological injury or death, neurosurgeons generally have avoided any attempts at surgical ablation of giant cerebral aneurysms. It has only been in the last 20 years that techniques have been developed to make this operative procedure safe enough to justify its application by experienced neurovascular surgeons working in selected centers. An important component in achieving a successful surgical outcome is the anesthetic care provided. The anesthetic management is complex and critically important to the ultimate outcome, and it should only be undertaken by anesthesiologists who are experienced in neurovascular anesthesia.

Giant aneurysms are particularly difficult surgical challenges because: (1) Their large size makes direct visualization of the vascular anatomy difficult. (2) The vascular branches essential to maintaining flow to normal brain may be an integral part of the giant aneurysm and cannot be included in the surgical ablation without causing permanent neurological injury. (3) Standard aneurysm clips may not occlude a large, turgid aneurysm or may move once applied. (4) They may rupture during dissection or ablation, resulting in severe neurological morbidity or mortality.

To improve the safety for patients during surgical ablation of giant aneurysms, special anesthetic and surgical techniques using isovolemic hemodilution, deep hypothermia to 16°C–18°C (achieved with femoral-femoral cardiopulmonary bypass [CPB]), and temporary circulatory arrest have evolved [1, 2]. These techniques decompress the aneurysm, making it easier to clip, and protect the brain during circulatory arrest, which may last as long as 45 minutes.

■ Preoperative Evaluation

Aneurysms are classified as giant when they exceed 2.5 cm in diameter (Fig) and represent about 5% of all new aneurysms diagnosed each year.

151

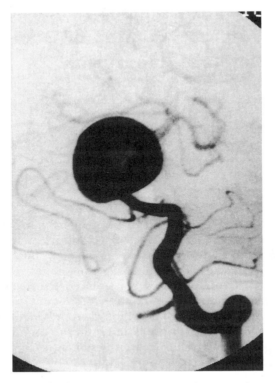

*Vertebrobasilar angiogram (A-P view) showing a giant
basilar trunk aneurysm. (Courtesy of Gary K.
Steinberg, MD, PhD, Stanford University.)*

Giant aneurysms occur two to three times more commonly in women than
men, but why this gender difference exists is not known. Although probably present from birth or early childhood as small aneurysms, most giant
aneurysms do not become symptomatic until the 4th or 5th decade of
life. When symptoms do occur, they usually take the form of intermittent
headaches or visual disturbances that are probably due to aneurysmal compression of adjacent neural tissue or increased intracranial pressure. If the
aneurysm should leak or bleed, neurological dysfunction will vary depending upon the site and magnitude of the hemorrhage. These patients
may complain of a severe headache, be confused and disoriented, have a
motor deficit of one or more extremities, or be comatose. The nature and
severity of any neurological deficits should be documented preoperatively.
Patients with giant aneurysms may have other smaller aneurysms as well,
and these may be the site of hemorrhage.

A major complication of an intracerebral hemorrhage is the development of cerebral vasospasm. This vasoconstriction of cerebral vessels may
be local or diffuse and may be mild or severe. If severe, it causes worsening

of the neurological deficits. It usually occurs in the first week after the hemorrhage, peaks at about 10 days, and is usually resolved within 2–3 weeks. The exact mechanism for the vasospasm is not known, but it is believed that the precipitating agent is free oxyhemoglobin, which causes release of vasospastic substances such as serotonin, prostaglandins, or potassium from brain tissue. If the neurosurgeon suspects that the patient may have focal cerebral edema or vasospasm from an intracranial hemorrhage, surgery usually will be delayed until the neurological symptoms and signs have stabilized or resolved and a computerized tomographic (CT) scan of the brain shows no evidence of further hemorrhage or edema formation. The current therapy for managing cerebral vasospasm, which includes the use of hypertension, hypervolemia, and hemodilution, presents substantial risk in patients with a giant aneurysm. However, they may be treated with epsilon-aminocaproic acid (20 mg/kg/hr) or a calcium channel–blocking drug (nimodipine or nicardipine) to relax cerebrovascular smooth muscle and steroids to decrease brain edema, although there is no convincing evidence that steroids are effective in the management of subarachnoid hemorrhage.

In some patients, recent attempts may have been made to decrease the size of the aneurysm by obliterating one or more of the major feeding vessels using interventional radiologic techniques. This procedure requires anesthesia, often for many hours, and may induce a new neurological deficit. Some of the same principles of anesthetic management outlined below apply during this anesthetic procedure. Most important is careful regulation of blood pressure to avoid sudden or severe episodes of hypertension that may induce aneurysmal rupture.

Because of their relatively young age, patients diagnosed with a giant aneurysm usually do not have other serious cardiovascular diseases. However, intracerebral aneurysms occur more commonly in patients with certain congenital disorders such as polycystic disease of the kidneys, coarctation of the aorta, fibromuscular hyperplasia, and Marfan and Ehlers-Danlos syndromes. Patients who have had a recent intracranial hemorrhage from a leaking giant aneurysm are prone to develop systemic hypertension, hypovolemia, and electrocardiographic (ECG) abnormalities. The hypertension is believed to be due to autonomic hyperactivity and is generally treated with antihypertensive drugs, which should be continued up to the time of anesthesia and surgery. The hypovolemia following subarachnoid hemorrhage may be due to the neurological impairment of vasomotor function or to the effects of prolonged bed rest. Electrocardiographic abnormalities occur in 50%–80% of patients who sustain an intracranial hemorrhage. Appropriate preoperative evaluation includes ECG characterization of the abnormality. If the patient has a history of ischemic or valvular heart disease, then echocardiography, cardiac enzyme studies, and cardiac catheterization may be helpful in determining whether the ECG changes are due to heart disease or intracranial hemorrhage.

Appropriate preoperative laboratory studies include determination of hemoglobin or hematocrit, prothrombin time (PT), and plasma thrombo-plastin time (PTT) because a coagulopathy will be induced during surgery and a chest roentgenogram, ECG, electrolyte panel, and a CT, magnetic resonance imaging, and cerebral angiogram to define the site, size, and surrounding effects of the giant aneurysm. The neuroanesthesiologist should review these studies well in advance of the proposed surgical date so that sufficient time is allotted for further analysis or treatment if either should be necessary. Whenever possible, the patient should be advised to donate as many units of autologous blood as possible for use during and after operation. A minimum of six units of autologous, donor-directed and/or bank blood should be typed, crossmatched, and available the day of surgery. In addition, the neuroanesthesiologist should place four 1000-ml bags or bottles of normal saline and eight 250-ml bottles of albumin 5% in a refrigerator at 4°C the night before surgery to be used for cooling during isovolemic hemodilution. Two or three citrate-phosphate-dextrose (CPD) bags should be obtained from the blood bank the day before surgery to use for collecting shed blood during isovolemic hemodilution.

The most important part of the preoperative preparation from the patient's point of view is a careful, thoughtful, unhurried discussion of the proposed anesthetic and surgical plan, the risks associated with the operation, how they will be handled, and the expected outcome. Each of these phases of discussion must be accompanied by appropriate reassurances that the anesthetic-surgical-nursing-perfusionist team will work efficiently and effectively together to minimize risk and maximize a favorable outcome. Because the risks of death range from 5%–15% and serious neurological injury from 15%–50%, these discussions with the patient and the obtaining of an informed consent must be conducted by the most senior and experienced neuroanesthesiologist and neurosurgeon and be reflected in the preoperative patient record. Generally, some premedication is desirable both the night before surgery and before coming to the operating room. A variety of sedative-hypnotic drugs (e.g., midazolam 2 to 5 mg intravenously) can be used for these purposes.

■ Intraoperative Management

The goals of anesthesia for this operation are threefold: (1) to provide satisfactory surgical anesthesia, (2) to decrease intracranial volume (blood and tissue) to optimize working space within the cranial compartment, thereby minimizing the need for surgical retraction of brain tissue, and (3) to increase tolerance of the brain to ischemia by decreasing cerebral metabolic rate of oxygen through the use of deep hypothermia, barbiturate therapy, and isovolemic hemodilution.

Obviously, general anesthesia with endotracheal intubation must be used. Following placement of the standard monitors (noninvasive blood pressure cuff, pulse oximeter, ECG, neuromuscular transmission), anesthesia may be induced with a variety of agents, including thiopental up to 20 mg/kg or propofol up to 8 mg/kg with or without midazolam 0.15 mg/kg, all in divided doses to permit evaluation of the pharmacological responses of the patient. If there is concern about hypovolemia or cardiovascular dysfunction, the doses of thiopental or propofol can be decreased and supplemented with lidocaine up to 2 mg/kg IV. Lidocaine appears to have effects on cerebral blood flow and metabolism that are similar to those for thiopental but without the cardiovascular depressant effects of thiopental. Once the patient is anesthetized, vecuronium 0.15 mg/kg or equivalent doses of other nondepolarizing neuromuscular-blocking drugs such as atracurium or rocuronium is administered to facilitate endotracheal intubation and subsequent positioning of the patient. We prefer to avoid pancuronium for neuromuscular blockade because of the associated tachycardia, and we do not use succinylcholine or mivacurium in order to avoid the fasciculations of the former and the short duration of action of both drugs. To provide analgesia in the early period following induction of anesthesia, we supplement the sedative-hypnotic with an opiate, usually meperidine up to 2 mg/kg, although equivalent doses of other opiates such as fentanyl, alfentanil, or sufentanil are also suitable.

Once anesthesia is induced and endotracheal intubation completed, anesthesia is maintained with thiopental by continuous infusion up to a total dose of 40 mg/kg (or the equivalent dose of propofol) over the next 2 hours, meperidine up to a total dose of 5 mg/kg (or the equivalent dose of fentanyl or its derivatives), and isoflurane up to 1% with oxygen. Nitrous oxide is not used because of its potential for reversing the protective effects of thiopental from focal ischemia. Additional doses of nondepolarizing neuromuscular-blocking drugs are given as needed to maintain no more than one twitch in a train-of-four, and an additional dose is given just prior to the start of CPB.

Ventilation is controlled throughout the operation, and tidal volume and respiratory rate adjusted to maintain moderate hyperventilation and arterial carbon dioxide tension between 25–30 mm Hg. The advantages of hypocarbia include: decreasing cerebral vascular volume to provide more surgical working space, thereby lessening the need for vigorous retraction of brain tissue; improving regional distribution of cerebral blood flow (CBF) by preferentially diverting blood to potentially ischemic areas of the brain; better buffering of brain lactic acid that may form as a result of focal ischemia; and decreasing anesthetic requirement.

Careful control of the patient's blood pressure is critical to a successful operation. Any substantial increases in blood pressure during induction of anesthesia or prior to CPB will increase transmural pressure across the aneurysm wall and increase the likelihood of rupture. Prior to CPB, the blood pressure is generally maintained in the normal-to-20%-below-normal range for that patient, using anesthetic agents alone or in combination with an esmolol infusion to decrease heart rate to a range of 50–60 beats/min. If the desired level of blood pressure is not achieved with this regimen, sodium nitroprusside (SNP) may be added. SNP also has the advantage that it facilitates both cooling and rewarming because of its vasodilatory effect. However, it must be administered cautiously in a very dilute solution or profound hypotension will occur suddenly. If a vasoconstrictor is needed, particularly during CPB while the patient is still cold, a pure alpha-adrenergic stimulant such as phenylephrine is preferred because of its minimal dysrhythmogenic potential. Responses to vasoactive drugs are much easier to regulate if a normal blood volume has been established and maintained throughout the anesthetic period.

Upon completion of anesthetic induction, additional vascular catheters and monitors are placed. We insert two large-bore (16–18 g) intravenous catheters for fluid and blood infusion; a triple-lumen central venous pressure (CVP) catheter for monitoring of CVP and infusing vasoactive drugs such as esmolol, SNP, or phenylephrine; and two radial artery catheters, one for continuously monitoring blood pressure and the other for drawing off blood to institute isovolemic hemodilution. An esophageal stethoscope and a bladder catheter, both with temperature monitoring capabilities, are also inserted.

Once the vascular catheters have been placed, isovolemic hemodilution is begun. Generally, about 1000 ml of blood are withdrawn into CPD bags and replaced with 1000 ml of cold albumin 5%. This usually results in a decrease in hematocrit to 22%–26%. Frequent intraoperative checks of hematocrit are made to avoid excessive hemodilution. Once blood is withdrawn and additional cold normal saline is infused, the hematocrit will usually decrease further to values of 18%–20%. The goal in isovolemic hemodilution is to decrease the hematocrit to approximately the same value as the expected decrease in body temperature. The withdrawn blood is held at room temperature for reinfusion at the conclusion of the operation. Although there is no evidence that the administration of glucose-containing solutions is harmful to patients undergoing this surgical procedure, we do not use glucose solutions and in general attempt to maintain blood glucose in the normal range.

Simultaneously, with the start of isovolemic hemodilution, patient cooling is begun. This is accomplished using surface cooling by convection in a cold operating room, having the patient lie on a water-circulating thermal blanket that is maximally cooled, applying properly insulated ice packs to the abdomen and legs of the patient, infusing cold fluids intravenously, and administering sodium nitroprusside as tolerated to induce cutaneous vasodilatation. It is important to initiate cooling as soon as anesthesia is established because surface cooling is a relatively slow method to decrease patient body temperature. Some advise irrigation of the bladder with cold saline to facilitate cooling; we have no experience using that modality in this setting.

While cooling is occurring, the neurosurgeons are occupied positioning the patient. Prior to positioning, it may be desirable to insert a lumbar subarachnoid drain to remove cerebrospinal fluid (CSF), thereby improving visualization of the aneurysm during surgery and avoiding welling up of CSF into the surgical field. Depending on the site of the aneurysm, the patient will be supine or tilted slightly laterally with the head in a Mayfield headrest, turned 30°–45° away from the aneurysm. The eyes are taped shut, all pressure points are well padded, and anti-embolism stockings and sequential compression devices are applied to the legs to minimize deep venous thrombosis. The operating table is positioned such that the neurosurgeons are at the patient's head, the cardiovascular surgeons are at the patient's chest and hips, and the anesthesiologist is at the patient's feet. All vascular and monitor lines and anesthetic hoses must have sufficient length to reach below the patient's feet. Because circulatory arrest is planned, the chest is prepped and draped in a sterile manner to permit defibrillation and access by the cardiovascular surgeon if that should be necessary. Both femoral regions are prepped and draped in a sterile manner for femoral artery–femoral vein cardiopulmonary bypass, in case one side has vessels that are too small for proper cannulation.

While the cardiovascular surgeon is preparing the femoral vessels for cannulation, the neurosurgeons are exposing the giant aneurysm. To limit brain swelling and facilitate exposure of the aneurysm, the anesthesiologist must institute measures to control brain size. These include: (1) hyperventilation with hypocarbia to induce cerebral vasoconstriction, thereby decreasing CBF and cerebral blood volume. While the blood volume change is relatively small, probably not exceeding 20–25 ml, this decrease may be helpful in a small compartment such as the brain. (2) Administration of thiopental or propofol will have a similar effect as hypocarbia and decrease CBF and cerebral blood volume. (3) Limiting the total crystalloid infusion volume to no more than 10 ml/kg plus replacement of urine output and limiting the dose of isoflurane to 1% or less will decrease the chances for brain swelling during or after the operation. (4) Generally, mannitol 1 g/kg and furosemide 0.3 mg/kg are administered before opening the dura, to induce osmotic diuresis and decrease brain size. Giving the diuretics simultaneously avoids the transient increase in cerebral blood volume that occurs if only mannitol is used. These doses will produce a substantial diuresis, necessitating monitoring of serum potassium and probable supplemental intravenous potassium therapy. We generally find it necessary to add potassium 20 mEq to 1 or 2 liters of normal saline during the course of surgery. (5) Once the dura is opened, the lumbar drainage catheter can be safely opened to remove unwanted CSF from the operative site. (6) Finally, some neurosurgeons believe that steroids may prevent brain swelling and request the administration of dexamethasone 8–12 mg or its equivalent.

Once the giant aneurysm is exposed, the neurosurgeons make the final determination if the aneurysm can be obliterated without resorting to CPB. If it cannot, the neurosurgeons optimize the position of the brain retractors, since they cannot be safely moved once systemic heparinization has been instituted. Systemic heparinization is then effected using a loading dose of 300 U/kg and maintained by an infusion of 100 U/kg/hr. Femoral-femoral CPB is then initiated and the patient is cooled to an esophageal temperature of 16°C–18°C. During CPB cooling, the heart will usually fibrillate between 22°C–26°C. Once 18°C is reached, the CPB unit is turned off. With no cerebral circulation, the aneurysm collapses, and surgical clipping or ablation by wrapping with or without acrylic cement is accomplished. It may be necessary to institute and stop CPB several times to apply several clips and ensure total occlusion of the aneurysm. However, total circulatory arrest time should not exceed 45 minutes at this temperature.

When the surgical ablation is complete, CPB is resumed and an intraoperative cerebral angiogram is obtained to confirm that the aneurysm is obliterated. If it is not, further attempts at surgical ablation during circulatory arrest may be attempted. Once the ablation is complete, warming is instituted. Partial CPB is continued until normal cardiac rhythm is established and the patient's body temperature is above 36°C. It is important to achieve this temperature because once partial CPB is discontinued, the patient's temperature will tend to drift lower unless vigorous efforts are made to maintain warmth. Warming the operating room and intravenous fluids and using warming lights and a hyperthermia blanket (Bair Hugger, Augustine Medical, Inc., Eden Prarie, MN) will facilitate the warming process. Activated clotting time (ACT) should be measured to ensure that heparin reversal is complete after careful protamine administration. If coagulation seems inadequate following heparin reversal, blood is sent for clotting studies, and platelets, fresh frozen plasma, and calcium gluconate are administered as needed. Hetastarch 6% is not used in these patients owing to its potential for inducing a coagulopathy. Once rewarming is begun, it is also necessary to begin to restore the hematocrit to a more normal value. Fluid infusion is changed from normal saline to the whole blood obtained at the start of the operation plus the autologous or donor-directed units of whole blood or packed cells available from the blood bank. In addition, the perfusate from the CPB unit is spun down and the packed cells returned to the patient.

When the desired body temperature has been achieved and the vital signs of CPB are stable, the femoral vessels are decannulated and the wounds closed. During this same interval, the neurosurgeons are closing the dura and cranial vault. Prior to leaving the operating room, one last set of laboratory values for hematocrit and electrolytes is obtained. If there is concern about undue oozing, the ACT is repeated, and if appropriate, measurements of PT and PTT are made. Owing to the length of the operation and the physiological derangements that have been induced, it is generally advisable to leave the endotracheal tube in place during transport of the patient to the intensive care unit, and for a time thereafter. During transport, the patients are breathing oxygen, and arterial blood pressure, ECG, and oxygen saturation are monitored.

■ Postoperative Care

If the anesthetic and operative events have gone smoothly and the patient has not sustained any neurological injury from the temporary circulatory arrest or ablation of the aneurysm, he or she should emerge from anesthesia promptly and have the endotracheal tube removed within a few hours. This will be the pattern for most patients. Vigilance must be maintained to avoid hypertension in the postoperative period. Usually the blood pressure can be maintained in the normal range with a combination of esmolol and SNP given intravenously using a constant infusion pump.

Other complications that may occur in the early postoperative period include: vasospasm; intracranial hemorrhage and stroke, particularly if the heparin or cold-induced coagulopathy is not fully corrected or recurs; hypothermia, if full rewarming is not accomplished before termination of CPB; hypervolemia, owing to the large fluid shifts that may occur from the use of isovolemic hemodilution, CPB, and blood loss; and seizures. In anticipation of the possibility of postoperative seizures, neurosurgeons will often request the administration of a loading dose of phenytoin (usually 15 mg/kg) during surgery followed by regular administration (usually 5 mg/kg/day) postoperatively. If any questions about neurological status arise postoperatively, a head CT scan and a coagulation panel should be requested. Another potential complication of concern is the possible development of deep venous thrombosis, thrombophlebitis, and pulmonary embolism from the hypothermia and circulatory arrest. Occasionally, patients may develop hydrocephalus as a late complication requiring insertion of a ventriculoperitoneal shunt.

A variety of drugs can be used to manage the pain postoperatively, including meperidine, morphine, dihydromorphinone, and in some cases codeine may suffice. Generally, the patients are discharged home after 10–14 days hospitalization if no neurological injury of consequence occurs. Mortality from this operation varies widely, and probably depends in part on patient selection and experience with managing these cases. While most reported series of surgical treatment of giant aneurysms are small (less than 100 cases), operative mortality rates vary from none [1] to 21% [3].

The incidence of major morbidity in the form of severe neurological deficits upon emergence from anesthesia, postoperative intracerebral hemorrhage, or delayed or late neurological sequelae is higher, and ranges from 17% [4] to 50% [5].

■ References

1. Silverberg GD, Reitz BA, Ream AK. Hypothermia and cardiac arrest in the treatment of giant aneurysms of the cerebral circulation and hemangioblastoma of the medulla. J Neurosurg 1981;55:337–346
2. Silverberg GD. Giant aneurysms: surgical treatment. Neurol Res 1984;6:57–63
3. Onuma T, Suzuki JL. Surgical treatment of giant intracranial aneurysms. J Neurosurg 1979;51:33–36
4. Whittle IR, Dorsch NW, Besser M. Giant intracranial aneurysms: diagnosis, management, and outcome. Surg Neurol 1984;21:218–230
5. Steinberg GK, Shuer LM, Adler J. Intracranial neurosurgery. In: Jaffe RA, Samuels SI, eds. Anesthesiologist's manual of surgical procedures. New York: Raven Press, 1994:6

Interventional Neuroradiology: Techniques, Applications, and Clinical Issues

Robert J. Singer, MD

Alexander M. Norbash, MD

Increasingly, anesthesiologists are called upon to provide their services in an interventional radiology facility. In this rapidly evolving field, it is important that anesthesiologists understand the nature of the various treatment modalities and requirements for anesthesia and sedation. Contemporary interventional neuroradiology occasionally seems to be the product of a fertile science fiction writer's imagination. Remarkable intracranial and intraspinal therapies are possible through small transcutaneous puncture arteriotomies. The specific therapeutic tools that have changed the most in the past decade include angioplasty, intravascular adhesive- and stent-related technologies, and even simple superselective vascular catheterization. Advances in the neurointerventional field have been a result of accelerated development in three areas: materials advances, imaging chain advances, and increased interdisciplinary cooperation.

The first of these areas relates to new manufacturing technologies, material engineering sciences, and polymer chemistry. These advances allow creation of catheters as small as 1.5 millimeters in diameter that can negotiate the vascular tree in the most sensitive portions of the brain. Here blood vessels can be selectively opened, closed, buttressed, and lasered. The second area relates to the improvement in the visual imaging chain, allowing the interventional neuroradiologists to confidently see the therapy being performed. The third area involves progress in microneurosurgical techniques and neuro–intensive care management that has broadened the scope and practical application of many neurointerventional developments. Success in this field depends on interdisciplinary support between neurointerventionalists, vascular neurosurgeons, anesthesiologists, stroke neurologists, and intensive care specialists.

■ Hardware Advances and Medications

Hardware

Hardware advances include improved catheter delivery systems and the materials that can be delivered through these catheters, the improved imaging chain, which allows visualization of pathology, the tools with which therapy is performed, and the delivery of therapy itself.

Microcatheters are used in small vessels such as those encountered above the skull base and above the origin of the external carotid artery. Various types of microcatheters exist, and microcatheter selection is application specific. Microcatheters are ordinarily placed telescopically through a larger guiding catheter called a coaxial introduction system, where the semirigid guiding catheter provides secure placement of the microcatheter, which by nature of its flexibility would otherwise tend to buckle in larger vessels. Two families of microcatheters exist: flow-directed microcatheters and microwire-directed microcatheters. Flow-directed microcatheters are extremely floppy and are pulled into the circulation passively by the onrushing flow of blood. The tip of flow-directed microcatheters may be slightly bulbous to enhance the flow-related pulling effect, and small syringe-controlled pulses are used as jets to redirect the slightly curved flow-directed catheter tips into specific branches of the circulation. Microwire-directed microcatheters are placed similarly to conventional catheters, with a floppy and relatively atraumatic wire used to selectively enter a chosen vascular branch; the microcatheter is then advanced into the vessel over this securely placed microguidewire. Advances in materials technology have created multisegment catheters with combinations of rigidity, flexibility, and torsional control.

Four broad families of therapeutic materials can be attached to or introduced through microcatheters. These families are comprised of inflatable balloons, which can either be detachable or nondetachable; particulate embolic substances; nonparticulate embolic materials, including liquid embolic agents such as cyanoacrylates or "glue" derivatives; and wire devices, including microcoils (controlled or uncontrolled release) and stents.

Two broad types of detachable and attached balloons exist. The first includes relatively atraumatic silicone balloons used to gently dilate spastic vessels, of which detachable versions have been used to block traumatic carotid cavernous fistulas and to seal aneurysms. The second type of balloon includes polytetrafluoroethylene-derived balloons, which are slightly more rigid than their silicone counterparts and are used for applications such as atherosclerotic angioplasty.

Particulate embolic materials include particulate and powdered gelfoam, a resorbable gelatin, and more permanent occlusive substances, including polyvinyl alcohol. These particulate substances are often sized to allow obstruction of chosen channel diameters without the undesirable side effects of parent vessel occlusion (from particles that are too large) or distal embolization into the venous limb (from particles that are too small and float through a malformation).

Liquid embolic agents include ethylene vinyl and cellulose acetate derivatives, and cyanoacrylate derivatives. Although the glue derivatives have become popularized for closure of high-flow vascular connections, they demand high operator expertise. Potential complications include accidental adhesion of catheters into the feeding vessel and accidental closure of critical draining veins by injection of suboptimal glue solutions or from suboptimal catheter positions. Such accidental venous closure may result in malformation rupture, in which the inflow is unaffected and accelerated central venous thrombosis with massive venous infarctions result.

Metallic intravascular hardware includes coils, stents, and braided occlusion devices. Coils promote thrombosis and may be placed by controlled or uncontrolled delivery. Controlled delivery examples include electrolytically and mechanically detachable coils. These allow the operator to reposition the coil within the chosen delivery site until satisfactory placement is seen, following which the coil is released. Uncontrolled coils are pushed through the distal end of a delivery catheter, where the conformational shape of the coil and the unpredictable three-dimensional shape of the cavity it is entering result in less controlled placement.

Metallic stents are an outgrowth of wire-related technologies. Two broad categories include balloon expandable and self-expanding stents. Such stents may conform to a manufactured shape and diameter, such as self-expanding stents, or may be malleable and conform to the size and shape of the vessel and deployment balloon chosen to place the stent. These stents act as tunnels to either restrict blood flow inside a selected channel or to mechanically buttress a vascular wall refractory to angioplasty.

Medications

Neurointerventional techniques hinge to a high degree on successful patient sedation, proper monitoring, and selective use of blood pressure/perfusion–controlling agents. Drugs are administered pre- or intraprocedurally to decrease the chance of thromboembolic complications, to alter vascular wall reactivity, to increase or decrease blood pressure to protect the vascular bed and aid catheterization (as with flow-directed catheters), or for a direct neurovascular effect. Systemic anticoagulation is often required during microcatheterization and embolization procedures to diminish the risk of thromboembolic complications.

Nimodipine and other calcium-channel blockers may be given prophylactically to minimize arterial vasospasm (which can result from direct catheter-induced irritation). In addition, calcium-channel blockers and nitroglycerin may be given intra-arterially during the procedure to treat focal arterial spasm. Intra-arterial papaverine is used to treat diffuse arterial spasm, such as that seen 7–10 days following subarachnoid bleeding.

Other vasoactive drugs are administered when there is a physiological need for decreased or increased perfusion pressure. The need to control perfusion pressure may be a result of altered inflow states, such as occurs following partial arteriovenous malformation (AVM) embolization prior to definitive second-stage embolization or surgery.

■ Endovascular Hemostasis

Endovascular hemostasis is performed to arrest life-threatening hemorrhage or, preoperatively, to decrease intraoperative hemorrhage from hypervascular lesions [1–3]. The majority of meningiomas are hypervascular and benefit from preoperative embolization. The traditional materials used for embolization include gelfoam and polyvinyl alcohol particles. The gelfoam particles are resorbed within 48 to 72 hours, and once they have led to intravascular thrombosis, there is a significant reduction in blood loss at surgical resection. The advantage of utilizing polyvinyl alcohol particles is that even if the entire tumor cannot be safely removed surgically, embolized portions of the tumor remain nonviable. The disadvantage of polyvinyl alcohol particles is the potential for accidental embolization of important anastomosing arterial branches or collateral vessels that may supply the retina or cranial nerves, resulting in loss of vision or stroke. Many collateral arterioles of the skull base and cranial nerves are under 100 microns in size, thus the chance of collateral and perforator vessel embolization may be decreased by using particle sizes greater than 100 microns.

Meticulous mapping of meningioma vessels allows evaluation of parasitized vessels that normally do not supply the intracranial circulation but are unusually prominent and have been recruited by angiogenetic factors elaborated by the meningioma. Traditionally, meningiomas are supplied by primary meningeal vessels such as middle meningeal artery branches from the external carotid circulation, periophthalmic meningeal collateral vessels, and posterior meningeal vessels from the vertebral circulation. Ordinarily, catheterization of these vessels is performed with microguidewire-directed microcatheters. Flow-directed catheters and liquid embolic materials may be utilized when there is significant intratumoral arteriovenous shunting or intratumoral fistula formation. We prefer that at least 72 hours elapse between preoperative embolization and surgical resection to promote maximal intravascular thrombosis and hemostasis.

Juvenile nasopharyngeal angiofibromas are hypervascular tumors arising in the posterior lateral nasopharynx, traditionally in adolescent males, and growing to large size with parasitization of the intracranial circulation. This may result in direct extension to the skull base and cranial vault. These tumors recur when large, and are extremely vascular. The concerns with preoperative embolization parallel those of meningiomas, although angiofibroma vascular supply is primarily nonmeningeal. The traditional vascular supply for juvenile nasopharyngeal angiofibromas also arises from the external carotid circulation, and the risk of accidentally embolizing perforating vessels that supply the cranial nerves of the skull base, as with meningiomas, may be diminished by injecting particles over 100 microns in size. These patients can occasionally present with tumor extending into the nasopharynx displacing the soft palate anteriorly and inferiorly, posing intubation and airway challenges. In spite of a greater than 50% reduction in surgical blood loss postembolization, these patients still average more than 1 liter of blood loss.

Following radiation therapy and surgery, many of these lesions recur with parasitization of intracranial circulation. When this occurs, the supplying vessels are usually very small and arise directly from the internal carotid artery. These vessels are small enough to preclude direct catheterization; therefore, hemostasis cannot be obtained with transcatheter therapies. Two alternate methodologies have been used. The first involves computed tomography (CT)-guided needle puncture of the nasopharyngeal angiofibroma with preoperative instillation of liquid adhesive into the angiofibroma. The second method places a balloon catheter in the internal carotid artery to temporarily occlude it above the origin of small perforator vessels. Into the static column of blood below the balloon a sclerosing agent (such as alcohol) is injected, which percolates through the small perforator vessels and results in small vessel thrombosis. The large-diameter internal carotid artery is not damaged due to dilution of the agent by the volume of contained blood. Following decompression of the balloon, the sclerosing agent dilutes further while traveling distally into the intracranial circulation.

■ High-flow Pathology

High-flow lesions can be divided into two types. The first type consists of abnormal direct connections at the dural compartmental level between arteries and veins [4–7]. The second type consists of high-flow AVMs of the brain (Figs 1A, 1B). These refer to networks of malformed arterial and venous vessels that result in rapid flow states with characteristic architectural and pathological features [8, 9].

Fistulas

Direct fistulas may be the result of high velocity deceleration injuries, typically associated with extensive midfacial and cranial fractures. Traditionally, the surgical repair of such lesions has been challenging for two reasons: the site of injury is difficult to access because it is at the skull base, and the injury has produced a high-flow situation that can result in

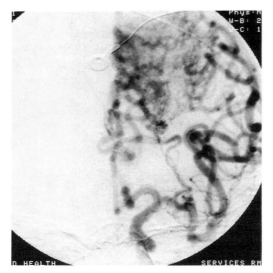

A

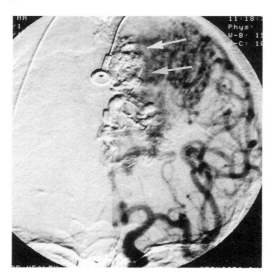

B

Fig 1. *(A) Frontal projection of a left internal carotid artery injection demonstrates dense vascular enhancement in the superior portion of the left supratentorial cerebral hemisphere due to the presence of a high-flow arteriovenous malformation. (B) post-embolization corresponding frontal digitally subtracted projection now shows "ghosted" adhesive material in the medial left frontal lobe (straight white arrows), corresponding with the site of adhesive cyanoacrylate embolization.*

significant blood loss during surgery. In lesions such as carotid-cavernous fistulas, a detachable balloon is partially inflated in the internal carotid artery at the rent, and the balloon is quickly and selectively pushed through the rent into the cavernous sinus, where it may be filled with a semisolid hydroxymethacrylate solution and then deployed. By placing an appropriate number of balloons within the cavernous sinus, the high-flow fistula can be closed. A similar approach is utilized when closing direct dural fistulas elsewhere in the meningeal circulation. This may be performed with detachable balloons, glue, or metallic coils incorporating either thrombogenic substances or Dacron fibers.

With dural fistulas, symptoms are due to passive congestion of the normal venous limb codrained by the fistulized vein. For example, carotid-cavernous fistulas may produce elevated venous pressure in the periophthalmic circulation producing glaucoma, since the normal intraocular circulation drains to the orbital venous system. Additionally, there may be transmission of venous pressure to the cortical draining veins, affecting cerebral circulation and producing altered mentation or venous hemorrhages.

Treatment of indirect dural fistulas is different than that of direct dural fistulas: rather than a single or small group of high-flow vessels, there is a cloud of small vessels directly supplying dural veins. Indirect carotid-cavernous fistulas occur with proliferation of skull base and meningeal artery branches directly feeding the hyperemic cavernous sinus. These small vessels require particulate substances for embolization. A dural component arising from the external carotid circulation can be embolized in the absence of a direct intracranial parenchymal or orbital/periorbital retinal supplies. Unfortunately, many examples of this specific pathology are found with vessels arising from the internal carotid artery, similar to post-radiation recurrent juvenile nasopharyngeal angiofibromas.

Often, with direct and indirect carotid-cavernous fistulas, there is a need for repeated embolization. Immediately following treatment, there may also be slight aggravation of the baseline symptoms, including temporarily augmented proptosis. As first-line treatment of indirect carotid-cavernous fistulas, most individuals advocate intermittent compression of the common carotid artery. This is performed as graded compressions for a duration of 15–30 seconds, 2–4 times per hour while the patient is awake. Compression is performed only by the patient, using the arm contralateral to the side of the fistula, so that in case hemispheric ischemia develops, the contralateral arm (which is controlled by the fistula-side hemisphere) develops weakness and releases compression before a frank infarct develops. The intention is to decrease flow in the common carotid artery, allowing propagation of thrombi in the abnormal small fistula supplying vessels. If conservative compression therapy is unsuccessful after 4 weeks, transarterial therapy is recommended. If transarterial therapy is unsuccessful, often retrograde transvenous therapy is necessary. In this case, coils are often employed to decrease the outflow from direct and indirect fistulas, thereby resulting in decreased inflow through the arterial supply. Unfortunately, venous-side occlusion may result in transient elevated pressures at the arterial and fistula sites, aggravating symptoms.

Arteriovenous Malformations

High-flow arteriovenous malformations are groups of abnormal connections between arteries and veins in the brain parenchyma (see Figs 1A, 1B). These malformations may grow to remarkable size, consuming much of a hemisphere. Patients with high-flow AVMs present with seizures, focal motor deficits, or hemorrhage. The seizures and focal motor deficits are partially attributed to "steal" phenomena, in which blood designated for a normal portion of the brain is "stolen" by low resistance AVM vessels that divert the blood supply. Many architectural features of AVMs have been correlated with the probability of hemorrhage and steal in order to identify patients at greater risk for hemorrhage and, consequently, in need of more expedient treatment. Such features include size of the AVM, paraventricular location, number and length of feeding and draining pedicles, and peripheral or central hemispheric location.

At our institution, many of these embolizations are performed with flow-directed catheters selectively pulled into high-flow pedicles, where liquid adhesives may be used to fill branches embolizing the AVM. Approximately 10% of AVMs that we have treated have been completely embolized. These procedures are ordinarily performed for preoperative hemostasis, although with increased utilization of microcatheters and increasing expertise in the use of liquid embolic agents, independent cures have been achieved. Embolization is considered an adjunctive modality for radiation and/or traditional surgical treatment of high-flow AVMs.

AVMs are fed by a myriad of abnormally dilated blood vessels, thus embolization of a single pedicle results in complex rerouting of blood through the remaining patent AVM compartments. This altered routing may result in transient increases in AVM compartment pressure. To diminish the risk of normal perfusion pressure breakthrough hemorrhage in portions of the AVM unaccustomed to the transient increases in flow normally seen following embolization, we embolize no more than 30% of the AVM volume during each embolization. We also separate embolic sessions by at least 1 week to allow the AVM and surrounding vascular bed to restore autoregulation. This approach cannot be followed when less than 3 feeding pedicles supply a single AVM. In these instances, attempts are occasionally made for complete single session cure. Cure is defined as the point at which early venous drainage from the AVM is no longer evident when compared with the normal surrounding parenchyma.

Transient elevations in blood pressure may be helpful in guiding the distal placement of flow-directed catheters. These pressure manipulations must be performed in a controlled manner to minimize the risk of hemorrhage. Following embolic therapy, induced hypotension is used to promote propagation of thrombus within the AVM, minimize the increased blood supply to unembolized parts of the AVM, and theoretically decrease the risk of breakthrough hemorrhage.

■ Ischemic Disease

Selective intra-arterial thrombolysis (Figs 2A, 2B) is performed with a variety of agents. For greatest success, the shortest possible time should elapse between onset of ischemic symptoms and intra-arterial thrombolytic administration [10–13]. Optimally, thrombolytics should be used within 6 hours following a defined event, although less than 4 hours is considered significantly more advantageous. With longer intervals, thrombolysis may convert a small bland infarct into a large hemorrhagic stroke by injuring a weakened vasculature. Before intra-arterial administration of thrombolytic agents, it is important to demonstrate that the infarct is ischemic and not hemorrhagic. This is ordinarily performed with a CT examination.

The first step in thrombolysis is systemic anticoagulation. Femoral arterial catheterization is performed with a micropuncture technique to minimize the risk of life-threatening retroperitoneal hemorrhage. The two most commonly used substances for intra-arterial thrombolysis are urokinase and tissue plasminogen activator. In the cerebrovascular circulation, prolonged treatment times are not possible due to the need for rapid thrombolysis. This need exists because cerebrovascular circulation must be restored to arrest continuing breakdown of the blood-brain barrier.

Intra-arterial thrombolytic agents are administered through microcatheters. Two schools of thought exist regarding microcatheter placement. The first believes that initial perforation of the clot with the microcatheter allows distal perfusion even if thrombolysis is prematurely terminated due to unforeseen complications. The second school of thought believes that clot perforation allows distal egress of the concentrated thrombolytic agent, which would be better utilized if kept in a static pool as close to the clot as possible. Perfusion catheters have been created that have multiple side holes and are otherwise identical to microcatheters. These perfusion microcatheters lace a linear internal portion of the clot with the thrombolytic administrated through the central catheter bore. Problems are encountered when addressing long clots. One may successfully thrombolyse the proximal clot, only to find the distal portion remaining. When the distal clot is lysed, proximal reclotting occurs. This may produce a back-and-forth thrombolysis while distal branch thrombi propagate, resulting in an unsuccessful outcome.

If an underlying atherosclerotic stenosis is found at the time of thrombolysis, definitive correction is delayed until the patient can recover from

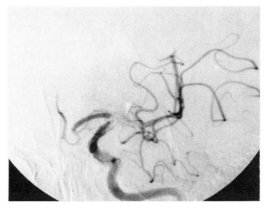

A

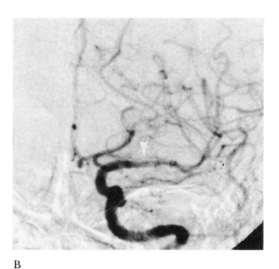

B

Fig 2. *(A) Frontal projection of the left internal carotid artery injection demonstrates a region of nonopacification in the proximal left middle cerebral artery (MCA) distribution. This represents thrombotic occlusion (white arrowhead), although there is distal MCA branch filling. (B) On similar projection, continuous column opacification of the previously thrombosed area (white arrowhead) is demonstrated following intraarterial tissue plasminogen activator instillation.*

the primary ischemic insult, and in the meantime, the patient is kept on full systemic anticoagulation. Significant morbidity and mortality are associated with therapeutic angioplasty of intracranial and craniocerebral vessels, thus angioplasty is usually reserved for patients that have failed conventional anticoagulation therapy. Additional functional studies may be performed to evaluate circulatory reserve. These studies include single photon emission CT, positron emission tomographic, and xenon CT examinations. These examinations may be performed before and after pressure challenges (including acetazolamide administration) to allow evaluation of vascular reserve in a challenged state. If there is evidence of poor cerebrovascular reserve, this may provide additional support for angioplasty or surgery for focal stenotic cerebrovascular lesions.

Intracranial angioplasty (Figs 3A, 3B) was first performed with soft silicone balloons inflated at low pressures to dilate vasospastic arteries following subarachnoid hemorrhage [14]. Microballoons were subsequently developed for intracranial high-pressure angioplasty applications, and balloons of various widths and diameters were designed for specific intracranial applications [15–17]. These balloons are guidewire directed and may be either single lumen (with occluding valve wires) or double lumen, with a secondary lumen used for balloon inflation and deflation. Unlike blood vessels of equivalent diameter elsewhere in the body, intracranial blood vessels lack an outer elastic lamina and may be more prone to lower pressure rupture. Not only are lower pressures utilized for intracranial angioplasty (<6 atm) when compared with extracranial angioplasty (up to 12 atm), but also overdilatation is not intentionally performed. Meticulous stenosis size measurements are performed, and ordinarily no more than two dilatations at each balloon size is performed. The goal is to increase the area of narrowing to greater than 60% of the native luminal diameter. Following these procedures, antiplatelet agents are used to decrease the risk of restenosis and thrombosis. Immediate procedural complications include dissection, rupture, thrombosis, and embolization.

When vessels are refractory to angioplasty, or when there is rapid restenosis, stent placement is a therapeutic alternative [18]. Two broad categories of intravascular stents exist: self-expanding stents, which assume a native conformation once deployed from their preloaded catheters, and balloon expanding stents, which are deformable and are expanded into place using a balloon-tipped catheter. The former stents are more difficult to place due to their less flexible placement catheters, while the latter type stent has the disadvantage of crimping and deforming if it is in a region in which outside compressive influences or mechanical impingements exist. Stents have found a variety of applications at the vertebral artery origin (Figs 4A, 4B), internal carotid artery origin, and in the central venous sinuses. Stents of sufficient flexibility and diameter for intracranial placement above the tortuous cervical vertebral artery or carotid siphon have yet to be designed. Stents have been successfully utilized with dissecting

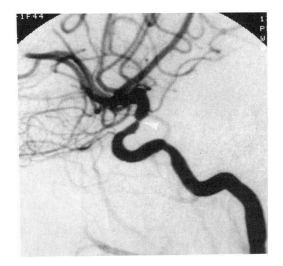

A

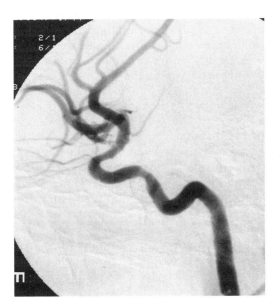

B

Fig 3. *(A) Lateral projection of a left internal carotid artery injection demonstrates a focal stenosis in the supraclinoid internal carotid artery (white arrowhead). (B) Corresponding postangioplasty image no longer demonstrates the previously seen focal stenosis.*

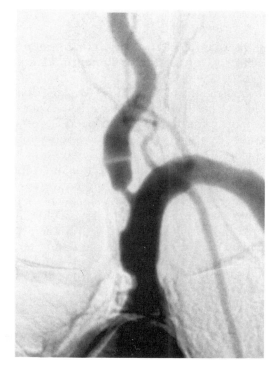

A

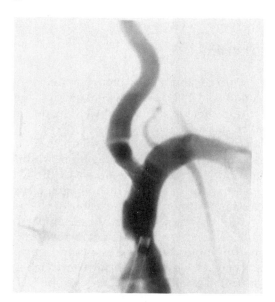

B

Fig 4. *(A) A focal stenosis is demonstrated at the origin of the left vertebral artery. (B) Postangioplasty and stenting, image demonstrates lattice-like structure transgressing the area previously showing focal stenosis.*

hematomas of the internal carotid artery. Here, intraluminal hemorrhage can cause encroachment on the native lumen, and may also create an embolic pocket.

Stent design modifications have been performed. Coatings and linings have been attached to stent frames. We have had experience placing two types of covered stents. The first type, an open-ended covered stent, is placed to reconstruct an artery with a pseudo-aneurysm. We have placed the second type of closed-ended covered stent in cases in which permanent artery occlusion is sought. If the distal aspect of the stent cover is closed, similar to a sock, expanding the stent in the native vessel allows abrupt and permanent feeding vessel occlusion. A similar maneuver may be performed with multiple coils or detachable balloons, although the occluding stent is more abrupt and less dependent on thrombic propagation.

Stents are permanent implanted devices and long-term concerns exist regarding their placement. The concerns deal with intimal hyperplasia with restenosis, incidence of distal stenosis beyond the stent location, and potential consequences of distal circulation microemboli. Elsewhere in the body, microemboli may result in minimal or no symptoms; however, in the cerebral circulation, small microemboli may result in potentially devastating complications. This issue has not yet been definitively addressed. At our institution, we place patients on antiplatelet agents following stent placement.

■ Aneurysm Therapy

Both acutely ruptured and stable aneurysms have been treated with endovascular techniques [19–24]. Aneurysm therapy centers on decreasing the pressure within the aneurysm, and thereby decreasing the chance of aneurysm rupture or further hemorrhage.

Aneurysms can be filled with substances that prevent blood from entering them or that allow thrombus propagation within the aneurysm. Thrombus propagation is promoted in two ways: the first is exposure of blood within the aneurysm to a large thrombogenic surface area, while the second involves interruption and alteration of intra-aneurysmal flow causing static flow eddies. Aneurysm filling has been performed in the past with detachable balloons and is currently performed with coils. The most promising advance for minimizing risk of inadvertent extra-aneurysmal coil migration has been the development of controllable microcoils. Two broad types of controllable coils have been developed. The first type is a mechanically detachable coil design, including such design elements as interlocking cylinders, balls, and springs attached to the controlled coil [22]. The second type of detachable coil includes an electrolytically detach-

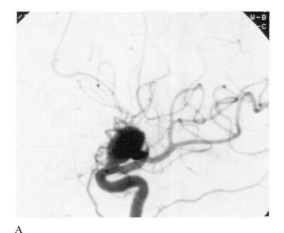

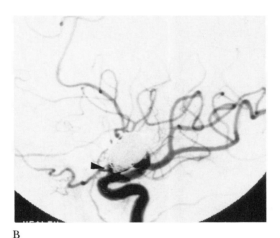

Fig 5. *(A) Lateral projection shows an ophthalmic-region giant aneurysm arising from the supraclinoid internal carotid artery. (B) Following placement of Guglielmi detachable coils (Target Inc., Fremont, CA), opacification of the aneurysm body is no longer appreciated, although there is residual opacification of the aneurysm neck (white arrowhead).*

able active portion (Figs 5A, 5B) that allows the ability to place the entire coil mass within the aneurysm prior to electrolytic detachment [23, 24].

Endovascular aneurysm therapy requires meticulous evaluation of the aneurysm's architectural characteristics. Foreign substances placed within the aneurysm for propagation of thrombus clearly depend on the ability of the substance to remain within the aneurysm lumen and not drift out of or protrude from the aneurysm into the parent vessel. Ordinarily this implies that the aneurysm neck must be narrow relative to aneurysm fundal width, therefore fusiform, or wide-neck, aneurysms cannot be successfully treated with these techniques.

Wide-neck aneurysms may be treated with alternative approaches. If there is supplemental flow into the parent vessel from a location more distal than the aneurysm origin, occlusion of the proximal parent vessel may be performed with preservation of distal branch flow through collateral supply. Such "protected vessel sacrifice" may be performed in many instances in which there is potentially duplicated circulation to a region that is also fed by a diseased vessel; the diseased vessel may be sacrificed without resultant vascular supply ischemia. With feeding-vessel aneurysm therapy, the decreased aneurysm pressure and flow allows for slow and gradual aneurysm thrombosis. Future techniques may include covered stents placed across the aneurysm neck in order to reconstruct the parent vessel; however, there is the risk of inadvertently occluding essential feeding vessels that may arise from the aneurysm neck region.

■ Monitoring

Neurophysiological monitoring can help predict and avoid neurological deficits resulting from vessel occlusion. The need for such monitoring is greatest in the setting of deliberate vessel occlusion, as in the embolization of tumors, AVMs, or fistulas. Additionally, such techniques are valuable when the parent vessel must be sacrificed, as with giant or surgically inaccessible aneurysms. Some neurointerventional procedures are conducted with only mild sedation, and repeated clinical examinations minimize the need for neurophysiological monitoring. Certain patients will require general anesthesia, however, and neurophysiological monitoring can be helpful in directing therapy in the unconscious patient.

A wide variety of noninvasive monitoring techniques are available and are discussed in the chapter by Lopez. The goal of this monitoring is to define vessels that are safe to embolize, realizing that a significant amount of the blood supply to a region may come from perforating vessels that are below angiographic resolution.

Two techniques have been particularly useful, the somatosensory evoked potential (SSEP) [25] and the electroencephalogram [26–28]. The use of SSEP monitoring in the angiographic suite provides additional information when selecting vessels for embolization. It is a useful tool, especially when correlated with clinical examination.

Electroencephalography is useful for predicting cerebral ischemia and tolerance to permanent vessel occlusion during neurointerventional procedures [26–28]. It is often used at the time of balloon test occlusion, in conjunction with pharmacological provocation and clinical examination. Its overall specificity and sensitivity have yet to be documented in neuroendovascular procedures. Although, like SSEP monitoring, it offers another physiological measure of cerebral tolerance to intervention.

■ Conclusion

The explosion of technology that has resulted in successful transvascular treatment of life-threatening cerebrovascular pathology is a result of strong interdisciplinary cooperation. This cooperation allows appropriate patient selection, meticulous intraprocedural monitoring and therapy, and judicious multimodality postprocedure follow-up and care. Without the benefit of this cross-pollination and teamwork, including radiology, neurointensive care, neurosurgery, and neuroanesthesia, many if not most of the developments discussed in this chapter would not be possible.

■ References

1. Valvanis A. Preoperative embolization of the head and neck: indications, patient selection, goals and precautions. AJNR 1986;7:943–952
2. Manelfe C, Lasjaunias P, Ruscalleda J. Preoperative embolization of intracranial meningiomas. AJNR 1986;7:963–972
3. Davis KR, Debrun GM. Embolization of juvenile nasopharyngeal angiofibromas. Semin Intervent Radiol 1987;4:309–320
4. Vinuela F, Fox AJ, Debrun GM, et al. Spontaneous carotid-cavernous fistulas; clinical, radiological, and therapeutic considerations. J Neurosurg 1984;60:976–984
5. Halbach W, Higashida RT, Hieshima GB, et al. Transvenous embolization of dural fistulas involving the transverse and sigmoid sinuses. AJNR 1989;10:385–392
6. Halbach W, Higashida RT, Hieshima GB, et al. Dural fistulas involving the cavernous sinus: results of treatment in 30 patients. Radiology 1987;163:437–442
7. Picard L, Bracard S, Mallet J, et al. Spontaneous dural arteriovenous fistulas. Semin Intervent Radiol 1987;4:219–240
8. Marks MP, Lane B, Steinberg GK, Chang PJ. Hemorrhage in intracerebral arteriovenous malformations: angiographic determinants. Radiology 1990;176:807–813
9. Marks MP, Lane B, Steinberg GK, Chang PJ. Vascular characteristics of intracerebral arteriovenous malformations in patients with clinical steal. AJNR 1991;12:489–496
10. Zeumer H, Freitag HJ, Grzyska U, Neunzig HP. Local intraarterial fibrinolysis in acute vertebrobasilar occlusion: technical developments and recent results. Neuroradiology 1989;31:336–340
11. Zeumer H, Hundgren R, Ferbert A, Ringelstein EB. Local intraarterial fibrinolytic therapy in inaccessible internal carotid occlusion. Neuroradiology 1984;26:315–317
12. Barnwell SL, Clark WM, Nguyen TT, et al. Safety and efficacy of delayed intraarterial urokinase therapy with mechanical clot disruption for thromboembolic stroke. AJNR 1994;15:1817–1822
13. Mori E, Tabuchi M, Yoshida T, Yamadori A. Intracarotid urokinase with thromboembolic occlusion of the middle cerebral artery. Stroke 1988;19:802–812

14. Newell DW, Eskridge JM, Mayberg MR, et al. Angioplasty for the treatment of symptomatic vasospasm following subarachnoid hemorrhage. J Neurosurg 1989; 71(Part 1):654–660
15. Brown MM, Butler P, Gibbs J, et al. Feasibility of percutaneous transluminal angioplasty for carotid artery stenosis. J Neurol Neurosurg Psychiatry 1990;53:238–243
16. Higashida RT, Tsai FY, Halbach VV, et al. Transluminal angioplasty for atherosclerotic disease of the vertebral and basilar arteries. J Neurosurg 1993;78:192–198
17. Kachel R, Endert G, Basche S, et al. Percutaneous transluminal angioplasty (dilatation) of carotid, vertebral, and innominate artery stenoses. Cardiovasc Intervent Radiol 1987;10:142–146
18. Marks MP, Dake MD, Steinberg GK, et al. Stent placement for arterial and venous cerebrovascular disease: preliminary experience. Radiology 1994;191:441–446
19. Weir B. Intracranial aneurysms and subarachnoid hemorrhage: an overview. In Wilkins RH, Rengachary SS, eds. Neurosurgery. New York: McGraw-Hill, 1985: 1308–1329
20. Debrun G, Fox AJ, Drake C, et al. Giant unclippable aneurysms: treatment with detachable balloons. AJNR 1981;2:167–173
21. Fox AJ, Vinuela F, Pelz DM, et al. Use of detachable balloons for proximal artery occlusion in the treatment of unclippable cerebral aneurysms. J Neurosurg 1987; 66:40–46
22. Marks MP, Chee H, Lidell RP, et al. A mechanically detachable coil for the treatment of aneurysms and occlusion of blood vessels. AJNR 1994;15:821–827
23. Guglielmi G, Vinuela F, Dion J, Duckwiler G. Electrothrombosis of saccular aneurysms via endovascular approach. Part 2: preliminary clinical experience. J Neurosurg 1991;75:8–14
24. Gugliemi G, Vinuela F, Duckwiler G, et al. Endovascular treatment of posterior circulation aneurysms by electrothrombosis using electrically detachable coils. J Neurosurg 1992;77:515–524
25. Misulis KE. Evoked potentials. In: Essentials of clinical neurophysiology. Boston: Butterworth-Heinemann, 1993:219–234, 245–264
26. Sharbrough FW, Messick JM Jr, Sundt TM Jr. Correlation of continuous electroencephalograms with cerebral blood flow measurements during carotid endarterectomy. Stroke 1973;4:674–683
27. Sundt TM, Sharbrough FW, Piepgras DG, et al. Correlation of cerebral blood flow and electroencephalographic changes during carotid endarterectomy, with results of surgery and hemodynamics of cerebral ischemia. Mayo Clin Proc 1981;56: 533–543
28. Astrup J, Siesjo BK, Simon L. Thresholds in cerebral ischemia—the ischemic penumbra. Stroke 1981;12:723–725

Postoperative Pain Management in the Neurosurgical Patient

■■■■■■■ Michael J. Cousins, AM, MD, FANZCA
■■■■■■■ Hamed S. Umedaly, MD, FRCPC

The postoperative neurosurgical patient presents a challenging pain management problem. Pain is common in these critically ill patients [1] and has often been undertreated for fear of masking recognition of surgical pathology and of depressing ventilation.

Untreated pain is associated with a physiological and neuroendocrine stress response [2] that may have particular deleterious effects on postoperative outcome, especially in patients with coexisting disease [3]. Although tremendous progress has been made in neurosurgical anesthesia [4], little effort has been invested in postoperative pain management [5]. Pain management regimens are often based on attitudes and biases developed early in the medical education of doctors and nurses. For example, intramuscular fixed-dose codeine remains a common, albeit irrational, approach to analgesia. It is important to understand that the effective treatment of pain may be associated with an improved safety profile, decreased morbidity, and thus lowered cost [3].

Significant advances have been made in the understanding of the processing and modulation of pain from the periphery, the afferent neurons, spinal cord, and brain, and many new analgesic agents and modalities have been developed. However, little has changed, with these advances still awaiting application in neurosurgical patients.

This chapter will focus on the potential effectiveness of existing pain assessment methods and management modalities. Ineffective analgesia is more likely related to shortcomings in assessment and in the manner in which analgesics are used, rather than to properties of specific agents [6]. A targeted review of exciting developments in pathophysiology and in pharmacology will be discussed to stimulate the reader to consider the problem of neglected pain management in the neurosurgical patient and to inspire creative strategies to prevent and control postoperative pain.

179

■ Causes of Undertreatment of Pain

Inadequate pain assessment and formulation of a poorly defined treatment plan are significant barriers to effective postoperative pain relief. Pain scoring systems should have a specially reserved place on the patient chart along with the vital signs and neurological status and should be as routine as the recording of heart rate, blood pressure, and temperature. Moreover, the response to the therapeutic intervention should be assessed; yet, in current practice, often no measurement of adequacy of pain control is made. Simple verbal or visual analogue pain scales are recommended, however, they are not entirely reliable.

Assessment of postoperative pain may be difficult due to a multiplicity of surgical and medical causes compounded by postoperative neuropsychologic impairment that compromises cooperation. However, simplified questions and observations are valuable when used with appropriate caution [7]. Agitation, restlessness, hypertension, and tachycardia all have multiple etiologies that must be considered but may be simply a manifestation of pain.

Neurosurgical patients, especially postcraniotomy patients, are usually monitored in critical care environments that allow close monitoring of responses to analgesic regimens. However, conventional therapy of prescribing intermittent doses of analgesics in response to patient demands is often ineffective and is recognized as suboptimal management for a number of reasons: the patient may not request it, the bedside clinician may not administer it, and the dose and interval may not be appropriate. This results in uneven blood concentrations, and undertreated pain, possibly alternating with excessive and unpredictable periods of sedation, respiratory depression, and other side effects [8].

■ Consequences of Undertreated Pain

Pain and its physiological and psychological consequences are difficult to define, measure, and validate. However, pain-related pathophysiology may be associated with increased morbidity, mortality, and costs of care [3]. Multiple stressors such as injury, hemorrhage, pain, and anxiety may contribute to the neuroendocrine and humoral response [9]. The concepts of plasticity, sensitization, and control have replaced the hardwired models of nociceptive transmission [10]. Afferent nociceptive traffic may be amplified at peripheral sites by various inflammatory mediators and cytokines and at central sites by physiological processes involving neurotransmitters, receptors, and postreceptor messengers, including gene regulation [10]. These complex peripheral and central sensitization processes outlast the injury and together produce a state of postinjury hyperresponsiveness.

This hyperresponsiveness amplifies the stress response and makes effective pain management difficult [10].

The effects of pain, compounded by the sensitization process, produce significant untoward effects on organ systems. Moreover, these effects may increase morbidity as a result of changes in intracranial pressure (ICP) and hemostasis; this is particularly apparent in patients with coexisting disease who lack physiological reserve [11].

The effects of stress include an increased sympathetic response, resulting in hypertension and tachycardia that may produce an inequity in myocardial oxygen demand and supply in patients potentially at risk for myocardial ischemia and infarction. These hemodynamic changes may also produce increased intracranial pressure, particularly if cerebral autoregulation is compromised. Also, hypertension increases the risk of hemorrhage and rebleeding from vascular anastomotic sites. Pain may be a source of anxiety and the development of delirium and acute psychosis, which exposes the patient to risks of direct and indirect injury [11]. The respiratory effects of stress may produce shunt and hypoxemia, with the potential for cerebral hypoxia [12]. Sodium and water retention caused by increased activity in the renin-angiotensin aldosterone axis, hypothalamic stimulation, and catabolic hormone secretion may produce unfavorable intracranial fluid shifts.

Hyperglycemia, a further result of the stress catabolic cascade, has also been shown to be associated with risk of cerebral injury following ischemia [13]. Untreated pain is also associated with a hypercoagulable state and a reduced fibrinolytic system, predisposing neurosurgical patients to further risk of thromboembolic complications [14]. Finally, undertreated pain may expose the patient to the risk of development of persistent postoperative pain [15].

There is significant controversy as to whether it is possible to eliminate the stress response and the degree of pain relief required [2]. Although it appears that effective analgesia may not eliminate subtle measures of stress response, analgesia at least blunts the major organ system responses to pain [9].

■ Methods and Rationale for Analgesic Delivery

Regional Analgesia

Neurosurgeons were leaders in advocating the use of regional anesthesia and analgesia for craniotomy. Indeed, neurosurgeons were the majority group in the American Society of Regional Anesthesia, first formed by Gaston Labat.

Wound infiltration for operative analgesia may decrease the need for general anesthesia, may potentially provide quicker recovery times [16], and may decrease the need for postoperative opioids. Is it possible to improve the effectiveness of local anesthetics? Although controversial, some studies [16] suggest improved postoperative analgesia by the pre-emptive use of local anesthesia. Certainly bupivacaine [17] produces longer-lasting analgesia than lidocaine. Top-up wound infiltration at the end of a long craniotomy would also likely provide enhanced postoperative analgesia. Development is proceeding on sustained-release bupivacaine from polymer microspores [18]. This modality has the potential to extend analgesia further into the postoperative period.

Ropivacaine, a newly launched enantioselective local anesthetic, has possibly lower cardiotoxicity than bupivacaine [17]. There is no advantage, in duration or toxicity, in adding epinephrine. Ropivacaine may become the local anesthetic of choice for wound infiltration because of its enhanced safety and similar local anesthetic properties to bupivacaine.

Regional blockade may be used for surgical procedures in the head and neck. Although extensively used in the past for operative anesthesia, its use has waned with the advent of safer general anesthesia with endotracheal intubation. However, a resurrection of regional techniques for postoperative analgesia may be prudent. Potential blocks for craniotomy include circumferential scalp infiltration, greater and lesser occipital nerve block, and auriculotemporal, trigeminal ganglion and trigeminal divisions, and superficial cervical plexus blocks [19]. Postoperative analgesia for neck incisions, including carotid endarterectomy and cervical decompressive surgery, may be enhanced by superficial cervical plexus blockade [19]. Although, not the scope of this chapter, the reader is referred to regional anesthesia sources, including Murphy [19] and Scott [20].

Opioids

Opioids continue to play a key role in the provision of postoperative analgesia. Pharmacokinetic advances have enhanced the understanding of drug effects, including concepts such as effect-site concentration and context-specific half life [21]. Significant progress has occurred in the development of more potent and shorter-acting opioids [22] as well as novel modes of delivery [23]. The traditional "as required" intramuscular techniques are being replaced by these more complex modes of delivery and appear to provide improved analgesia and patient satisfaction with potential for improved outcome. This trend has not occurred in neurosurgery, probably due to concerns of the potential untoward effects.

Despite trends toward the use of potent opioids and total intravenous anesthesia, there appears to be a barrier to their rational use in neurosurgical patients in the postoperative period. As discussed above, patients monitored in critical care areas are ideal for intensive approaches to analgesia. However, it has been suggested that opioids under certain circumstances may increase intracranial pressure [24]. This effect of opiate analgesic agents is not irrelevant, but rather constitutes one factor among many involved in intracranial pathophysiology. Certainly, intracranial pressure considerations remain foremost in patients with ICP-related cerebral ischemia and obtundation caused by severe head injury or the mass effects of hemorrhage or tumor. However, these considerations are often generalized to all neurosurgical patients and sometimes even to those with no intracranial pathology.

Despite inconsistencies in the literature, it appears that opioids have very little effect on cerebral blood flow (CBF) and cerebral metabolic rate (CMR) in the normal unstimulated nervous system [24]. Most studies involve the concomitant use of other agents that affect arousal; therefore, the specific properties of opioids are difficult to delineate.

High-dose morphine (1 mg/kg) produces no effect on CBF and a 40% reduction in CMR for oxygen [25]. This effect on CMR is absent in the presence of nitrous oxide. No studies of the effect on ICP are available; however, autoregulation appears to remain intact in the normal range. Fentanyl appears to produce minimal changes in CBF and CMR for oxygen [26] and no effect on autoregulation and CO_2 responsiveness [23]. Alfentanil and sufentanil have been studied extensively with regards to their effects on CBF, CMR for oxygen, and ICP. There is some evidence that the increased ICP and decreased cerebral perfusion pressure that occurs when large bolus doses are given may represent a normal autoregulatory response to the sudden reduction in mean arterial pressure [27].

Overall, the considerable advantages of opioids in neuroanesthesia, including the promotion of systemic and cerebrovascular stability, should extrapolate to advantages in the postoperative period, in which much lower doses can be used and rapid boluses can be avoided [23].

The effects of opioids on pupil size are well known and precipitate concern regarding interference with the neurological examination. The effect produced by stimulation of the Edinger-Westphal nucleus in the midbrain is related to opioid plasma level, and equianalgesic concentrations produce similar effects on pupil size [28].

Respiratory depression is another unwanted effect. All mu-receptor agonists depress respiration, produce a right shift in the CO_2 response curve, and blunt the hypoxic drive for ventilation. However, these effects are dose-site and effector-site–concentration dependent, mediated by the mu_2 receptor in the medullary respiratory center. Equianalgesic concentrations produce equal respiratory depressant effects [29]. Therefore, the advantages of specific opioid agonists depend on their pharmacokinetic characteristics. For example, minimal changes in arterial CO_2 tension ($PaCO_2$) were seen with alfentanil infusion for postoperative pain [30]. Tramadol, an atypical opioid available in Europe, may have clinical potential due to its mixed effects on mu receptors and its inhibition of reuptake of serotonin and norepinephrine, thereby producing less sedation and, since the opioid effect is less than with pure mu agonists, less respiratory depression [31].

Codeine is considered a weak opioid and is associated with considerable nausea and vomiting. Ventilatory depression may occur late. Codeine (methylmorphine) is a pro-drug metabolized to morphine by o-demethylation. This process is essential for its analgesic effect and is catalyzed by a genetic polymorphic enzyme, cytochrome P-450 IID6 (CYP2D6) [32]. Two major genotypic forms of this enzyme exist rendering patients phenotypically extensive metabolizers (em) or poor metabolizers (pm). Approximately 8% of the Caucasian population are poor metabolizers and thus have no analgesic response to codeine [32]. Coadministration of several antiarrhythmics (e.g., quinidine) and antidepressants (e.g., fluoxetine), also potent inhibitors of CYP2D6, result in conversion from an em to pm, a process called phenocopying, thereby further decreasing the population of patients with a potential therapeutic effect from codeine [33]. Absorption by the intramuscular route is variable with up to a fivefold difference in peak blood levels, with time to peak at approximately 30–60 minutes. Plasma elimination half life is approximately $3\frac{1}{2}$ hours [34]. Using a patient-controlled paradigm for codeine administration, a ninefold variation in minimum effective analgesic concentration was observed, while a portion of patients experienced no analgesic effect of codeine. A sixfold variation in effective dose was found [34]. Thus, codeine by the intramuscular route is an unpredictable pro-drug with variable metabolism to an active drug. This does not equate to a safe, effective method of providing analgesia in the postoperative period.

■ Routes of Systemic Opioid Administration

The intramuscular route involves the deposition of a bolus into tissue followed by absorption and redistribution according to regional blood flow. The intravenous route is preferable with continuous infusion to avoid wide swings in drug concentration [35]. Rational use involves titrated frontloading followed by a maintenance infusion with monitoring of effects and appropriate adjustment to maintain the minimum effective analgesic concentration. Suboptimal analgesia requires retitration and adjustment of the infusion rather than just adjustment of the infusion, as this will cause delayed (4–5 half lives) effects with the potential for delayed respiratory depression and sedation [35]. Accumulation potentially can occur with resultant adverse effect, therefore, close monitoring is essential. Very effective nurse-controlled infusion rivaling patient-controlled analgesia (PCA) has been shown [36]. Continuous alfentanil infusion for pelvic surgery [37] showed effective analgesia and only transient elevation of arterial CO_2 associated with initial bolus administration. Short-acting opioids like remifentanil should be ideal for infusion and will be discussed later.

Patient-controlled analgesia involves the self-controlled administration of small boli of opioids when pain is experienced. It was conceived and designed to minimize the effects of interpatient pharmacokinetic and pharmacodynamic variability [38]. It is based on the concept that a negative feedback loop exists (and is intact) such that when pain is experienced analgesia will be demanded and when pain is reduced the demand will cease. It appears that quality of analgesia is superior and patient satisfaction is higher than with traditional intramuscular use. However, the absence of an intact feedback loop such as in the early postoperative period may become a liability. It is also evident that patients may use PCA to some other endpoint and may tolerate considerable pain. The safety of PCA appears to be comparable to intramuscular opioids; factors associated with respiratory depression include advanced age, concurrent background infusion, sedative medication, and pre-existing obstructive sleep apnea syndrome [39–41]. PCA may have a role only in selected postcraniotomy patients and only with appropriate adjustment of the dosage, but there is a larger role in noncraniotomy postoperative pain management.

Computer-assisted continuous infusion, or target-controlled infusion, has undergone significant development in the operative environment. Although there is limited experience, it may be logical to extend this technique with appropriate modification into the postoperative period for analgesia. These systems use a computer program incorporating a pharmacokinetic model to control an infusion pump to maintain a selected effect-site concentration. Excellent results were obtained using alfentanil for aortic surgery [42] and major orthopedic surgery [43], providing effective and safe analgesia.

Passive transdermal fentanyl has shown to be effective for postoperative pain; however, its use is limited due to slow absorption, prolonged time to reach steady state, and prolonged effects caused by cutaneous deposition of the drug [44]. An active titratable device, utilizing a battery-powered iontophoretic transdermal application of fentanyl is undergoing development and may have significant advantages with respect to rapid production of analgesic plasma concentrations [45], rapid decrease in plasma concentration with no depo effect after cessation of the current, and extreme portability, allowing mobilization where appropriate.

■ Remifentanil

An interesting development in opioids has been a new synthetic opioid, remifentanil. It contains an ester linkage allowing inactivation by blood and tissue esterases [46]. This results in a very short half life of 9–10 minutes and a small volume of distribution. This pharmacokinetic profile describes a drug that can be given by constant rate infusion with the advantage of rapid up titration and rapid down titration effects. The context specific half life, defined as "the time required for a 50 percent reduction in effect site concentration," is short (in the range of 3–4 minutes), a constant over time, and constant over a 15-fold variation in effect-site concentration [47].

Thus, remifentanil may be the ideal opioid analgesic when given by an intravenous infusion to patients in whom effective analgesia needs to be balanced by the necessity for constant neurological monitoring. Its pharmacokinetic properties make it a titratable drug, forgiving of under- and overdose. Target-controlled infusion pumps are probably of no further benefit given remifentanil's predictable pharmacokinetic profile. Investigation of its effects on CBF, ICP, and CMR for oxygen at analgesic concentrations are required. However, its properties may make it an ideal agent for intraoperative and early postoperative use.

■ Nonsteroidal Anti-Inflammatory Drugs

Nonsteroidal anti-inflammatory drugs (NSAIDs) interfere with the inflammatory process and attenuate the process of peripheral sensitization [48]. NSAIDs targeted for perioperative pain may provide useful coanalgesia with opioid-sparing properties, but use can be limited by adverse effects [49]. The potential adverse effects of gastric mucosal ulceration, renal dysfunction, and increased bleeding appear to occur mainly in susceptible patients with history of peptic ulceration, bleeding or anticoagulant therapy, or renal dysfunction possibly associated with hypovolemia and concurrent use of nephrotoxic agents [49].

Acetaminophen may have a useful role as an adjunct to analgesia and may be administered by the oral or rectal route. Acetaminophen, thought to have mainly central effects, with low toxicity has recently been shown to have its analgesia at least partly mediated by N-methyl-D-aspartate (NMDA) receptor and nitric oxide pathways [50].

There would be significant advantages to the development of agents that selectively inhibit the effects of inflammation on pain while leaving intact the cytoprotective effects of the eicosanoids. Recently two isoforms of the cyclo-oxygenase enzyme that dissociate the constitutive and inflammatory effects may lead to the development of selective cyclo-oxygenase inhibitors with an improved side effect profile [51].

■ Neuroprotection and Analgesia

The NMDA receptor has been linked to excitotoxic ischemic neuronal death [52] and amplification of nociceptive stimuli [53]. Therefore, NMDA antagonists may provide a unique opportunity to improve the effectiveness of pain management while providing neuroprotection. The NMDA-receptor complex is an ionophore in which a regulated ligand-gated ion channel capable of passing calcium into the cell producing effects on coupled second- and third-messenger systems such as nitric oxide and cyclic guanosine monophosphate [54]. Nociceptive stimulation can cause a persistent enhancement of the excitability of the spinal cord. This appears to be mediated by the excitatory amino acids acting on the NMDA receptor and has been termed central sensitization or "wind up" [53]. The process of wind up mediated by the NMDA receptor produces changes in wide dynamic range dorsal horn neurons; this causes a loss of tonic inhibitory block, calcium influx, and enhanced sensitivity to subsequent nociceptive stimuli by increased automaticity, magnified responses, and enlargement of receptive fields. These processes appear to amplify postoperative pain and render its management more difficult.

Regulation of the release and reuptake of excitatory neurotransmitters is impaired during ischemia. Surges of glutamate trigger massive calcium influx, with second- and third-messenger activation stimulating increased metabolic activity and toxic-free radical formation, thereby producing an exacerbation of the already unfavorable oxygen demand-supply inequity [52].

There appear to be beneficial opioid-sparing effects of ketamine and dextromethorphan, both noncompetitive NMDA antagonists [55]. Also, improved outcome appears to be evident for focal cerebral ischemia with NMDA blockers [52] such as dextrophan, a metabolite of dextromethorphan. A significant evolution of pharmacological agents has occurred, which holds promise for more selective and less toxic competitive inhibitors of the excitatory amino acid pathway [56].

Although the effects of ketamine on cerebral blood flow, cerebral metabolic rate, and intracranial pressure are unknown, especially in the postoperative period, recent evidence [57] suggests that it does not produce deleterious effects on ICP during anesthesia. Overall, modulation of excitatory amino acid pathways may have simultaneous beneficial effects on pain management and neuroprotection.

■ Pain Management for Specific Neurosurgical Procedures and Problems

The goal for this section is to outline the problems and to provide suggestions to further optimize pain management, rather than to specify treatment plans.

Craniotomy

The occurrence and severity of postoperative pain after craniotomy has not been formally studied but considered by many to be mild to moderate [58]. However, there are reports of persistent postsurgical pain [59];

whether this occurrence is preventable by improved postoperative pain management or a modified surgical approach is unclear.

The effects of undertreated pain have been discussed above. It will be emphasized that codeine by the intramuscular route in the postoperative period does not seem rational. This is based on unpredictable absorption, variable and delayed metabolism to morphine, wide variation in minimum effective analgesic concentration, and delayed effects. Furthermore, at equianalgesic doses the effect on pupillary signs, respiratory depression, sedation, and cerebral hemodynamics appears to be comparable to morphine. Thus, it seems preferable to utilize a more titratable opioid in low doses.

Maintenance analgesia depends on several factors, including patient and monitoring parameters. Indeed, some patients may be candidates for PCA while others may require intermittent injections or continuous infusion. Continuous infusions are not dangerous provided that simple principles are understood regarding the pharmacokinetics. Blood gases can be used to assess the effects on $PaCO_2$. The use of shorter-acting opioids with constant context-specific pharmacokinetics such as alfentanil and remifentanil allow more rapid up titration, are more forgiving of relative overdose, and allow rapid termination of effects to assess neurological status. Target-controlled infusions extended into the postoperative period may improve effectiveness and safety [42].

The use of longer-acting local anesthetics such as bupivacaine and ropivacaine either as local infiltration or regional blockade at the end of the surgical procedure [17] may further enhance analgesia and reduce the requirement for opioids. Acetaminophen may also be useful to decrease opioid requirements.

Carotid Revascularization

These patients often have coexistent cardiovascular disease and are at particular risk from the hemodynamic changes of uncontrolled pain, but they also require early and close neurological evaluation. Thus, titration of low doses of opioid and subsequent appropriate maintenance analgesia should be considered. Furthermore, local infiltration or superficial cervical plexus block may significantly benefit these patients by decreasing postoperative opioid requirements. Unilateral carotid surgery may be carried out with a combination of superficial and deep cervical plexus block as the sole means of anesthesia [59a].

Spinal Cord Injury

Acute and persistent pain following spinal cord injury (SCI) is under-recognized [60] and presents as a difficult management problem. There are few studies that indicate a rational and effective approach to pathophysiology, classification, and management. These patients, apart from other injuries and respiratory compromise, are at risk for musculoskeletal pain, visceral pain, and neuropathic pain at and below the level of injury. Although mechanisms of neuropathic pain are largely unknown, proposals include [60]: (1) local irritation at the site of injury, (2) activation of alternate intraspinal pathways, (3) loss of descending or intraspinal inhibitory mechanisms, and (4) effects of deafferentation.

The management is largely empiric. Opioids may be somewhat helpful for musculoskeletal and visceral pain but are ineffective for neuropathic pain [61]. Various modalities, including noradrenergic tricyclic antidepressants, anticonvulsants, and membrane-stabilizing systemic local anesthetics, have been used with some success [61]. Other more interventional techniques such as intrathecal administration of morphine, clonidine, and gamma-aminobutyric acid agonist baclofen appear to have some benefit in selected patients [62]. Stimulation techniques such as dorsal column stimulators may be beneficial to a subpopulation of SCI patients with an incomplete thoracic lesion and neuropathic pain [63]. Surgical procedures such as dorsal root entry zone radiofrequency lesions are most effective for radicular pain [64].

Spinal Decompressive Surgery

Although the incidence of postoperative pain following decompressive surgery for spinal stenosis and root lesions is highly variable, these patients often have pre-existent pain with sensitization, may have residual neuropathic pain, and may be opioid tolerant. Thus, decompression may not immediately alleviate their pain. Indeed, a study by Joshi and colleagues [65] that compared epidural fentanyl versus PCA intravenous morphine showed that visual analogue pain scores after lumbar laminectomy, even with PCA, were a mean of 5/10 for the first 24 hours. Moreover, they showed an enhanced postoperative analgesia with epidural fentanyl, with a favorable side effect profile, albeit with a small group of patients. Other studies have shown the analgesic advantages, including decreased hospital stay, of single shot or catheter application of epidural opioids [66, 67] and intrathecal opioids [68]. Delayed respiratory depression is a potential problem and requires increased monitoring for the first 24 hours.

Significant controversy and reassessment of the management of back pain has occurred recently. The merits of reoperation are debated [69]. Nevertheless, a significant proportion of patients, in whom the correct surgical procedure was carried out by an experienced surgeon, have persistent symptoms. This group of patients, "the failed back," probably have either arachnoiditis or significant nerve damage such that peripheral and central neuropathic changes have occurred. In this group, further surgery is unlikely to succeed and a nonoperative approach should be considered [69].

Because the effects of chronic pain on the entire biopsychosocial status of patients can be devastating, early referral to an experienced multidisciplinary pain clinic may improve outcome by the use of pharmacological, musculoskeletal, and psychological therapy. This early involvement may be preferable to end state consultation, after the devastating effects on function and deconditioning have occurred [67, 70].

▪ Summary

We hope to have inspired an interest in approaching the pain management issues in this challenging group of patients. Despite significant progress in understanding the pathophysiology of pain, the development of therapeutic options, and the publication and dissemination of guidelines, this progress does not seem to have been adopted into clinical practice. Bonica has stated "for many years I have studied the reasons for inadequate management of postoperative pain, and they remain the same. . . . Inadequate or improper application of available information and therapies is certainly the most important reason" [71]. Let us accept the challenge to re-evaluate pain management in the postoperative neurosurgical patient.

Future development may provide enhanced multimodal analgesia with the development of enantioselective NSAIDs and peripherally acting opioids that do not cross the blood-brain barrier. Targeted inhibition of the central neuroplasticity that underlies sensitization, rather than attempts to use pre-emptive analgesics, may be more fruitful. Inhibition of excitatory amino acids may prove beneficial for perioperative neuroprotection and pain management. In addition, longer-acting local anesthetics show significant promise. The importance of understanding the specific benefits available and matching these characteristics to the particular patient is emphasized.

Evaluation of outcomes, including morbidity and patient satisfaction, will determine if effective and rational provision of analgesia may indeed be safer than withholding analgesia. However, it is clear that re-evaluation and refinement of conventional therapy is necessary.

▪ References

1. Oden RV. Acute postoperative pain: incidence severity and etiology of inadequate treatment. Anesthesiol Clin North Am 1989;7:1–15
2. Dahl JB, Kehlet H. The value of preemptive analgesia in the treatment of postoperative pain. Br J Anaesth 1993;70:434–498
3. Yeager MP, Glass DD, Neff RK, et al. Epidural anesthesia and analgesia in high risk surgical patients. Anesthesiology 1987;66:729–736
4. Todd MM, Warner DS, Sokoll MD, et al. A prospective comparative trial of three anaesthetics for elective supratentorial craniotomy: propofol/fentanyl, isoflurane/fentanyl, isoflurane/nitrous oxide and fentanyl/nitrous oxide. Anesthesiology 1993; 78:1005
5. Cousins MJ, Mather LE. Relief of postoperative pain. Advances awaiting application. Med J Aust 1989;150:354–356

6. Collins JG. Acute pain management. Int Anesthesiol Clin 1991;29:25–36
7. Srivatanakul K, Weis OF, Alloza JL, et al. Analysis of narcotic analgesic usage in the treatment of postoperative pain. JAMA 1983;30:69–78
8. Austin KL, Stapleton JV, Mather LE. Multiple intramuscular injections: a major source of variability in analgesia response to meperidine. Pain 1980;8:47
9. Kehlet H. Modification of responses to surgery and anesthesia by neural blockade: clinical implications. In: Cousins MJ, Bridenbaugh PO, eds. Neural blockade in clinical anesthesia and management of pain. 2nd ed. Philadelphia: J.B. Lippincott, 1987:145–188
10. Woolf CJ. Somatic pain-pathogenesis and prevention. Br J Anaesth 1995;75: 193–200
11. Osborn I. The neurosurgical patient in the postanesthesia care unit in post anesthetic care unit problems. Anesthesiol Clin North Am 1990;8(2):355
12. Bernauer EA, Yeager MP. Optimal pain control in the intensive care unit, in recent advances in critical care medicine. Int Anesthesiol Clin 1993;31(2):201–219
13. Lam AM, Winn HR, Cullen BF, et al. Hyperglycemia and neurological outcome in patients with head injury. J Neurosurg 1991;75:545
14. Hamilton MG, Hall RD, Pineo GF. Venous thromboembolism in neurosurgery and neurology. J Neurosurg 1994;34(2):280–292
15. Cousins MJ. Prevention of postoperative pain. In: Bond MR, Charlton JE, Wolf CJ, eds. Proceedings of the VIth World Congress on Pain. Amsterdam: Elsevier, 1991:41–52
16. Dahl JB, Moinche S, Kehlet H. Wound infiltration with local anesthetics for postoperative pain relief. Acta Anaesthesiol Scand 1994;38:7–14
17. Cederholm I, Ajermau B, Evers H. Local analgesic and vascular effects of intradermal ropivacaine and bupivacaine of various concentrations with and without adrenaline in man. Acta Anaesthesiol Scand 1994;38:322–327
18. Malinovsky J, Bernard J, Corre P, et al. Motor and blood pressure effects of epidural sustained-release bupivacaine from polymer microspores: a dose-response study in rabbits. Anesth Analg 1995;81:5, 19–24
19. Murphy TM. Somatic blockade of the head and neck. In: Cousins MJ, Bridenbaugh PO, eds. Neural blockade in clinical anesthesia and management of pain. 2nd ed. Philadelphia: J.B. Lippincott, 1988
20. Neil RS. Head, neck and airway. In: Wildsmith JAW, Armitage EN, eds. Principles and practice of regional anaesthesia. New York: Churchill Livingstone, 1987: 168–176
21. Shafer SL, Varvel JR. Pharmacokinetics, pharmacodynamics and rational opioid selection. Anesthesiology 1991;74:53–63
22. Egan TD, Lemmen HJ, Fiset P, et al. The pharmacokinetics of the new short-acting opioid remifentanil in healthy adult male volunteers. Anesthesiology 1993;79: 881–892
23. Davies FW, White M, Kenny GNC. Post operative analgesia using a computerised infusion of alfentanil following aortic bifurcation graft surgery. Int J Clin Monit Comput 1992;9:207–212
24. Albanese J, Burbee O, Viviarand X, et al. Sufentanil increase/intracranial pressure in patient with head trauma. Anesthesiology 1993;79(3):493–497
25. Jobes DR, Dennel EM, Bush GL, et al. Cerebral blood flow and metabolism during morphine-nitrous oxide anesthesia in man. Anesthesiology 1977;47:16
26. Jung R, Shah N, Reinsel R, et al. Cerebrospinal fluid pressure in patients with brain tumours: impact of fentanyl versus alfentanil during nitrous oxide—oxygen anesthesia. Anesth Analg 1990;71:419
27. Marx W, Shah N, Long C, et al. Sufentanil, alfentanil and fentanyl: impact on cerebrospinal fluid pressure in patients with brain tumours. J Neurosurg Anesth 1989;1:3
28. Ashbury AJ. Pupil response to alfentanil and fentanyl. Anaesthesia 1986;41:717

29. Shook JE, Watkins DB, Camporesi EM. Differential effects of opioid receptors in respiration, respiratory disease, and opiate induced respiratory depression. Am Rev Respir Dis 1990;142:895

30. Camin F, Debucquoy B. Alfentanil infusion for post operative pain. A comparison of epidural and intravenous routes. Anesthesiology 1991;75(2):171–178

31. Raffa RB, Fredericks E, Reimann J, et al. Opioid and nonopioid components independently contribute to the mechanism of action of tramadol, an atypical opioid analgesic. J Pharmacol Exp Ther 1992;260:275–285

32. Eichelbaum N, Gross AS. The genetic polymorphism of debrisoquine/spartame metabolism—clinical aspects in Kalow. Pharmacogenetic of drug metabolism. Munich: Springer-Verlag, 1992:625–648

33. Knemer HK, Eichelbaum M. Molecular basis and clinical consequences of genetic cytochrome P450 2D6 polymorphism. Life Sciences 1995;56(26):2286–2288

34. Persson K, Sjostrom S, Sigurdardottir E, et al. Patient controlled analgesia with codeine for postoperative pain relief in ten extensive and one poor metaboliser of dextromethorphan. Br J Clin Pharmacol 1995;39(2):182–186

35. White PF. Clinical use of intravenous and analgesic infusions. Anesth Analg 1989; 68:161

36. Murphy DF, Grazzioti P, Chalkiadis G, et al. Patient controlled analgesia: a comparison with nurse-controlled intravenous opioid infusion. Anaesth Intensive Care 1994;22:589–592

37. Camu F, Debucquoy F. Alfentanil infusion for postoperative pain: a comparison of epidural and intravenous route. Anesthesiology 1991;75(2):171–178

38. Ferrante FM, Orau EJ, Rocco AG. A statistical model for pain in patient-controlled analgesia and conventional intramuscular opioid regimes. Anesth Analg 1988;67:457

39. Etchers RC. Respiratory depression associated with patient controlled analgesia: a review of eight cases. Can J Anaesth 1994;41:15

40. Shug SA, Torrie JJ. Safety assessment of postoperative pain management by an acute pain service. Pain 1993;55:387–391

41. Ashburn MA, Love G, Pace NL. Respiratory-related critical events with intravenous patient-controlled analgesia. Clin J Pain 1994;10:52–56

42. Davies FW, White M, Kenny GN. Postoperative analgesia using a computerised infusion of alfentanil following aortic surgery. Int J Clin Monit Comput 1992;9: 207–212

43. Van den Niewenhuzen MCO, Engbers FM, Burm AGL, et al. Computer controlled infusion of alfentanil for post-operative analgesia. A pharmacokinetic and pharmacodynamic evaluation. Anesthesiology 1993;79:481–492

44. Sandler A, Baxter A, Samson B, et al. Postoperative analgesia with transdermal fentanyl: analgesic and respiratory effects. Can J Anaesth 1993;40:A51 (Abstract)

45. Ashburn MA, Streisand J, Zhang J, et al. The iontophoresis of fentanyl citrate in man. Anesth Analg 1994;78:512 (Abstract)

46. Egan TD, Lemmans HJ, Fiset P, et al. The pharmacokinetics of the new short-acting opioid remifentanil (G187084B) in healthy adult male volunteers. Anesthesiology 1993;79:881–892

47. Westmoreland CL, Hoke JF, Sebel PS, et al. Pharmacokinetics of remifentanil and its major metabolite in patients undergoing elective inpatient surgery. Anesthesiology 1993;79:893–903

48. Woolf CJ. Somatic pain-pathogenesis and prevention. Br J Anaesth 1995;75: 169–176

49. Souter AJ, Fredman B, White PF. Controversies in the perioperative use of nonsteroidal anti-inflammatory drugs. Anesth Analg 1994;79:1178–1190

50. Bjorkman R, Hallman KM, Hedner J, et al. Acetaminophen blocks spinal hyperalgesia induced by NMDA and substance P. Pain 1994;57:259–264

51. Rang HP, Urban L. New molecules in analgesia. Br J Anaesth 1995;75:146–156

52. Albers GW, Atkinson RP, Kelley RE, et al. Safety, tolerability and pharmacokinetics of the N-methyl-D-aspartate antagonist Dextrophan in patients with acute stroke. Stroke 1995;26(2):254–258

53. Woolf CH, Thompson SWN. The induction and maintenance of central sensitization is dependent on N-methyl-D-aspartic acid receptor activation implications for the treatment of post injury pain hypersensitivity states. Pain 1991;44:293–299

54. Mayer ML, Miller RJ. Excitatory amino acid receptors, second messengers and regulation of intracellular Ca^{+2} in mamalian neurons. Trends Pharmacol Sci 1990; 11:254–260

55. Roytblat L, Korotkorucko A, Katz J, et al. Postoperative pain: the effect of low dose ketamine in addition to general anesthesia. Anesth Analg 1993;77:1161–1165

56. Dray A, Urban L, Dickenson A. Pharmacology of chronic pain. Trends Pharmacol Sci 1994;15:190–197

57. Mayberg TS, Lam AM, Matta BF, et al. Ketamine does not increase cerebral blood flow velocity or intracranial pressure during isoflurane/nitrous oxide anesthesia in patients undergoing craniotomy. Anesth Analg 1995;81:84–89

58. Agency for Health Care Policy and Research, US Department of Health and Human Services. Acute pain management: operative or medical procedures and trauma. Feb 1992

59. Schessel DA. Pain after surgery for acoustic neuroma. Otolaryngol Head Neck Surg 1992;107(3):424–429

59a. Davies MJ, Mooney PH, Scott DA, et al. Neurologic changes during carotid endarterectomy under cervical plexus block predict a high risk of postoperative stroke. Anesthesiology 1993;78:829–833

60. Siddall PJ, Cousins MJ. Post spinal cord injury pain: mechanisms and treatment options in anesthesiology and pain management. In: Stanley TH, Asburn MA, eds. Anesthesiology and pain management. Amsterdam: Kleuver-Academic, 1994:237–251

61. Siddall PJ, Taylor D, Cousins MJ. Pain associated with spinal cord injury. Curr Opin Neurol 1996;8:447–450

62. Siddall PJ, Gray M, Rukowski S, Cousins MJ. Intrathecal morphine and clonidine in the management of spinal cord injury pain: a case report. Pain 1994;59:147–148

63. Cioni B, Meglio M, Pentimalli L, et al. Spinal cord stimulation in the treatment of paraplegic pain. J Neurosurg 1995;82:35–39

64. Sampson JH, Cashman RE, Nashold B, et al. Dorsal root entry zone lesions for intractable pain after trauma to the conus medullaris and cauda equina. J Neurosurg 1995;82:28–34

65. Joshi GP, McCarrol SM, O'Rourke K. Postoperative analgesia after laminectomy: epidural fentanyl infusion versus patient controlled intravenous morphine. Anesth Analg 1995;80:511–514

66. Ray CD, Bagley R. Indwelling epidural morphine for control of postlumbar spine surgery. Clin J Pain 1988;4:209–212

67. Gibbons KJ, Barth AA, Badny SL, et al. Lumbar discectomy: use of an epidural sponge for postoperative pain control. Neurosurgery 1995;36(6):1131–1135

68. Ross DA, Drasner K, Weinstein PR, et al. Use of intrathecally administered morphine in the treatment of postoperative pain after lumbar spinal surgery: a prospective, double blind, placebo-controlled study. Neurosurgery 1991;28(5):700–704

69. Wynn Parry CB. The failed back. In: Wall PD, Melzack R, eds. Textbook of pain. 3rd ed. New York: Churchill Livingstone, 1994:1075–1094

70. Bonica JJ. Neural blockade in the Multidisciplinary Pain Clinic. In: Cousins MJ, Bridenbaugh PO, eds. Neural blockade in clinical anesthesia and management of pain. 2nd ed. Philadelphia: JB Lippincott, 1988:1119–1138

71. Bonica JJ. The management of pain. Lea & Febiger, 1990

A Primer of Malpractice Law for the Neuroanesthesiologist

Lawrence Molton, JD

During my work with physicians, I have found a wide disparity of knowledge about the nature of the US civil justice system. Some clinicians include expert witness testimony as a significant part of their professional practice, others avoid anything to do with lawyers at all costs, and most fall somewhere in between. It appears that many clinicians lack sufficient knowledge about legal principles and process and are often frustrated when their work is scrutinized by courts. Increased sophistication about the legal system by anesthesiologists will serve the interests of doctors and patients alike.

The first part of this paper describes the anatomy of malpractice law and addresses some of the basic components of negligence cases: scientific and legal proof, the standard of care, causation, and the stages of litigation.

The second part focuses on certain types of errors that give rise to malpractice suits and considers ways in which changes in the organization of data gathering may improve the results for anesthesiologists in malpractice cases.[a]

Malpractice Law and Anesthesia

Malpractice: The Issues

In modern law, actions for malpractice are negligence actions, structurally similar to slip-and-fall or other negligence cases, with only a few key differences. In malpractice law, the basis for the standard of care is different and there are special statutes in some states limiting the amount that can be recovered for certain categories of damages.

[a]I am indebted to Karen Posner, PhD, and the compilers of the ASA Closed Claims Study at the University of Washington for the use of their claims survey.

195

The elements of a negligence action include causation, duty, proximate cause, breach of the standard of care, and the possible negligence of the victim. Most of these elements are not pertinent to the usual malpractice case. Unlike pedestrians, drivers, and users of power tools, surgical patients are not capable of contributing to the intraoperative problems they experience: they are unconscious. Hence the plaintiff's conduct is not an issue. While there is a line of malpractice cases that specifically turns on the duty issue, it does not apply to hospital-based medicine. Proximate cause is fascinating but rarely relevant, and so in the tradition of legal writing it will be relegated to a footnote.[b] The issues that dominate any malpractice case are breach of the standard of care and sometimes causation.

Causation and Injury

A brief summary of legal causation shows how differently it is analyzed in the law than in medicine. The core concept in negligence law is called "cause in fact." A is defined as the cause in fact of B if but for the occurrence of A, B would not have happened. As applied to the operating room, it means that if the patient would not have suffered the injury B if the doctor had not done action A, then action A caused injury B. But if B would have occurred irrespective of action A, then there is no cause in fact and the injured person cannot recover even if the doctor was negligent.

A case in the American Society of Anesthesiologists' (ASA) Closed Claims database illustrates this well. An ASA 5 patient underwent emergency craniotomy for an acute intracranial bleed. The anesthesiologists documented bilateral breath sounds heard by at least two people. The patient died during the surgery. The autopsy found the endotracheal tube in the esophagus. The autopsy concluded that the brain lesion caused the patient's death and that the esophageal intubation was not a contributing cause. Therefore, there was no liability for negligence.

In the situation in which there are multiple causes, the traditional test is that the conduct must have been a "substantial factor" in bringing about the result for liability to be imposed.

The legal approach differs from the medical one in that assessments of causation are totally retrospective in law but not in medicine. A physician with a complex differential diagnosis will frequently include elements in his or her treatment plan designed to deal with more than one potential

---

[b]"Proximate cause" is one of those strange legal terms for which the meaning is not what it appears to be. It actually deals with the boundaries of foreseeable results. It arises when a chain of events has come together to produce a strange result (think of the Rube Goldberg machine). Although the negligent act that started the chain is the cause in fact of the injury, at some point, the series of intervening steps between original act and ultimate result reaches the point at which the law will find the original act too remote from the result to give rise to liability.

The law imputes liability only for negligent acts for which consequences are in some manner a foreseeable result of the type of carelessness that occurred. Drawing the boundaries of foreseeability is one of the most revered academic exercises in the law. However, it is not too important here, because physicians are rarely sued for a remote event.

source of the problem and may adjust that treatment at any point to reflect improved information, as disease is a dynamic process. After the patient's condition has resolved, it may be clear that there was an identifiable cause, but a good result may be obtained even if there was not.

The legal system must decide whether or not there was an identifiable cause, and it must do so in a single proceeding with no opportunity to revise its ruling later on. Unlike in medicine, the choice of cause controls the outcome. If the ruling is that something other than the defendant (e.g., pre-existing disease, a non-negligent surgery) was the cause, the patient receives no compensation. This is why the legal system forces physicians to opine about cause even when there is no way to do so.

Setting the Standard of Care

Most physicians are aware that they are judged by a more deferential standard than are other citizens. While the usual definition of negligence is conduct falling below what is expected of the "reasonable person," a physician can only be found negligent if his conduct was inferior to the customary practice of other physicians in his locality and specialty.

A special rule of negligence law that is relevant here is called *res ipsa loquitur* (the thing speaks for itself). This rule is applied to a case when: there was an accident caused by an instrumentality under the exclusive control of the defendant, and the event that occurred is one that does not occur in the absence of negligence. When *res ipsa* is applied, the burden of proof is reversed, and the defendant will be found liable unless he can prove that his actions were not the cause of the injury.

One of the textbook cases on this, familiar to all first-year law students, happens to be an anesthesia case. *Ybarra v Spangard,* 25 Cal.2d 486 (1944). During an appendectomy, the anesthesiologist, a Dr Reser, pulled the plaintiff's body to the head of the table and laid him back against two hard objects at the top of his shoulders. He then administered general anesthesia. When Ybarra awoke, he felt sharp pain halfway between the neck and the point of the right shoulder. The pain spread to the lower arm and grew worse. Ybarra developed paralysis and atrophy of the muscles and required a splint. Expert testimony stated Ybarra had traumatic paralysis due to pressure or strain applied to the area of pain.

The California Supreme Court held: "where a plaintiff receives unusual injuries while unconscious and in the course of medical treatment, all those defendants who had any control over his body or the instrumentalities which might have caused the injuries" are inferred to be negligent, and must prove themselves not to be so. Thus, the physician will be liable in this situation, because no one can prove what actually happened.

There are no studies on jury deliberations to prove this, but actual jury verdicts may reflect the use of this standard in anesthesia cases even if the court has not explicitly instructed the jurors on *res ipsa*. People believe medicine can do wonders, as it certainly can, and they like explanations. If juries hear about a bad outcome and the defense has no plausible explanation as to the reason for it, the jury is likely to find the defendant negligent.

Scientific Thinking and Legal Analysis

One of the most troublesome facets of the legal system for clinicians is its apparent lack of scientific rigor. Physicians are used to quality assurance meetings, mortality/morbidity conferences, tumor boards, and peer-reviewed journals. If adversarial hearings are needed, such as before the state medical board, the audience is an expert one. In contrast, lawsuits are handled by judges and lawyers who are not trained in scientific thinking and often struggle to understand it.

The concept of proof is very different in the tort system than in science. Courts make rulings on scientific issues that are not always based on a degree of evidence that a physician or scientist would find acceptable. The usual scientific rule is that the probability of the observed result being due to chance must be less than 5% for a study to be statistically significant. Breadth of the confidence interval, size of the relative and absolute risk, and other measures are also used to assess the probative value of the data. But there is no requirement in law that a finding of causation be based on data of a specified strength.

Physicians are also trained to regard causation as a combination of biological mechanisms, temporal sequence, and epidemiological correlations. The legal system is willing to hear most any evidence that an expert is willing to testify to and has no hard and fast rule about how much of what type of evidence is required to prove a fact.

This major difference in approach is a result of the very different goals of the professions. Any reputable scientist is comfortable publishing a paper that states that the data are insufficient to answer the question or that it cannot be determined which of the competing explanations is most compelling. The goal of the scientist is to advance knowledge, to sort out what is known and what is still uncertain, and to facilitate the design of studies that will answer the next question. The confidence in the finding is more important than the nature of the finding.

The goal of the court system is to settle disputes. Every trial must produce a winner on every issue and on the ultimate outcome. The law does not have the luxury of saying there is no answer; further study is needed. Whatever evidence exists is by definition sufficient to answer the question. One of law's most famous aphorisms is from Robert Jackson, the prosecutor at Nuremberg and Supreme Court Justice, on the source of the Supreme Court's authority: "We are not final because we are infallible; rather, we are infallible because we are final."

Each element of the plaintiff's case must be proved by the plaintiff. Thanks to the detailed news coverage of a well-known matter that shall remain nameless, I suspect everyone is now aware that while a criminal conviction requires proof beyond a reasonable doubt, a judgment in a civil case requires only proof by a "preponderance of the credible evidence." That phrase simply means that there is more evidence supporting a proposition than opposing it.

From Deposition to Trial

I recall a deposition of a resident in which the first question elicited a look of terror, even though this was not a malpractice case. Physicians need to know that depositions are not specialty board exams or competency hearings. Depositions are a search for information about every detail anyone can remember about the day of the incident, most of which will prove to be pretty unimportant. At a trial, the attorneys already know what happened (the oldest rule of trial cross-examination is never ask a question you don't know the answer to). At a deposition, the attorneys do not know much of what has happened, and the questioning will continue on whatever path the responses lead. They are supposed to be exercises in logic, so that the witnesses are required to articulate the reasoning behind actions they took or the progression of their state of mind in response to the stream of data they received.

The discovery phase of a lawsuit involves an attempt to reconstruct the events that took place in the operating room. The most important part is of course the deposition of the anesthesiologist(s). The attorneys will ask for a moment-by-moment description of events. To provide this information, the anesthesiologist studies the written record and then describes the sequence of events, orally and sometimes in writing. Because of the long interval, often years, between the incident and the deposition, it is problematic how much of this account will be true memory and how much will be interpretation of his or her notes combined with hazy recollections.

Depositions are not conducted under the same evidentiary rules as trials. Any question can be asked that is likely to lead to the discovery of relevant evidence, which allows very broad questioning. As there are no jurors, judges, or journalists present, there is usually no showboating or gratuitous flamboyant rhetoric. When an attorney asks an improper question, the witness answers anyway; an objection is made so that a judge can later rule on whether the question was improper and thus inadmissible at the trial. In some cases, the depositions are under a special order that forbids anyone not involved with the lawsuit from reading them. The best thing about depositions is that they make it possible for 90% of civil cases to be settled without a trial.

An aspect of the litigation process that I think is counterintuitive to most outsiders is that its capriciousness increases rather than decreases as a case progresses.

Evaluation of a case is done by attorneys whose professional success depends on their ability to accurately gauge both what happened and how a jury will react to the evidence. Before a suit is filed, the injured person's attorney usually has an expert review of the facts to evaluate the strength of the case. During the discovery process, both sides often have experts studying the medical records and the depositions of the physicians to assess the situation. Later, experts on both sides are deposed, and their testimony is again evaluated by various attorneys and their expert consultants who judge the credibility of those witnesses.

If no settlement is reached, the case will be argued in front of judges with no scientific training and decided by juries that may have no education or experience at all. Little wonder then that a leading torts scholar who was an advocate of no-fault systems in the 1960s coined the phrase "the negligence lottery" to describe how the current system handles large claims.[c] The analogy is apt: the range of results is remarkably wide, and random variables such as jury composition and geographic location appear to dominate. For the attorneys, the trial is a bit like entering the commodities market, with the futures prices in the hands of 12 people who may or may not understand the scientific testimony.

I would argue that this system is fair but not just. That is, it is free of systemic biases, corruption, or malice, but it decides cases in an extremely imprecise and irrational manner.

Of Damages, Trials, and the Lottery

Trials are difficult to study because one cannot design controlled studies of courts the way one can for cancer treatments. I present an anecdotal account of one case, from Southern California in 1990, to illustrate the difficulty of assigning fair value to a case in trial. The report of the case comes from *Jury Verdicts Weekly,* a publication that summarizes the results of jury trials.

The Lifeguard's Ankle Mr Chavez, a young, healthy lifeguard, broke his ankle in an accident and later underwent surgery to remove the pins from the ankle.[d] He may have had a pre-existing heart condition. During the procedure, Chavez suffered a cardiac arrest and lapsed into a coma for 3 weeks. He suffered cortical blindness, memory lapse, perception deficits, and loss of fine manual coordination.

---

[c]Mare A. Franklin, "Replacing the Negligence Lottery: Compensation and Selective Reimbursement," U. Virginia Law Review 53:774(1967).
[d]*Chavez v Altig* (Super. Ct. of Orange Cty. 1990), Jury Verdicts Weekly 1991;35:27.

The plaintiff alleged that the anesthesiologist was negligent for using the wrong mix of gases and failing to ventilate properly, while the defense argued that Chavez' heart problem and an electrolyte imbalance as well as hypersensitivity to the release of catecholamines caused the disaster. The defense also testified that Chavez might have had an allergic reaction to the drugs he was given.

The trial lasted 17 days. It is important to note that California has a statute limiting damages for general pain and suffering to $250,000: the variation in result comes from attempts to calculate the wage loss and estimate the cost for future medical care. In this case, the past medical bills were agreed to be $223,000.

Before trial, the plaintiff asked for $1.5 million, while the defense offered $570,000 combined cash and annuity. Before the trial, the plaintiff lowered his demand to $900,000 (not coincidentally the amount of the insurance policy), but it was not accepted. Once the trial began, the offer was withdrawn. As the testimony progressed, the perceived value of the case rose. During the trial the defense twice raised their offer, first to $720,000 and then to $1 million, but the offers were not accepted. After the case went to the jury, the plaintiff raised his demand to $2 million. The defense did not accept.

Given that malpractice cases are handled on a contingency fee, so that the plaintiff's lawyer receives no fee if he loses but a large percentage of any award that is received, the case is very much a lottery. After nearly 6 hours of deliberation, the jury came back with a total award of $13 million. Converting that to present cash value, it came to $3.8 million plus accrued interest, for a total of $5,009,000. The verdict was of course appealed.

Predicting a jury's view on liability is no easier.

The Dangerous Asthmatic   A 44-year-old asthmatic went into bronchospasm during surgery and suffered brain damage.[e] She alleged an improper intubation, a choice of agents that was more likely to cause bronchospasm in asthmatics, and a failure to respond properly to the problem. The defense argued that there was no negligence and that such a patient could lapse into bronchospasm even if no one is negligent.

It is very difficult to predict whether a jury will find the doctor liable in such a case. The defense offered zero, and the plaintiff asked for $800,000. The jury came in with $1.285 million! After a trial, the usual course is for the defense to ask the judge to lower the verdict as excessive, and then one or both sides appeal. Before the judge could rule, the parties settled for a package of cash and annuity worth $1 million present value. Both sides, it is safe to say, wished they were more accurate.

---

[e]*Metheney v Rowland-Smith* (Super. Ct. of Tulare Cty. 1990), Jury Verdicts Weekly 1991;35:11.

■ Improving Anesthesiologist Performance in Malpractice Litigation

Anesthesia Recordkeeping and the Malpractice Suit

Are there procedural steps that anesthesiologists can take that are likely to improve their outcome in malpractice suits? To identify these changes, I have categorized the types of errors that occur during neurosurgery into three types: physical error, protocol error, and data gathering error. I believe there are suggestive empirical data that indicate that reducing errors in the data gathering category will improve malpractice outcomes.

One of the frustrations of research in this field is the paucity of data on malpractice litigation. Attorneys are not social scientists, and there is no central source of data on lawsuits. Many cases of permanent injury do not result in a suit being filed, and many lawsuits are dismissed or settled very early on, and thus never appear in surveys. Thus, I can make no claims for comprehensiveness or statistical significance for the conclusions in this paper.

To search for empirical evidence I have reviewed the case summaries of claims involving neuroanesthesia dating back to 1978, provided by the ASA Closed Claims Study, which include the opinions of their reviewer as to what happened. I have excluded from my sample those cases in which no recovery was paid to plaintiffs. Although this probably excludes some instances of substandard physician conduct, it also should reduce the effect of frivolous or very weak lawsuits on the data.

Qualitative Analysis of Error

Physical error refers to inadvertently damaging the patient while doing the right thing. This would encompass surgical dissection of something not meant to be dissected, setting a dial to an unintended number, IV site damage, and many similar things. It also includes the most common error in anesthesia, failure to intubate or ventilate the patient properly.

Another category of error would be the choice of treatment protocol. This encompasses the physician response to sudden major threats to patient survival such as cardiac arrest, malignant hyperthermia, or a vasovagal response to physical stimulus. It also includes the choice and dose of agents used and many other patient management decisions. Here the courts scrutinize the sequence of steps taken and compare it to the customary practice, such as, was the dose and dose rate of lidocaine appropriate for the patient in fibrillation.

The third category is data gathering error. This includes failing to use a monitor, having it malfunction during use, failing to look at or process the data coming from the monitor, and failing to appropriately record the data after receiving it. It also includes errors of vigilance, in which the anesthesiologist failed to react properly to various signs that were apparent by direct observation without the need for a monitor.

The first two types of error relate to the core physical and intellectual skills that make up the practice of anesthesia. Obviously a reduction in the frequency of these errors may lead to fewer malpractice suits as well as higher quality of care. A discussion of possible ways to achieve that is beyond the scope of this paper. The third type of error can be addressed more easily, by changing routines and increasing awareness.

It is important to realize that unlike the many changes in clinical decision making that are driven more by legal than medical considerations (i.e., "defensive medicine"), what is discussed here are information management changes that should improve legal performance without necessarily affecting treatment. Improved data on physiological parameters such as short-term changes in blood pressure or agent uptake is legally useful whether or not it would affect intraoperative decisions and/or clinical outcomes.

Monitors

From a legal perspective, there is a benefit to the use of additional monitoring. The custom of the profession clearly has evolved toward ever more intensive use of monitors, such as the progression of pulse oximetry from a novel device to a universal standard in only a few years. (Introduction of this device also produced the biggest drop in malpractice premiums of any change in anesthesia practice.) It is tempting to say that since a new device cannot be considered standard of care until it has obtained sufficient market penetration, a physician takes no legal risk by ignoring it. This approach is fraught with danger. The influence of an implicit doctrine of res ipsa loquitur is too great. There are a significant number of cases in which trials or settlements have awarded money to people in part because of the absence of monitoring data.

The ASA sample that comprises the database for this paper includes 62 neurosurgical cases in which money was paid to an injured person. Of those cases, 16 included failure to monitor or failure of a monitor. This does not mean that the failure to monitor caused the injury, although it may have in some cases. However, this number implies that failing to monitor looks terrible to the litigators. It drives up the value of the case and increases the dollars paid out.

Using specific cases from the ASA database as anecdotal evidence, we see that failure to monitor or failure to record can adversely affect the legal outcome for the neuroanesthesiologist.

In one case, an ASA 1 young woman underwent transsphenoidal hypophysectomy for a pituitary adenoma, under general anesthesia with cocaine and epinephrine. She experienced premature ventricular contractions and wide complex dysrhythmias, and an end-tidal nitrogen spike and a flattened end-tidal CO_2 curve were noted. When the drapes were removed, the patient was cyanotic, and she arrested and suffered severe brain damage. The etiology remained unclear. The use of a low flow technique, an air embolus, and allergic reaction were considered as causes. But the defense was unable to produce as experts several witnesses who might have exculpated the defendant, because those witnesses considered failure to use a precordial or esophageal stethoscope (in 1987) to be unacceptable. The failure to monitor significantly impaired the defense independent of the value of the monitoring; there is no way to know whether use of the stethoscope would have prevented the adverse outcome.

Thus, there is a strong argument to be made in favor of using Doppler monitors, an arterial line, and a central venous pressure (CVP) line in many of the procedures typical in neurosurgery and using pulse oximetry, precordial and/or esophageal stethoscopes, an end-tidal CO_2 monitor, agent monitor, and other standard monitors in all cases.

Data Collection Standards

The core document that will always define an anesthesia malpractice case is the anesthesia record. Although the forms vary from institution to institution, the record always contains a basic grid that allows the physician to chart vital signs over time. Other areas record the delivery of agent, the monitors in use, the drugs given, and the names of personnel.

Using the best possible monitors can only help the physician in a lawsuit if he makes certain to record the data they provide. In a second case from the ASA database, the patient underwent a craniectomy in a sitting position for acoustic neuroma. The surgeon tore the venous sinus while opening the dura and announced air entrainment. Bradycardia, hypotension, and Doppler changes were noted. Atropine and vasopressors were given, and the air was removed by a CVP catheter. After the blood pressure (BP) and pulse stabilized, the surgery was completed uneventfully. The patient awakened with significant incapacity, attributed to paradoxical air embolism. The doctor testified he turned off the N_2O during the event, but this does not appear in the record. The reviewer concluded that the anesthetic management was appropriate and that the lawsuit was settled for a large sum primarily because the record was weak.

The use of the 5-minute grid in anesthesia records presents another legal challenge. When reconstructing the incident, it is necessary to interpolate to fill the gaps in the record. For example, it is common for the BP to be tracked by an automatic device every 5 minutes and charted accordingly. Although the device continues to display the last BP, there is no measurement of the actual BP for the 4 intervening minutes. In a case in which a sudden deterioration in the patient's status occurred, inquiry will be made as to whether there was warning of trouble on the horizon. Similar gaps are possible in the heart rate, electrocardiographic record, and pulse oximeter even though they may record each beat. No one stares continuously at a monitor, and witnesses may not recall what they saw at each moment they were looking. Reconstruction of the data may be more difficult if the physicians had elected to reduce the aural clutter by turning off the audible signal from the monitoring device(s).

Again, it is not possible to know how the anesthesiologist would have acted in the face of additional information, or whether the outcome would have been altered. But gaps in the data are clearly prejudicial to the physician in a lawsuit because they facilitate an inference that more frequent monitoring would have warned of an impending problem, thus enabling the physician to intervene in time to forestall the unfavorable result.

What changes in record-keeping procedure might improve the outcome of a lawsuit for an anesthesiologist without being so burdensome as to interfere with clinical care? It is tempting to argue for a totally comprehensive and reliable automated record of the data generated by all monitors. In most cases, these data should enable the physician to defeat the inference that the injury could have been avoided by greater physician vigilance. For example, in the case of a patient who complained of awareness during surgery due to being "too light," if the continuous monitoring record showed that blood pressure and heart rate rose for only a few seconds before the problem began, this would support the anesthesiologist's view that he or she acted as rapidly as possible.

Such a system is practical in many hospitals today. In some institutions, all of the data from the operating room monitors can be reviewed in real time by anyone on the computer network. Even without this "live" viewing option, computers can store complete records of all clinical monitoring data. To have any probative force, such a record must be tamper-proof, so that any alteration in the raw data would be detectable. If not, the attorneys would have to consider the possibility that unfavorable readings had been removed, making the record of little value.

At second glance, however, this solution may not be so wonderful. The usual handwritten record is self-censored: the anesthesiologist does not write every entry as it happens, but makes entries when the pace of the surgery allows it. He or she is free to omit obviously erroneous readings from the printed page. This is necessary because of the frequency of artifactual readings. Electrical interference from the electrocautery or other sources can jam monitoring equipment, light can interfere with the pulse oximeter and produce a false reading, and any monitor is capable of malfunctioning at any moment.

To the lay reviewer, the existence of a record full of strange readings, blanks, or corrections will seem suspicious. Because they only see the one case with a bad outcome and not the thousands of others, lawyers and juries might conclude from purely artifactual readings that problems were obviously occurring throughout the case and the physicians were derelict in not recognizing them.

Several other approaches exist that might be capable of delivering more credible data in the event of a lawsuit. Vital information could be recorded more frequently, such as, every 1 minute, thus reducing the ability of the attorneys to argue that there were undetected dangerous conditions brewing. Continuous recording could be configured on a standby basis, ready to be activated at the first sign of a potential intraoperative event. This would address the issue of lawsuits for improper management of cardiorespiratory failure during anesthesia. Or the anesthesiologist could use a pen-based system for recording in real time, which would automatically provide precise unalterable time tags for each entry. Artifactual entries could either be deleted from the system, or never recorded at all.

All of these systems clearly mandate improved equipment quality. If unalterable records or a more intensive recording system are to become standard, monitor malfunction must be minimal. If random artifactual numbers appear with significant frequency, every record will have some strange components that reduce its value and probably lead to the demise of the system.

A challenging obstacle to these approaches is the desire of some physicians to intentionally reduce the amount of information they are bombarded with to avoid data overload. Do some clinicians prefer not to have a surfeit of data because that streamlines their thinking process? If so, does that approach improve their clinical decision making? It may well impair their legal performance.

It is also unfortunately true that in the situation in which the quality of care is low, the legal system provides disincentives to increased data gathering. A physician whose vigilance was poor, or whose understanding of the risk posed by a complex cluster of factors was limited, can escape liability more easily if the result appeared unknowable and unforeseeable. In those situations, fewer monitors (unless they are clearly required by the standard of care in that locality) are better.

It is unlikely there will be empirical data that can determine if these changes would be effective. When a new monitoring device or record-keeping program first appears, studies will be done to compare the clinical outcome of the new approach to the old one, not the number of lawsuits filed within 1 year of, for example, using propofol versus alfentanil. Nevertheless, it is instructive to look at the potential effects of changes in recording, monitoring, and other aspects of the surgical environment on legal outcomes.

I wish to acknowledge the extensive contributions of Professor Richard Jaffe, MD, PhD, of the Department of Anesthesia at Stanford University Medical School, whose intellectual guidance and clinical insights were invaluable in preparing this paper.

Index

Future Issues

Volume 35, 1997

Winter (No. 1)

MECHANICAL VENTILATION

Spring (No. 2)

ENDOCRINE DISORDERS AND ANESTHESIA

Summer (No. 3)

ACUTE AND CHRONIC PAIN

Fall (No. 4)

AIRWAY MANAGEMENT IN PEDIATRIC ANESTHESIA